Todung Mulya Lubis is an Indonesian lawyer, human rights activist, the founder of the Lubis Santosa & Maramis law firm, honorary professor at the Melbourne Law School and, from 2018, Ambassador of Indonesia to the Kingdom of Norway and the Republic of Iceland. He has held the position of deputy chair of the Human Rights Investigation Commission for East Timor, and member of the Asian Human Rights Commission in Hong Kong. He has also served as chair of the Indonesian Crisis Group (ICG) International Foundation; and chairperson of the Indonesian Corruption Watch (ICW) Ethical Council. From 1980–1983, he was director of Indonesia's famous dissident NGO, the Legal Aid Foundation, where he worked for many years. His influential 1983 book *In Search of Human Rights: Legal–Political Dilemmas of Indonesia's New Order 1966–1990* played an important role in defining democratic thinking about human rights in Indonesia.

WAR ON CORRUPTION
AN INDONESIAN EXPERIENCE

TODUNG MULYA LUBIS

MELBOURNE UNIVERSITY PRESS

MELBOURNE UNIVERSITY PRESS
An imprint of Melbourne University Publishing Limited
Level 1, 715 Swanston Street, Carlton, Victoria 3053, Australia
mup-contact@unimelb.edu.au
www.mup.com.au

First published 2023
Text © Todung Mulya Lubis, 2023
Design and typography © Melbourne University Publishing Limited, 2023

This book is copyright. Apart from any use permitted under the *Copyright Act 1968* and subsequent amendments, no part may be reproduced, stored in a retrieval system or transmitted by any means or process whatsoever without the prior written permission of the publishers.

Every attempt has been made to locate the copyright holders for material quoted in this book. Any person or organisation that may have been overlooked or misattributed may contact the publisher.

Typeset by J & M Typesetting
Cover design by Peter Long
Cover image: The ruins of what was once the neighbourhood of Pasar Ikan in Jakarta, Indonesia, 2016.
© Oscar Espinosa / Getty Images

Printed in Australia by McPherson's Printing Group

Asia Law and Society Series Editor: Jeremy Kingsley

 A catalogue record for this book is available from the National Library of Australia

9780522879643 (paperback)
9780522879650 (ebook)

In memory of Muhammad Hatta and Pramoedya Ananta Toer
For my family, Cici, Oriza, Tondi, Yurika, Azzira, Aeera and Norge

Contents

Tables and figures	viii
Foreword by Tim Lindsey	ix
Preface	xv
1 Political corruption in Indonesia	1
2 Historical perspective	37
3 KPK: a superbody?	74
4 State capture corruption	110
5 Political corruption cases and criminalisation	132
6 Conclusion	163
Notes	174
References	204
Index	232

Tables and figures

Table 1: Corruption by type of case, 2004–18   10
Table 2: Corruption cases handled by the Attorney General's Office and state funds recovered   12
Table 3: Corruption cases handled by the Supreme Court (Cassation)   13
Table 4: Ten most corrupt world leaders in recent history   112
Figure 1: Political dynasty of Ratu Atut Chosiyah (Banten Province)   114

Foreword

Todung Mulya Lubis has dedicated his life and career to the realisation of the rule of law (*negara hukum*) in Indonesia. One of Indonesia's most eminent and respected lawyers, he is recognised there and abroad for his resolute commitment to human rights, social justice and the fight against corruption. Beginning his career in the highly restrictive environment of Soeharto's 'New Order' regime, Mulya committed himself to defending citizens from state oppression. Since the fall of Soeharto in 1998 after thirty-two years of oppressive rule, Mulya has worked to promote reforms to deliver the rule of law as promised by Indonesian's Constitution, now amended to reflect long-repressed aspirations for liberal democracy. He has also continued to fight for the rights of the marginalised and has become a leading campaigner against the death penalty.

Mulya was born in the small village of Muara Botung, North Sumatra, in 1949 and in 1969 enrolled in the Faculty of Law at the prestigious University of Indonesia. After graduating in 1974, he was offered a scholarship to pursue a Master of Laws at the University of California, Berkeley, which he did from 1977 to 1978.

At the University of Indonesia, Mulya was a prominent student activist, leading demonstrations against the New Order, protesting undemocratic elections and systemic corruption – in particular, the misuse of state funds for the construction of Soeharto's wife's vanity project, the Beautiful Indonesia in Miniature Park (*Taman Mini Indonesia Indah*). In 1974, he organised a major anti-regime protest that led to the cancellation of the licences of several media publications and the detention of a number of activists. As a result of his activism, he too was detained and interrogated by the military, and twice had his passport confiscated to prevent him from speaking out overseas against the New Order.

While still at the University of Indonesia, Mulya also began volunteering at the new Indonesian Legal Aid Foundation (LBH), one of the few non-governmental organisations willing to openly oppose President Soeharto and the military regime that supported him. At LBH, he worked under, and then alongside, Adnan Buyung Nasution, the charismatic founder of the organisation. His time at LBH was to prove instrumental. It was here that Mulya's activism grew into a commitment to the rule of law and the pursuit of justice.

Mulya worked with LBH for eighteen years, travelling across Indonesia defending the rights of the poor and marginalised, regardless of their ethnicity, faith or gender. He defended labourers who had been unfairly laid off, poor farmers and urban residents who had been evicted from their land, political prisoners, and East Timorese and Acehnese activists, regarded as subversive separatists by the Soeharto regime.

While at LBH, Mulya helped develop the concept of 'structural legal aid', which recognises that, to be effective, legal aid must also address the root causes of human rights violations and work to address the structural causes of inequality in society. He also founded LBH's Human Rights Department and began the tradition of publishing an annual Human Rights Report in 1979, initiatives that became hallmarks of the LBH approach. Mulya went on to serve as director of the Jakarta Legal Aid Foundation from 1980 to 1983.

For his defence of social justice and human rights, Mulya often received intimidating messages and phone calls, as well as abuse and threats of violence—even death threats. His work with LBH also provoked the ire of the Soeharto government, and he was eventually banned from speaking at public events, writing and teaching.

As a form of political exile, he was therefore offered another scholarship in 1987 to study in the United States. There he undertook a second Master of Laws at Harvard Law School, focusing on international human rights, before returning to the University of California, Berkeley, where he completed his PhD in 1990. His doctoral dissertation, 'In Search of Human Rights: Legal-Political Dilemmas of the New Order 1966-1990', proved to be a major and influential text. It was the first systematic scholarly study of human rights in Soeharto's Indonesia and played an important role in fashioning democratic thinking about human rights and the rule of law in Indonesia.

Since the collapse of the New Order regime in 1998, Mulya has continued to make vital contributions to the process of democratic reform, including by supporting public participation in policy formation and implementation. In that same year, he was, for example, one of the founders of the influential and highly regarded human rights NGO, the Commission for the Disappeared and Victims of Violence (KontraS). Today, Mulya maintains a strong belief in the crucial role of civil society in deepening reform and promoting transparency and accountability in the justice sector.

For Mulya, the root causes of corruption are the same as those that lead to abuse of human rights. He was therefore also instrumental in guiding the early years of important anti-corruption organisations Transparency International Indonesia and Indonesia Corruption Watch, coming to believe that corruption and the weakness of rule of law are intertwined problems, as he shows so clearly in this book.

Mulya has also served as the Chair of the Indonesian International Crisis Group (ICG), a member of the board of trustees for the Tifa Foundation (Open Society Foundation), and a member of the board of trustees of the Center for Electoral Reform (CETRO).

Although Indonesian governments have often been annoyed, and even threatened, by Mulya's determination, outspokenness and independence, some have come to respect him for these same qualities. In 1999, for example, Mulya was appointed as the Deputy Head of the Elections Supervisory Committee for Indonesia's first democratic elections after the fall of Soeharto. The reforms instituted by the Committee set the essential foundations for subsequent elections in the country, which is now recognised for having among the most free and fair elections in the region.

In 1999, Mulya was also selected as a member of the Commission for the Investigation of Human Rights Violations in East Timor, and visited the newly independent country to document abuses by the Indonesian military. More recently, he was appointed by the government to selection committees for the leadership of the Corruption Eradication Commission (KPK), senior justices of the Constitutional Court, and members of the Witness and Victims Protection Agency (LPSK). In 2018, he became ambassador to Norway and Iceland.

Mulya is a founder and senior partner of Lubis, Santosa and Maramis Law Offices, a corporate law firm, but has also been lead counsel in a number of important human rights cases, often on a pro-bono basis. In one of his most prominent cases, Mulya defended *Time* magazine in a defamation case brought by Soeharto. The former president sought $US27 billion in compensation because of a 1999 story alleging that he and his family had amassed US$73 billion during his time in power. Underpinning Mulya's defence of *Time* was a sense of obligation to defend the hard-won (and then very new) freedom of the press. Following a ten-year struggle, the Supreme Court ruled that *Time*'s reporting was in the public interest, and that reporting such findings was the job of the press. This was an important moment in the long struggle to build the rule of law in Indonesia.

In recent years, Mulya's name has become synonymous with the struggle against the death penalty in Indonesia. Mulya acted for two members of the Bali Nine, a group of Australian drug traffickers arrested in Denpasar airport in 2005, who had been sentenced to death. Despite a deep personal opposition to narcotics, he took the cases of Andrew Chan and Myuran Sukumaran because of a belief that the death penalty contravenes the right to life, guaranteed by the Indonesian Constitution.

As was widely reported, Mulya's efforts over almost a decade to save the Bali Nine members were ultimately unsuccessful. Following the execution by firing squad of Chan and Sukumaran in April 2015, he was devastated. With emotion running high, he tweeted: 'I failed. I lost.' He felt that he been able to do little more than 'delay defeat', the title he later gave to a fictionalised account of his experiences in this case.

But Mulya's struggle, and that of the Indonesian and Australian legal teams that worked with him, was not futile. They attracted global attention and reinvigorated the anti-death penalty movement in Indonesia. In fact, Mulya's eloquent and level-headed defence of human rights made a major contribution to shifting the debate in Indonesia, creating space for an alternative vision of the Indonesian legal system where the death penalty no longer has a central place. At the time of writing, the national legislature was even considering a proposal to amend the Criminal Procedure Code to ensure that death row inmates who demonstrate good behaviour for ten years can receive commutation of their sentence to a term of imprisonment.

Mulya is a poet and a prolific writer, and his main theme has been the ongoing struggle to implement the rule of law in Indonesia. He is widely respected for his critical analysis of the persistent challenges facing the justice sector as it struggles to reform itself to meet the needs of the aspirational democracy that began to emerge after Soeharto resigned in 1998.

As he points out, despite greater attention to human rights and the establishment of important legal institutions, such as the Constitutional Court, the Corruption Eradication Commission and the Judicial Commission, recent years have seen stagnation in reform, and even democratic regression. Mulya has maintained an acute focus on a series of core problems that he sees as causing this backsliding. They include persistent and deep-rooted corruption, particularly in the judiciary, the failure of reform in most law enforcement institutions, particularly the police and prosecution service, and overlapping and conflicting laws and regulations. These are all themes Mulya explores in detail in this book, which builds on lectures he delivered at his alma mater, the University of Indonesia.

He teaches at several other universities too, and in 2014 was made an Honorary Professor of Law by the University of Melbourne in recognition of his work on advancing the rule of law.

Todung Mulya Lubis has spent his career working to advance and secure reforms to the troubled Indonesian legal system for the benefit of all Indonesian citizens, often at great risk to himself. This book is one result of that long struggle.

Tim Lindsey
Melbourne
November 2022

Preface

Reformasi in 1998 opened many doors for social activism in Indonesia, and as one of its activists I became obsessed with the issue of corruption. My background as lawyer has dictated my instinct that there have been millions of irregularities, unlawful acts and abuses of power in robbing the wealth of the nation, illegally enriching power holders, businessmen and their cronies. The insane display of wealth in cities throughout Indonesia has angered the people, leading to a widespread anti-corruption movement against Korupsi, Kolusi and Nepotisme (KKN). These three social ills, namely corruption, collusion and nepotism, must be cured, if necessary by confiscating their ill-gotten wealth and sending the 'corrupts' to prison.

Anti-corruption organisations, such as Masyarakat Transparansi Indonesia (MTI), Indonesian Corruption Watch (ICW) and Transparency International-Indonesia (TI-I), were established mostly by civil society. At the same time, the need to set up a special agency to eradicate corruption is widely and openly discussed by various groups, intellectuals, academics, politicians, lawyers and social activists. The police and prosecutors who, by law, are in charge of corruption eradication were perceived as part of the problem because of the culture of corruption within their own organisations. If Indonesia is serious about fighting corruption, the task must be assigned to a new agency with all necessary authority to investigate, prosecute and adjudicate the alleged corruption. The establishment of Komisi Pemberantasan Korupsi (KPK) and Pengadilan Tindak Pidana Korupsi (Pengadilan Tipikor) must be seen as a logical outcome of the anger of the people, to which the political elite (executive, legislature and judiciary) have responded positively.

As a lawyer and activist, I was in the middle of efforts to combat corruption. On one hand I was involved in leading ICW and TI-I as, respectively, head of the ICW Ethical Board and Chair of TI-I. I was not part of the leadership in KPK, but I regarded myself as 'outside counsel' of KPK, given the fact that KPK summoned me many times to exchange ideas or to advise them about particular legal problems. In addition, the government also commissioned me to be involved in selecting the leadership of KPK as well as mediating the conflict between KPK and the police. In the eyes of many people, I have been perceived as too close to KPK—as '*orang dalam KPK*' (KPK insider).

It is not an overstatement to say that my engagement with corruption eradication has fascinated me more and more. It always reminded me of my late father, who taught me to play by the rules all the time, not to steal even one single penny. I was taught to be grateful every day for what I have. I feel an adrenaline rush every day when there is an outbreak of corruption cases. I gained an abundance of information and knowledge about corruption and corruption eradication, which inspired me to write a book on political corruption because I saw political corruption as the mother of all corruption. I wanted people to understand corruption and its complexities from an interdisciplinary perspective, and I thought my book would open their eyes to endemic, systemic and widespread corruption. Furthermore, I wanted to teach a course on the 'sociology of corruption', which I already started at Gajah Mada University.

In 2013 I joined Harvard Kennedy School as a visiting fellow with the intention of doing my research and writing a book on political corruption in Indonesia. I finished writing the first chapter, but in the middle of my research I was called home to assist the campaign team of Joko Widodo, who at that time was running for

President. Joko Widodo, whom I was acquainted with when he was mayor of Solo, had a good reputation as a no-nonsense public official, and I thought he would have accepted the torch to fight corruption if he was elected President. I agreed to return to Indonesia with one promise: that I will be back at Harvard Kennedy School to continue my research. As it turned out, I was stuck in Jakarta. And the book idea was abandoned. I no longer had time to do my research.

In 2018 I was appointed Ambassador of Indonesia to the Kingdom of Norway and the Republic of Iceland. Frankly, I had no thought of continuing to write a book owing to my super-busy schedule in my new career. But when the COVID-19 pandemic began in March 2020, most people had to work from home, and suddenly I found that I had a lot of time again. So I revived my book project and started writing in my spare time. Eventually I managed with great difficulty to finish writing my book on political corruption in Indonesia. I am not completely satisfied with my writing because I want to add more and more, but at the same time I know that no one will be satisfied with one's writing because of constant changes in one's surroundings. I decided to send the manuscript to a publisher and let the readers read and react. The book will speak for itself.

Many people influenced my thinking about corruption and corruption eradication, and I would like to express my sincere appreciation and indebtedness to them: Adnan Buyung Nasution, Erry Riyana Hardjapamekas, Arief Soerowidjoyo, Teten Masduki, Natalia Soebagyo, H.S. Dillon, Ismid Hadad, Daniel Dhakidae, Mardjono Reksodipuro, Rizal Malik, Mas Achmad Santosa, Bambang Widjoyanto, Abraham Samad, Busro Muqqodas, Bambang Harimurty, Alexander Lay, Emmy Hafid, Zaenal Arifin Mochtar, Saldi Isra, Denny Indrayana, Laode Syarif, Lelyana Santosa, Smita Notosusanto, Erwin Natosmal Omar and Rachman Tolleng. Young anti-corruption activists from ICW and TI-I have given me their enthusiasm, which swept away my occasional despair. Numerous people from the academic community and media outlets kept reminding me that the fight against corruption must be continued.

Special thanks go to my good friend Tim Lindsey for his constant encouragement and who despite his busy schedule still found time to read and edit my manuscript to make it more systematic and readable. His valuable comments make the book sharper in the historical and analytical context. Another good friend is David Dapice, who when I was at Harvard Kennedy School gave me an economic perspective on corruption. In addition Gustav Papanek, who spent a lot time in Indonesia and knows about the culture and economics of corruption, also took time to read my first chapter and offered some suggestions.

During the writing of this book I have been generously assisted by my secretary in Jakarta, Ingrid Juliana, who compiled materials that I needed to read. In Oslo, my personal assistant, Agung Sudrajat, has been instrumental in organising my time and writing. He also assisted me in doing additional research, including compiling the book's tables. One other name that I should mention here is Julie Willie, who helped me with the initial editing of my manuscript. My sincere thanks to all for your assistance.

Final editing of this book has been done by Cathryn Game, who in her meticulous way worked word by word and came up with questions and suggestions. Perhaps it has been hard for Cathryn because I might have written the book in Indonesian-language style. But after reading the final edited version of the book I found it much more readable. My appreciation and thanks go to Cathryn. In addition I extend my appreciation to Nathan Hollier, publisher at Melbourne University Publishing, and legal scholar Jeremy Kingsley of Swinburne Law School, who have responded positively upon reading my manuscript and included it in MUP's Asia Law and Society Series.

My acknowledgements would not be complete if I did not mention my wife Damiyati and daughter Oriza, who have been watching and supporting my work night and day. They know that writing a book on political corruption is my obsession, and they let me spend long hours working on it almost every night. Long-distance support also came from my small family in Jakarta: Tondi, Yurika, Azzira Aeera and Norge. I thank you and love you all.

Todung Mulya Lubis
Oslo, December 2022

Chapter 1

Political corruption in Indonesia

Pak, I am so afraid that you intend to corrupt.
　　　　　　　　　　　Pramoedya Ananta Toer, *Korupsi*

Toward Corruption-Free Indonesia.
　　　Komisi Pemberantasan Korupsi, *Annual Report 2011*

Pramoedya Ananta Toer, a celebrated Indonesian author, published a novel titled *Korupsi* (Corruption) in 1954. Although not his best novel, *Korupsi* caught my attention. It was published less than ten years after the fierce struggle for Indonesian independence.[1] The novel explores the tensions within a family, between husband, wife and children. Bakir, the husband and father—a kind and caring family man—is the head of a governmental agency in Jakarta. He is touted as a man of integrity. Sadly, his meagre governmental salary is far from sufficient. He is forced to live in poverty, despite his government position. Bakir had worked in this job for more than ten years with little or no improvement in his financial condition. He grows tired of his inability to create a good life for his family, including providing his children with a good education. Meanwhile, his friends become rich and affluent. Bakir decides to upgrade the quality of life of himself and his family. He ultimately determines that he must acquire more money and, if necessary, unscrupulously use his power to do so. The entire family dreams of having a better life. Bakir's wife, however, wants nothing to do with affluence if it comes at the expense of his integrity and the law. Integrity is a principle she is not ready to compromise. For this reason, she cries and says, 'Pak, I am so afraid that you intend to corrupt.'

As early as 1954, Pramoedya Ananta Toer accurately predicted that the young Indonesian nation would be damaged by widespread corruption. Toer astutely discerned the stark beginnings of a weakening value system, undermining what the founders had fought for when they declared independence. The desire to create a clean and healthy government with social justice for all is an Indonesian dream. This dream now seems to be a delusion amid a growing landscape of corruption. In fact, corruption is systemic and endemic in Indonesia.

Democracy returned to Indonesia after the end of the thirty-two-year authoritarian rule of Soeharto's government, but democracy has not yet succeeded in eliminating corruption, collusion and nepotism (*korupsi, kolusi dan nepotisme* or KKN). According to the Corruption Perceptions Index (CPI) published by Transparency International, a global coalition against corruption, Indonesia's score has consistently been 30 (out of 100)[2] or higher for the last twenty years; a score that has steadily been increasing from 2012 and 2019, only with the latest development in 2020, when it fell back to 37 after reaching 40 in 2019. Looking at South-East Asia more broadly, Indonesia has a slightly better score than Myanmar, Cambodia and Laos, but sits far below Singapore, Malaysia and even Thailand.[3]

Although statistics obtained for the period 2004–20 indicate that the rank has improved each year, corruption in Indonesia has not diminished at all. Rather, it has inflated or spread, and is becoming more decentralised. There are no longer any provinces or regencies that are free of corruption.[4] Every year, the Indonesian Corruption Eradication Commission (Komisi Pemberantasan Korupsi; KPK) publishes an annual report. In its Annual Report for 2012, KPK announced its mission: 'Toward Corruption-Free Indonesia',[5] reflecting the bold campaign theme of various anti-corruption agencies: a zero-tolerance policy against corruption. In

2018, the KPK Annual Report made it clear that this mission—which it abandoned in 2012[6]—had not been achieved. In fact, the report provided a complete picture of how widespread corruption had become throughout the country. In fact, the KPK Annual Report of 2018 recorded 330 corruption cases prosecuted directly by KPK that year involving national and regional parliamentarians, ministers, governors, mayors, regents, commissioners of several state auxiliary agencies, or directors of state-owned enterprises, among others.[7]

Corruption has long been a part of human history, the dark human vice that tempts individuals in society to live in luxury, join the affluent and aristocratic, and break the chains of poverty. Under Soeharto's authoritarian government, corruption seemed to be the rule, not the exception.[8] For him, maintaining corruption from the top down was the essence of his brutal strategy to foster loyalty and unity within his government, the New Order (*Orde Baru*). Various shady businesses and social schemes were set up to exploit loopholes within the law, but even so demonstrated blatant non-compliance with the laws by which all were formally bound.[9] At this time, corruption was centralised within the government and Soeharto's extended family became key players in bridging, structuring and restructuring corrupt business ventures. Thus, businessmen, whether local, national or foreign, came to consider corruption as a vital component of their business plans.[10]

In 1998, Indonesia was in the midst of profound economic strife due to the Asian Financial Crisis that began the previous year. The economy was paralysed and the Indonesian currency, the rupiah, had dropped to its historically lowest level, approximately Rp 16 000 to the US dollar. Banks and conglomerates, which served as Indonesia's economic backbone, collapsed, and capital flight brought Indonesia to a state of political and economic panic,[11] called *Krisis Moneter* (monetary crisis) or *Krismon*. The government and political elite inevitably disintegrated, and many quickly found political shelters to distance themselves from the disgraced Soeharto. Ironically, some emerged as vocal critics of Soeharto. Even one of his closest protégés, Harmoko, who at that time was the Speaker of the Dewan Perwakilan Rakyat (DPR, or People's Representative Assembly), the national legislature, straightforwardly asked Soeharto to resign the presidency. Several ministers in charge of economic development also tendered their resignations, leaving Soeharto no choice but to step down.

Outside the presidential palace, massive student-led demonstrations engulfed Jakarta and other major cities. They demanded not only Soeharto's resignation but also the national eradication of KKN (which in fact seemed to be the principal unifying factor that bound the demonstrators together). Thereafter, the fight against corruption, collusion and nepotism has been politically adopted by successive governments as a route to legitimacy and a means to reconcile the nation after a very costly and bloody conflict had torn it apart.

The next president, Habibie (1998–99), despite being a member of Soeharto's inner circle and his close confidante, launched bold new policies that were completely different from his predecessor's. He reintroduced freedom of the press by revoking the law that mandated a licence for all media publications.[12] He allowed new political parties to be set up and proposed a draft bill, the Eradication of Corruption Act, to be used as a basis to fight endemic corruption. Credit is often given to Habibie for his resolute determination to lay the foundations for a new Indonesia that could be more democratic and freer from corruption.[13] Despite the short period of his incumbency as president, Habibie did far more than was ever expected of a once-obedient crony of Soeharto.[14]

The political point of no return had now been reached. No one was contemplating a return to authoritarian government, although that was certainly possible under the 1945 Constitution.[15] Instead, amendments to the 1945 Constitution were undertaken annually between 1999 and 2002. The Reformasi (Reform) movement emerged, led by students, workers and intellectuals, who took initiatives intended to design a new political architecture for Indonesia that would uphold democracy, the rule of law, human rights and social justice. Even though many wanted to maintain the original

1945 Constitution, the amendments made succeeded in completely reinventing it. Only a few basic provisions were retained from the original text. Where the original 1945 Constitution was known for its short and simple form, the amended 'new' Constitution is much more comprehensive, clear and in alignment with universal principles of democracy, the rule of law, human rights and social justice.[16] For instance, the term of the President is now limited to two terms of five years (Art. 7), thereby preventing anyone from holding office for life. Additionally, in order to strengthen judicial checks and balances, several 'state auxiliary agencies' were introduced: the Constitutional Court (Art. 24c), the Judicial Commission (Art. 24B), the Regional People's Representative Assembly (Ch. VIIA) and others. Many more of these 'state auxiliary agencies' were then set up by new legislation.

One such agency is the Komisi Pemberantasan Korupsi (KPK), established on 27 December 2002 by virtue of Law No. 30 of 2002, on the Commission for the Eradication of Criminal Acts of Corruption.[17] Modelled on the Independent Commission Against Corruption (ICAC) in Hong Kong, the KPK was initially an *ad hoc* institution intended to confront systemic and endemic corruption.[18] Legally, the task of eradicating corruption before the establishment of the KPK had always fallen within the domain of the Attorney General's Office in cooperation with the police. However, instead of fighting widespread corruption, both the Attorney General's Office and the police copiously engage in corrupt practices. As a result, the Attorney General's Office and the police have long been considered obstacles to social justice and human rights, and major contributors to the problem of corruption itself, rather than part of any eradication effort. They protected corrupt officials and worked with them to achieve their corrupt purposes, enriching themselves in the process. Thus the establishment of the KPK was primarily a response to the dissatisfaction of the *rakyat* (the people, excluding the ruling elites) with the inadequate performance combating corruption of the Attorney General's Office and police, which reflected the deep distrust they have towards those institutions.

Anti-corruption legislation was enacted as early as 1999, when Law No. 31 of 1999 on the Eradication of Criminal Acts of Corruption (Law No. 31 of 1999) was promulgated.[19] This replaced Law No. 3 of 1971 on the Eradication of Criminal Acts of Corruption (Law No. 3 of 1971). Law No. 31 of 1999 is a far more complete and comprehensive law both in scope and in substance, as it provides a broader definition of 'corruption' and encompasses a wide range of different types of systemic corruption. Law No. 31 of 1999 was later amended by Law No. 28 of 2001, making the definition of corruption even broader, extending its reach to a greater number of acts, including—but not limited to—bribery, gratification, extortion, conflict of interest, and other illicit enrichments.[20] Moreover, the scope of the law is no longer limited only to public officials but also to non-public officials, such as politicians, businessmen and social activists. Indonesia's anti-corruption legislation became the most comprehensive in its history, reflecting Indonesia's signature (2003) and ratification (2006) of the United Nations Convention against Corruption (UNCAC).[21] Since corruption is closely linked to money-laundering, Law No. 8 of 2010 on the Eradication of Acts of Money Laundering was also promulgated, replacing previously ineffectual laws on money-laundering, namely Law No. 15 of 2002 and Law No. 25 of 2003.[22]

In implementing these comprehensive laws, the government also issued a number of Presidential Decrees, Presidential Determinations and Presidential Instructions (Perpres, Penpres and Inpres). Inpres No. 1 of 2013 is the most recent of these; it details actions that must be taken by governmental agencies, state auxiliary agencies and local governments to combat corruption. Its appendix lists 265 preventive and eradication actions that must be implemented by all governmental agencies, state auxiliary agencies and local governments.[23] In 2018, Presidential Decree No. 54 of 2018 was promulgated, setting out a National Strategy for Corruption Prevention. Although it focuses on prevention, it does not preclude the investigation, prosecution and trying of corruption cases.

Once established, the KPK became the *conditio sine qua non* of Indonesian social justice. The public was impressed by the success stories of the Independent Commission Against Corruption (ICAC) in Hong Kong, and as they lost all confidence in the Attorney General's Office and police, a powerful movement calling for the establishment of a similar agency in Indonesia emerged. Hence the Indonesian government had no choice but to swiftly establish a new institution to combat corruption. The KPK was born out of the public's pressing demands, and it is therefore appropriate to note that the KPK is a key outcome of Reformasi.

The KPK is an independent institution, which is required by law to execute its duties and authority free from interference from any power or agency. In combating corruption, the KPK has the functions of coordinating, supervising, investigating, prosecuting and monitoring suspicious financial activity. Law No. 30 of 2002, under which the KPK was born, granted significant power to the KPK to eradicate corruption through a variety of methods, including (non-exhaustively) investigating, prosecuting, freezing bank accounts, wire-tapping, imposing travel bans and detaining suspects.[24] No other law enforcement agency in Indonesia's history has ever possessed authority akin to that of the KPK, which explains the common use of the term 'superbody' as a descriptor of it (as described in chapter 3).

Both the Attorney General's Office and police still hold anti-corruption powers as their authority was never fully dismantled. However, cases where the amount at stake exceeds Rp 1 000 000 000, or in cases where there is significant public interest, or that may involve law enforcement officers (judges, prosecutors, police officers and advocates), may by law be taken over by the KPK at its own discretion (although in practice this has sometimes been difficult).[25] The KPK decides what to take on or not, on the basis of political importance and the availability of its own resources, such as the readiness of its investigators and prosecutors.[26] Therefore its purpose is not to undermine the Attorney General's Office nor the police but to assist and complement them; nevertheless, the KPK often finds itself in direct conflict with these agencies, seeing that both are plagued with systemic corruption, as will be explained below.

Legally, Indonesia has all necessary laws and regulations required to combat corruption. In fact, it has perhaps the most comprehensive anti-corruption laws in South-East Asia. Indonesia's failure to properly implement this legislation shows a lack of determination and coordination between various agencies in managing the various resources to devise the right strategy and action plan. In this regard, Indonesia suffers from an imbalance between law and enforcement action.

From an institutional point of view, Indonesia has almost every type of institution or agency designed to combat corruption. In addition to the Attorney General's Office, the police and the KPK, there is, for example, the Pusat Pelaporan dan Analisis Transaksi Keuangan (PPATK, or the Financial Transaction Reports and Analysis Center), which deals mainly with anti-money-laundering activities.[27] Another important agency is the Komisi Yudisial (KY or Judicial Commission), which among other things is tasked with overseeing judges to identify judicial corruption.[28] A third is the Lembaga Perlindungan Saksi dan Korban (LPSK or Witness and Victim Protection Agency), which supports whistleblowers and justice collaborators.[29] These state auxiliary agencies are legally independent institutions and are required to be free from interference from any powers, whether state or non-state. Legally, they are accountable only to the people through the DPR by way of submitting annual reports, summarising their programs and activities.

There are two other important state anti-corruption institutions, namely, Badan Pemeriksa Keuangan (BPK, or the Financial Audit Body)[30] and Badan Pemeriksa Keuangan Pemerintah (BPKP, or the Financial and Development Audit Body).[31] The first agency audits all governmental institutions, central and regional, as well as state auxiliary agencies, and in this respect the audit reports may uncover unaccounted amounts of money, or manipulated and corrupted accounting. These reports are then submitted to parliament and can be used by the other anti-corruption agencies to launch investigations. The second agency also does financial auditing, but is an instrument under the auspices of the government and therefore not considered a fully independent agency. However, its findings have, in many cases, also been used by anti-corruption agencies to commence investigations.

Outside the government, the existence of a vibrant civil society and free press strengthened the anti-corruption movement.[32] This type of support is an unprecedented phenomenon for Indonesia, considering that before Reformasi, civil society and the press were not allowed to participate in public political debate. Reformasi gave Indonesia a golden opportunity to work out new political strategies and courses of action to fight corruption, to translate into action what has been stipulated in anti-corruption legislation. Combating corruption has been a long sought-after activity. Even since the early years of independence, the Indonesian government established various governmental programs and bodies for this purpose,[33] but none were successful because there was never strong political commitment to eradicate corruption. They were launched as populist tools, often designed to please critics and students, who would occasionally engage in demonstrations, demanding the government take firmer action against corrupt officials and businessmen.

From around 2003, when news of corruption was published by the media and discussed openly, the government began to see widespread corruption as a serious crime. The government's newfound seriousness was most clearly demonstrated by the establishment of the KPK. Between the years 2004 and 2018, the KPK handled approximately 887 corruption cases concerned with the improper procurement of goods and services, corrupt licensing, bribery, money-laundering, budget abuses and obstruction of justice, as detailed in table 1.[34]

The number of cases, 887, is a relatively small total on a nationwide scale. The total number of corruption cases nationally is quite high if all prosecutions and investigations conducted by both the Attorney General's Office and police are included. Most corruption cases handled by the Attorney General's Office and the police are

Table 1: Corruption by type of case, 2004–18

Cases/Year	2004	2005	2006	2007	2008	2009	2010	2011	2012	2013	2014	2015	2016	2017	2018	SUM
Public procurement of goods and services	2	12	8	14	18	16	16	10	8	9	15	14	14	17	17	188
Issuance of permits or licences	0	0	5	1	3	1	0	0	0	3	5	1	1	2	1	23
Bribery	0	7	2	4	13	12	19	25	34	50	20	38	79	93	168	564
Illegal levies	0	0	7	2	3	0	0	0	0	1	6	1	1	0	4	25
Misuse of public budget	0	0	5	3	10	8	5	4	3	0	4	2	1	1	0	46
Money-laundering	0	0	0	0	0	0	0	0	2	7	5	1	3	8	6	31
Obstructing justice	0	0	0	0	0	0	0	0	2	0	3	0	0	2	3	10
Sum	2	19	27	47	37	37	40	39	48	70	58	57	99	121	199	887

Source: Komisi Pemberantasan Korupsi [Anti-Corruption Clearing House], web.kpk.go.id/id/publikasi-data/statistik/penindakan-2

typically petty corruption. Generally, it is the KPK that pursues major corruption charges, and the number it takes on is limited by its resources. The numbers are therefore disappointing compared to other countries with better-resourced anti-corruption watchdogs. In China, for instance, more than 1.1 million corruption cases were handled between 1980 and 2006, 30 000 of which involved senior officials, including roughly sixty high-ranking officials such as deputy ministers.[35]

Even so, the fact that the KPK prosecuted 887 corruption cases over a fourteen-year period is quite an achievement for Indonesia—unprecedented in its history, in fact. Many people lauded the establishment of the KPK in 2003, although there were some who were sceptical and felt only guarded optimism. However, it proved to be a success as it investigated cases considered unwinnable in the past. Gradually, the Indonesian people began to appreciate it and often expressed genuine support for its activities. For instance, when the KPK named Aulia Pohan, brother-in-law to then incumbent President Susilo Bambang Yudhoyono, as a suspect and subsequently prosecuted him, many people realised that it was an entirely new class of anti-corruption agency, one not easily intimidated by power.[36] The prosecution of the former Governor of the Bank of Indonesia, Burhanuddin Abdullah, was an example of yet another high-ranking official successfully pursued by the KPK for alleged financial corruption, despite huge political pressure to let him go.[37] Importantly, a former Chief Justice of the Constitutional Court, Speaker of the DPR and a Speaker of the Regional Representative Council (DPD) have now also been convicted of corruption.[38] There are now also several ministers from the cabinets of both Presidents Susilo Bambang Yudhoyono and Joko Widodo who have also been successfully prosecuted by the KPK.

Arguably, it is not institutions that are corrupt, but those engaged in corruption are often the very people responsible for managing the institutions or leading their operations. Indeed, 887 people tried and sentenced on corruption charges held office within national institutions, including ministers, members of the DPR, governors, mayors, regents, commissioners and directors of state-owned enterprises. (It is possible that in some corruption cases, there is more than one defendant so the actual number may be higher.) The number is relatively small in a nation of 270 million, but they stand as compelling evidence that the Indonesian government is serious about fighting corruption. This is a dramatic improvement from the thirty-two-year period of Soeharto's regime, during which not one single high-ranking official was ever brought to justice for corrupt practices.[39]

Table 2 provides the number of corruption cases handled between 2004 and 2018 by the Attorney General's Office, which both investigates and prosecutes corruption offences. The majority of cases concerned are only petty, small- or medium-sized corruption.

Table 2: Corruption cases handled by the Attorney General's Office and state funds recovered

No.	Year	Examination (number of cases)	Prosecution (number of cases)	State funds recovered (Indonesian rupiah)
1	2004	523	460	12.824.741.850.645,00
2	2005	546	542	
3	2006	588	515	
4	2007	636	512	
5	2008	850	849	
6	2009	1530	1824	
7	2010	2315	1715	No data
8	2011	1491	1169	198.210.963.791,00
9	2012	1401	1511	302.609.167.229,00
10	2013	1653	2023	403.102.000.215,00
11	2014	1537	2225	390.526.490.570,00
12	2015	1785	2446	642.612.382.187,00
13	2016	1527	2434	331.048.686.281,07
			Total	15.092.851.540.918,07

Source: 2004–09 Attorney General's Annual Report 2011; Year 2010 Attorney General's Annual Report 2012, Attorney General's Annual Report 2012–16. (Attorney General's Annual Reports from 2017 until 2020 could not be accessed)

The police investigated corruption cases before the KPK's establishment, and even now the police still undertake corruption investigations. However, the data is not well organised and corruption cases are often mixed with non-corruption cases, making it difficult to identify relevant cases with confidence. The same problem arises when researching data on corruption cases examined and decided by the Supreme Court. This is because corruption charges are considered 'special crime' (*pidana khusus*), a category that also includes banking and drug cases. However, and despite the incomplete data available, table 3 gives at least an approximation of the number of corruption cases handled by the Supreme Court between 2004 and 2019.

Table 3: Corruption cases handled by the Supreme Court (Cassation)

No.	Year	Cassation
1	2004	No data
2	2005	No data
3	2006	499 cases
4	2007	323 cases
5	2008	No data
6	2009	No data
7	2010	No data
8	2011	963 cases
9	2012	No data
10	2013	821 cases
11	2014	689 cases
12	2015	811 cases
13	2016	611 cases
14	2017	546 cases
15	2018	662 cases
16	2019	655 cases

Source: Supreme Court Annual Reports. For 2004 and 2005, there is no data available. For 2008–10 and 2012, data could not be retrieved owing to the Supreme Court inclusion of corruption in special crime cases together with drug-related crimes and crimes by minors

What is corruption?

There is an array of definitions of corruption. Scholars and practitioners often come up with definitions that reflect their own disciplines and backgrounds. There are those based on legal principles, as stipulated in laws and regulations. There are also more popular definitions, which approach corruption from a public interest perspective by evaluating the act as a matter of public opinion. Conversely, there are definitions that align with economic considerations affecting agency relationships.[40] Additionally, there are anthropological definitions, which see corruption as an anthropological and cultural event or deviation.[41]

Rose-Ackerman, a legal theory scholar, views corruption from a political–economic perspective. She argues that corruption is an elusive phenomenon that is difficult to capture in a single crisp definition. Each definition has its own difficulty. Furthermore, Rose-Ackerman states:

> One set of definitions conceptualizes corruption as deviation from some standard, such as the public interest, legal norms, or legal norms and moral standards sanctioned by the people. The second set associates corruption with system-level attributes, such as patrimonialism (as opposed to rational legal bureaucracy), primordial notions of the public interest (as opposed to the civic notion), or systems in which bureaucrats regard public office as a private business.[42]

Rose-Ackerman adopts the first approach; that is, that corruption belongs in the moral and legal categories. The definition she uses is: 'corruption is the misuse of public office for private or political gain'.[43] This is the definition commonly used by anti-corruption organisations and institutions such as the World Bank, the Asian Development Bank (ADB) and the International Monetary Fund (IMF), albeit with slightly altered wording.[44]

Another scholar, Klitgaard, offers a more technical definition of corruption, stating: 'Corruption equals Monopoly, plus Discretion, minus Accountability', or $C = (M + D) - A$.[45] This definition has been referred to by many activists and anti-corruption organisations as an ideal working definition, although it is narrow in scope, as it is limited to corruption committed by bureaucracies or public officials. In other words, private sector corruption might not be covered by Klitgaard's definition.

The word 'corruption' does not derive expressly from the English language, as many people may presume.[46] In fact, it comes from the Latin, *corruptio*, which means moral decay, wicked behaviour or rottenness. There is no such word in original Bahasa Indonesia. If *korupsi* is now in the Indonesian Dictionary, it is undoubtedly borrowed from its English equivalent. Other Asian cultures also do not recognise the word 'corruption', perhaps because Asian cultures are more receptive to the practice of giving and receiving gifts as an expression of appreciation. Even if this practice has become warped by corruption, it does not necessarily follow that Asian values are incompatible with the values of liberal democratic societies.[47]

One classification repeatedly mentioned in the literature on corruption is the distinction between grand corruption and petty corruption. Grand corruption refers to large amounts of corruption committed by public officials, politicians and businessmen, while petty corruption is small amounts of corruption committed by low-ranking civil servants, clerks, teachers, police or drivers and so on, in order to support their basic necessities. Petty corruption involves modest sums of money.[48] The former is often described as 'corruption by greed' and the latter as 'corruption by need'.

David C. Kang, a political scientist, uses the terms 'top-down corruption' and 'bottom-up corruption', meaning:

> Top-down corruption has been best explicated by the notion of a 'predatory' state. The predatory state is one in which the state takes advantage of a dispersed and weak business sector. Political elites pursue outright expropriation; they also solicit donations from businessmen who in turn are either shaken down by the regime or who volunteer

bribes in return for favors, and employ other means as well. In contrast, bottom-up corruption occurs when social actors have the power to overwhelm the state.[49]

Heidenheimer has classified corruption using colours: black, white and grey. 'Black corruption' is corruption that the majority of people condemn and would want to see severely punished on grounds of principle. Interestingly, 'white corruption' seems to be a more tolerated version, where there is no vigorous support for punishment. This may be the type of corruption that serves as a lubricant for economic development and trade.[50] 'Grey corruption' seems to elicit mixed reactions, as some forms require punishment and others do not.[51] Undoubtedly, this is a hazy reflection of a moral ambiguity within Indonesian society, which is one that still tolerates both white and grey corruption. This explains why corruption still exists and might perhaps be with us forever.

There is yet another term for corruption that is more sophisticated and morally complex than any other forms; that is, 'state capture corruption'. State capture corruption is the most highly sophisticated corruption as it occurs only when the entire state is hijacked and dominated by corrupt individuals. Legvold, who writes about corruption in the post-Soviet period, describes state capture corruption aptly as:

> ... occur[ring] when, in contrast to mere bribe-making, to secure access to a good or an exception to existing rules, interested parties exploit the malfeasance of officials to change the rules (laws, judicial rulings, or bureaucratic regulations). Rather than state officials and bureaucrats extorting business firms or ordinary individuals, powerful individuals or groups use material rewards or physical threats to reshape the state ...[52]

The United Nations Development Programme generated a more straightforward description: 'State capture: This refers to a situation where the private sector has effectively taken over certain state functions, a type of corruption generally less understood by the public or by the media. One example is when an international mining company is largely determining the contours of a country's mining policy.'[53]

The list of definitions and classifications can be added to, but most are already encompassed by the approaches just described.

Indonesia's approach to defining corruption is stipulated in Law No. 31 of 1999, as amended by Law No. 20 of 2001. Article 2 defines corruption as an unlawful act by an individual to enrich himself/herself, another person or a corporation, creating losses to the state finance or state economy.[54] The four elements of corruption that must be fulfilled to be classified as corruption are therefore: (1) an unlawful act; (2) involving an individual; (3) self-enrichment (or enrichment of another person or corporation); and (4) state financial and/or economic losses. This is a legal concept, but a more general understanding of corruption would be an abuse of power for personal gain, or misuse of public office or other forms of entrusted power for private or organisational benefit. This legal concept, as is understood in Indonesia, seems to be generally similar.

The legal element of 'abuse of power' is made clearer in Article 3 of Law No. 31 of 1999, which stipulates that abuse of power is performed by an individual in order to enrich either himself/herself, another person or a corporation, creating losses to the state finance or state economy.[55] Article 3 is arguably not all that different from 'abuse of power for private gain' or 'misuse of public office or other forms of entrusted power for private or organizational benefit'.

There are seven unlawful acts that may be linked to corruption: creating financial losses to the state, bribery, gratification, embezzlement, extortion, unfair acts, and conflicts of interest. These are generally referred to as corrupt acts and are delineated clearly in Law No. 31 of 1999, as amended. The only other crime that is not mentioned here is money-laundering, which is a relatively new form of corruption. Money-laundering is, however, regulated by other specific laws.[56]

Indonesia has also ratified the UN Convention against Corruption (UNCAC),[57] and this complements the existing anti-corruption law regime. There has never before been a comprehensive anti-corruption law regime in the entirety of Indonesian history. However, many laws—whether anti-corruption laws or other laws enacted from time to time—relate to the fight against corruption, both directly and indirectly.[58] Legally, there is no room for any individual to engage in corruption, given the laws and anti-corruption agencies in place. According to current laws, even a small token of appreciation, such as gift or souvenir, may be considered as gratification or facilitation of payment. Article 12B Law No. 31 of 1999, as amended, stipulates that any gratification for a civil servant or state employee, shall be considered as a bribe, when it has something to do with his/her position, and is contrary to his/her obligations or tasks. When the gratification amounts to Rp 10 000 000 (ten million rupiah) or more, the recipient must prove that it is not a bribe. But if the gratification is less than Rp 10 000 000, the public prosecutor must prove that it is a bribe.[59] In other words, the common cultural notion that a gift or small token of appreciation is not corruption is no longer accepted under the current anti-corruption law regime.

Chapter III of the UNCAC stipulates that corruption includes bribery (of both national public officials and foreign public officials, including officials of public international organisations), embezzlement, trading in influence, abuse of function, illicit enrichment, laundering the proceeds of crime, concealment, and obstruction of justice.[60] All states and state parties to the UNCAC are now obliged to adjust their anti-corruption law regimes to comply with the UNCAC. Those who do not have anti-corruption laws are to enact them immediately.[61]

The United Nations Development Programme describes the most common forms of corruption as bribery, embezzlement, extortion, abuse of discretion, favouritism, nepotism, clientelism, exploiting a conflict of interests, and improper political contributions.[62] There may be other forms, depending on circumstances and localities.

Types of corruption
The following types of corruption are stipulated by Indonesia's anti-corruption laws:
- causing state losses
- bribery
- gratification
- embezzlement
- extortion
- unfair act
- conflict of interest.

The UN Convention against Corruption specifies the following types of corruption:
- bribery
- embezzlement
- trading in influence
- abuse of function
- illicit enrichment
- laundering of proceeds of crime
- concealment.

The absence of political corruption
Under Indonesia's anti-corruption laws, there is no distinction between political and non-political corruption. However, political corruption has a special place within the subject of 'corruption' and is a more specific form of corruption. In the past and in many cases, the definition of corruption has been limited to simply 'petty corruption'—corruption by need—so, understandably, 'petty corruption' is already covered by the term 'corruption'. Conversely, 'grand corruption' relates very much to what is known as political corruption; that is, corruption by the holders of power such as politicians, their cronies and the ruling elite. This is more than white-collar crime. This type of corruption is not necessarily characterised by large amounts of money, but rather relates first and foremost to the controlling and perpetuation of power itself.

Historically, this is not new. With new and emerging states, the struggle against corruption itself is a political struggle about the form of the state.[63]

Defining political corruption simply as electoral corruption—that is, 'money politics' and vote-buying—is far from comprehensive.[64] Electoral corruption is only a small part of overall political corruption, although it is the most visible.[65] Detecting political corruption is more complex than merely calculating how much money is spent by each electoral candidate. Because political parties struggle to generate campaign financing, candidates are often forced to finance their own election campaigns. Only a small number of candidates have the personal wealth and resources necessary to finance their own campaigns. Instead, most candidates must solicit funds from various sources, by fund-raising, and this is how electoral corruption finds its insidious gateway.[66]

Mietzner has written on party financing in the post-Soeharto era, arguing that political corruption has become widespread and transparent. Parties that lost their state subsidies in 2005 therefore had to seek new funding sources.[67] In this respect, political parties made efforts, both legally and illegally, to finance their parties. One of the most notorious of these efforts was to increase salaries and allowances of members of the DPR by up to 82 per cent. This increase in salaries and allowances included payments for electricity, telephone, spouses, children, housing and intensive communication systems.[68] In reality, members of the DPR did receive part of the increase; however, most of it was meant to be a contribution for party fund-raising. In short, political parties, through their representatives in the DPR, compensated for losses in party subsidies by increases in salaries and allowances. This increase was not sufficient, however, to meet the demands of a party's operational expenses, and that explains why parties sought other opportunities. Here, too, is where political corruption comes into play. Mietzner states: 'To be sure, political corruption in Indonesia's Parliament had been rampant even during the period of generous public party financing between 2001 and 2005, but the subsequent reduction in legal subsidies provided an additional impetus (and, in the eyes of the parties, justification) for illicit fund-raising.'[69]

Similar practices can be found in other countries where democracy is not yet rooted in society. Yadav compares similar practices of fund-raising by political parties who abuse their controlling powers in legislative bodies:

> [I]n Tanzania, parties passed a legislative bill that legalized the practice of *takrima*, giving and receiving gifts in good faith. This was then used to justify both obtaining such gifts from businesses and giving them to voters in exchange for vote during elections ... In Romania, faced with voters and members too poor to contribute significantly to party coffers, party leaders went through the accounts of state banks, identified businesses who had borrowed from them, and then extracted donations for passing legislative bills and decrees rescheduling their debts ...[70]

Della Porta and Vannucci offer more detailed explanations about how party corruption works by controlling positions within the government as a minister, for instance. This opens the door to craft a transaction or contract in order to raise funds for the party. Della Porta and Vannucci state: 'Controlling the nominations to public bodies and the career of political actors, the parties can generalize the kickback, transforming corruption from exception into an established practice with accepted norms, at the same time guaranteeing the continuity of the system over time despite changes in the political personnel of the public administration ...'[71]

Allowing parties to raise funds through illicit fund-raising means that parties should explore every opportunity to access money, and in doing so, being near, or part of, those who wield political power is an absolute requirement. This explains why parties insist on having members in their cabinet: a seat in cabinet—political power—creates numerous opportunities for more fund-raising. Various transactions can then be entered into, using all sorts of seemingly legitimate schemes as camouflage.[72] Two cases involving the former Minister of Youth and Sports, Andi Malarangeng, and the former Minister of Agriculture, Suswono, are perfect examples of ministerial positions being used to raise funds for political parties. The Minister of Youth and Sports represented the Partai Demokrat (Democrat Party), the ruling party that led the government coalition, while the Minister of Agriculture represented Partai Keadilan Sejahtera (Prosperous Justice Party), a member of the government coalition. The Minister of Youth and Sports administered and supervised the construction of Wisma Atlet, an athletic facility in Jakabaring, Palembang, South Sumatra, while the Minister of Agriculture issued import licences for meat from Australia. Allegedly the two ministers received kickbacks or commissions from the companies that won the construction contract and import licences respectively. While each party denied receiving money from various projects and procurements granted by their ministries to their own party cadres, court proceedings and the media explicitly revealed that a significant part of the commissions, bribery and kickbacks obtained by these two ministers were distributed to their political parties.[73]

To understand more about political corruption, Legvold offers three distinct concepts to aid in understanding the specific nature of corruption in the post-Soviet region. Legvold develops the concepts of 'criminal state', 'criminalised state' and 'public corruption'.[74] The criminal state's core activities amount to criminal behaviour. Here, the state depends overwhelmingly on the returns from illicit trade and other illegal transactions or activities. 'Public corruption' arises where bribery works with some agencies or where 'bad apples' among public officials turn up more sporadically, while state institutions remain uncontaminated.[75] Indonesia is neither a criminal state nor a state with public corruption. Referring to Legvold, Indonesia might have been part of what he called the criminalised state, which 'implies a qualitatively different level of corruption, one in which the state itself is suffused with corruption. The state's core activity may not be corrupt, but the process by which the state acts is.'[76]

To further explain the operational meaning of 'criminalized state', Legvold considers the concept of 'state capture', as introduced by the European Bank for Reconstruction and Development Bank and the World Bank:[77]

> State capture occurs when, in contrast to mere bribe-making, to secure access to a good or an exception to existing rules, interested parties exploit the malfeasance of officials to change the rules (laws, judicial rulings, or bureaucratic regulations). Rather than state officials and bureaucrats extorting business firms or ordinary individuals, powerful individuals or groups use material rewards or physical threats to reshape the state. Alternatively, the criminalized state can be thought of as one where much, if not most, state activity has been privatized, that is, where either those in power or those with leverage over those in power use state agency to advance their private interest at the expense of the broader public good.[78]

Legvold explains the two other concepts of corruption: first, systemic and non-systemic corruption, and second, centralised or decentralised systemic corruption.[79] While these two concepts may have an additional emphasis on the operational side, in general they are in line with the criminalised state in operation.

The criminalised state in operation may be more severe than has been imagined. In a globalised world, where connectivity can easily be manufactured, the rise of what is called 'crimes of globalisation' should not be underestimated.[80] These crimes of globalisation may involve elements of state crimes, political crimes, white-collar crimes, state-corporate crimes and financial crimes.[81] This means that elements of a criminalised state may also be linked to crimes of globalisation in one way or another.

Greenhill describes the marriage of politics and illicit profits, arguing that there exists what he terms 'kleptocratic interdependence'.[82] The criminalised state in this perspective not only operates within the state but also inevitably travels beyond state borders. Greenhill eloquently describes what he means by kleptocratic interdependence as being 'characterized by four key features':

> 1) a division of political, functional, and social control between state and non-state actors i.e., the sharing of some of the sovereignty functions traditionally viewed as residing with the state; 2) a privileging of private gain over public good—although, in cases where states are particularly weak or poorly run, the public may in fact benefit from existence of such relationships; 3) an absence or dearth of legal and juridical accountability; and 4) some measure of fusion between the licit and illicit economic realms—although what each of these comprise will vary across cases ...[83]

Greenhill also uses the term 'transnational criminal organisations' (TCOs), an advanced form of organised crime.[84] If organised crime had ever been bound by national territories, our globalised world with its non-existent boundaries needs laws that prevent TCOs from doing business, legally or illegally. There are many states, both developing and developed, engaged in joint business activities with other states and transnational criminal organisations, complementing one another. States also engaged in international businesses may belong to, or be complicit in, this category of TCO. This feature of economic globalisation creates an entrance for TCOs and, in a legally justified form, to do legitimate business with states. This leaves an indirect opening for a marriage between international politics and illicit profits.[85]

To say there are no transnational criminal organisations in Indonesia might not be correct; however, many are not very organised and sophisticated. Illegal fishing and drug trafficking have always been run by transnational criminal organisations. Many illegal fishing operators have engaged in corruption and human and drug trafficking as well as arms smuggling.[86] Although it has not been convincingly proven, suspicion does exist that transnational criminal organisations do indirectly have connections with certain individuals who are also senior members of certain political parties.

On the surface, Indonesia has no national indications or political symptoms of an association or networks with other notorious transnational criminal organisations. Therefore political corruption in Indonesia can be analysed as a criminalised state in which many processes and acts are tainted with corruption. The players who are involved in corruption might not act for or on behalf of the government, but most are connected to, or interact with, the government in some capacity. Capturing, hijacking or abusing the government for private or political gain is therefore the ultimate in corruption since it appears proper and legal at the outset, but is substantially more dishonest, immoral and illegal than all other forms of corruption.

A common perception of corruption is that it is detrimental to societal well-being.[87] Corruption may take several forms but essentially is a form of business, as Harris argues:

> Indeed, political corruption is itself a form of business activity—since corrupt politicians require partnership with businesspeople to maximize the utility of their posts. Corrupt politicians may act as patrons of those below them or clients of those above them; most probably will do both, operating in a chain of corruption wherein the strength of one link determines that of the next ...[88]

In reality, business partnerships may also be criminal organisations that act as business entities, individually or as a group. The bottom line, as Funderburk argues, is that corruption is more than just immorality and dishonesty; it is a process that destroys or subverts honesty and integrity and, in the end, undermines the systemic integrity of legitimate governments and the rule of law.[89]

The ramifications of political corruption can manifest in various forms such as rent seeking, 'structural adjustment', privatisation, public sector procurement and natural resource exploitation. Initial economic growth amid political corruption may provide an economic lubricant to modernisation, which may provide immediate, specific and concrete benefits to society.[90] In fact, according to Huntington, corruption can cultivate modernisation, which can then give rise to new groups within society.[91] Although there may be truth to this, Huntington disregards the prevailing logic subscribed to by most legitimate governments: that corruption is a leading factor in social decay.[92]

Indonesia, for one, certainly views corruption and political corruption as a public enemy. Corruption deprives the people of their legitimate rights to have a better life in a broad sense. In the wake of corruption, poverty and marginalisation ensue and remain. A small elite group of politicians, businessmen and criminals controls most national resources, individually or jointly. They embrace any and all opportunities to preserve their control and possession over natural resources, while preaching good governance, democracy, social justice and the rule of law. The epidemic of political corruption is also assisted by the considerable increase in size of the public sector, economic growth and an awkward process of democratisation that neglects the institutionalisation of transparency and accountability.[93]

Conversely, the KPK does not use the term 'political corruption', although the majority, if not all, of the cases handled by it are undoubtedly cases of political corruption. In its many reports and statements, the KPK indicates that it will prioritise 'grand corruption' in strategic sectors that contain elements of national interest without using the term 'political corruption'. Three major sectors related to the national interest are particularly relevant here: industries related to food security (including agriculture, fishery and forestry), energy, and state revenues (taxes).[94] These three sectors are, according to the KPK, controlled by corruption, where all processes have been captured by those close to power. Several notorious cases investigated recently by the KPK dealt with these three sectors: tax manipulation (the Gayus Tambunan case), imported beef (the Luthfi Hasan Ishaaq case), and oil and gas (the Rudi Rubiandini case).[95]

This is not to suggest that other political corruption cases were not pursued—the KPK has certainly pursued a variety of complicated and high-profile political corruption cases.

Each instance of political corruption is naturally also grand corruption, but not every act of grand corruption involves political corruption. Despite this, there is a major difference in magnitude between political corruption and grand corruption. Grand corruption encompasses parliamentarians, governors, regents and mayors, and in most cases involves spectacularly high amounts of money. There is also judicial corruption, which involves judges, prosecutors, police and lawyers. Again, there are relatively few of these cases, but they must not be overlooked. It is not wrong to argue that the KPK has touched a nerve, making the country tremble in the face of the aggressive corruption investigations it has spearheaded.[96]

Quantifying the total cost of corruption is impossible.[97] To calculate the cost of corruption simply on the basis of economic loss would not measure the entirety of its ramifications. Empirically, there is tangible damage felt to the state, the government and society. As Bhargava and Bolongaita put it: 'There is a growing international realization that corruption cripples development in many ways. It worsens income inequality and poverty, reduces investment rates, lowers economic growth, diminishes democratization and weakens representation.'[98]

For Indonesia, Goodpaster describes how '[c]orruption ... is immensely costly to the state and society' and in fact: 'There are enormous economic efficiency losses and huge costs arising from misallocation of resources. There are competitiveness costs, as corruption is a principal reason for Indonesia's notoriously high transactions costs economy. There are large lost opportunity costs from all the investors, both domestic and foreign, that withdraw or forgo investing in Indonesia because of corruption and its associations.'[99]

The cost of corruption is in fact incalculable, going far beyond mere economic loss. Among other things, political corruption can destroy the legitimacy of political institutions, including the rule of law.[100] Mietzner uses the severe phrasing 'institutional defects in the democratic system'.[101] To put it differently, political corruption jeopardises the values of democracy, weakening the principles of quality, transparency and accountability.[102] There are irreparable costs to state and society unless a systematic overhaul and comprehensive process is administered to disinfect it of political corruption. The institutional integrity of the state and even the security of the state itself is in danger when the state is captured by widespread corruption. In the long term, it is the people who will suffer the most.[103] In new states, in particular, political corruption may progressively corrode the institutional character of the state, and that can eventually undermine sovereignty.[104]

The *modus operandi* and impact of political corruption, as explained above, reveals that Legvold's 'criminalised state' has indeed existed in Indonesia. The Indonesian state, as a matter of public policy, has never condoned corruption or political corruption but at the same time has not prevented itself from being hijacked and controlled by the players of political malfeasance (such as political parties, businessmen and cronies). This happens both at national and regional levels. In many instances, the practice of corruption appears outrageously blatant. While not much is done to prevent this, the apparatus of the state has been co-opted and inveigled by corruption. In countries where the free press and civil society are weak and scattered, state corruption emerges victorious. Ironically, the players of corruption have often managed to appear as generous benefactors with flashy donations and other charitable acts. It is disappointing that many people have not yet realised that the sheer fabric of society, the sturdy cohesiveness of the state, and the strong sense of belonging to community are gradually and insidiously eroded by corruption. The survival of the state is ultimately at stake.[105] A comprehensive, firm and consistent program of corruption eradication must be high on the agenda. War on corruption must be launched.

What has been done? What next?

The KPK as an institution has accomplished much since its establishment in 2003. More than 957 corrupt politicians, high-ranking officials, judges, police, prosecutors, advocates and businessmen have been investigated, prosecuted, tried and sentenced. Funds have certainly been recovered; however, the KPK has not recovered all amounts corrupted and laundered. Various schemes have been engineered by corrupt individuals with the assistance of professionals to hide their wealth, mostly in other countries. Even if the wealth is still within the country, the likelihood that the wealth has been diverted or spent is very high. Nonetheless, with all the power and authority vested in the KPK (by Law No. 30 of 2002 as amended by Law No. 19 of 2019),[106] it should have recovered far more than the amount reported. It is not wrong to argue that there have been obstacles in going after the wealth and assets of the corrupt.

As mentioned, and as discussed in chapter 3, the KPK has been described as a 'superbody'. A great deal of power and authority not vested in other law enforcement agencies has been invested in it.[107] For example, Article 1 (3) Law No. 30 of 2002 stipulates: 'The eradication of criminal acts of corruption is in the form of a chain of actions with the purpose of preventing and eradicating criminal acts of corruption through coordinated efforts, supervision, monitoring, investigations, indictments, prosecutions, and examinations (trials) at courts, all to be done with as much participation on the part of the general public as the Law allows.'

However, with this tremendous authority and power, expectations are high for the success of the KPK. As a 'superbody', the KPK should have accomplished more to bring all grand corruption cases, especially political corruption cases, to trial, in addition to recovering more state funds domestically and internationally. Unfortunately, the KPK has not yet been able to fulfil the expectations of the people. In a country where corruption is so endemic, systemic and widespread as it is in Indonesia, the amount of funds corrupted by certain elites is surely spectacular. If allegations that state losses amount to 30 per cent of the state's budget annually, then the KPK should reasonably have recovered a much higher amount than it has.[108] Sadly, the influence and power of the status quo and corrupt elite are still major impediments to corruption eradication. Popular support for the KPK does not always mean that the political elite fully supports it.

Six categories of corruption cases are handled by the KPK: procurement of goods and services; licensing; bribery and illegal levies; money-laundering; obstruction of justice; and misuse of public budget.[109] Of these, procurement and bribery seem to make up the majority of reported cases by the KPK—188 and 564 cases respectively. There were only 23 cases of licensing, 25 cases of illegal levies, 31 cases of money-laundering, 10 cases of obstruction of justice and 46 cases of budget abuse. However, these principal categories do not cover the full range of cases, as there are others that relate to money-laundering, concealment, trading in influence, obstruction of justice and conflict of interest.[110]

These 957 cases have brought down more than 957 politicians, high-ranking public officials, judges, prosecutors, police and businessmen. These include the former Minister of Social Affairs Bachtiar Chamsah; former Minister of Interior Hari Sabarno; Governor of North Sumatra Syamsul Arifin; Deputy Senior Governor of Bank Indonesia Miranda Swaray Gultom; politicians Nazaruddin, Angelina Sondakh, Wa Ode Nurhayati, Panda Nababan, Nunun Nurbaiti, to name just a few who have been sentenced to imprisonment.[111] In 2013, there were high-profile corruption cases involving the former Minister of Youth and Sports Andi Alfian Malarangeng; the head of the Special Task Force for Upstream Oil and Gas (SKK Migas) Rudi Rubiandini; the head of Driving Simulation for the police Djoko Susilo; the Governor of Riau Province Rusli Zainal; politicians Emir Moeis and Luthfi Hasan Ishaaq; and the Chief Justice of Constitutional Court Akil Mochtar.[112] Most of these high-ranking officials and businessmen belong to political parties so their actions can be considered political corruption, while Mochtar's case involved his receipt of bribes in election dispute cases. Other corruption cases handled by the KPK are often also legitimately political corruption cases, whether the corruption benefits a political party or an individual or both. Perhaps arguing that these cases ought to be considered political corruption is apt, simply because they are committed by politicians, even though the acts committed seem mostly to enrich themselves, their families and cronies. Even so, it is still possible for political parties to benefit indirectly from these corrupt politicians.

Existing anti-corruption regimes do not regulate corporate corruption, which is a major inadequacy. In a country with a multi-party system such as Indonesia, where political corruption is widely practised, corporations or even social foundations are used by political parties to channel funds unlawfully to their parties.[113] The cases of the Hambalang and Wisma Atlet sports facilities, involving the Treasurer of the Democrat Party Nazaruddin, are examples of corporations raising funds to be channelled to a party and even some key people within that party.[114] It is no secret that corporations awarded state-funded projects will usually have shared some revenue with politicians who had assisted them, as a kickback or commission. There is nothing unusual about this practice—it happens in many countries in various forms, although in some cases, the practice is carried out by transnational criminal organisations.[115] Worse yet, according to Greenhill, the practice of collaborating with these organisations has seen some states being dubbed 'bandit states' or 'criminal states'.[116]

Indonesia's anti-corruption law regime must be reformed with new laws that deal specifically with corporate corruption. This is not difficult since corporate crime is not new to Indonesia,[117] but in practice, corporate corruption is rarely pursued. To be sure, the Attorney General's Office has recently investigated, indicted and prosecuted some alleged corporate corruption cases involving a telecommunications company, IM2, and the oil company Chevron.[118] These two corporate corruption cases have generated significant controversy; however, they do not belong to what is traditionally deemed political corruption. Thus, to the extent that corporate corruption occurs, there is a need to challenge existing understandings of the *modus operandi* of political corruption.

The UNCAC states that corruption in the private sector must be dealt with seriously. All countries party to the convention must take measures to prevent corruption involving the private sector and impose civil and criminal sanctions if the corporation fails to comply with the measure.[119] Among others, the UNCAC identifies certain acts that may be considered offences of corruption: the establishment of off-the-books accounts, the making of off-the-books or inadequately identified transactions, the recording of non-existent expenditures to 'make up the books', the entry of liabilities with incorrect identification of their object, the use of false documents, and the intentional destruction of bookkeeping documents earlier than foreseen by the law.[120]

Furthermore, Articles 21 and 22 of the UNCAC deal with two possible offences by corporations: bribery and embezzlement. (In addition, offences of corporations may also be in the form of money-laundering, misappropriation and concealment.) This is too limited in scope since corporations are also capable of money-laundering, misappropriation, concealment and even entering into illegal trading activities such as illicit drug trafficking, illicit weapons transfers, human trafficking, tax evasion, gambling and prostitution.[121] Thanks to globalisation and the internet,[122] criminal acts are no longer restricted to a particular country but have expanded beyond traditional national boundaries to create transnational crimes.[123]

The KPK is not the only agency combating corruption. Every governmental agency, including state auxiliary agencies, has been tasked with combating corruption by building a more transparent and accountable system of governance. Corruption can only be fought by strengthening governance, so that it provides no room or opportunity for corruption. Both Presidents Susilo Bambang Yudhoyono (2004–14) and Joko Widodo (since 2014) issued a series of governmental regulations and presidential instructions outlining six long-term and short-term strategies for tackling corruption:[124] (1) prevention; (2) law enforcement; (3) governmental regulations; (4) international cooperation and stolen assets recovery; (5) education and anti-corruption culture; and (6) reporting mechanisms.[125]

On the basis of these strategies, the government introduced the 2013 Actions for Prevention and Eradication of Corruption and the 2018 National Strategy to Prevent Corruption, in which no less than 265 separate actions were listed, with specific objectives for and measurements of success. Those 265 actions must be implemented by all governmental agencies, executive, legislatures and judiciaries, together with all other state auxiliary agencies.[126]

The list contains actions related to transparency, accountability, access to information, complaint mechanisms, whistleblowers, justice collaborators, conflicts of interest, codes of ethics, supervision, bureaucratic reform, strict prohibition of off-budget, e-procurement, punishment, regular reporting and monitoring, law enforcement, law reform, reversed burden of proof, extraditions and mutual legal assistance agreement, assets forfeiture, and education and socialisation of anti-corruption.[127] The ultimate objective of all these actions is to enhance system integrity in order to generate a zero-tolerance policy against corruption. Maintaining a standardised system of integrity will enhance anti-corruption efforts if all actions are implemented in accordance with all the guidelines.

The KPK acknowledges that it aims to build up the national integrity system whereby all government agencies, state auxiliary agencies, business sectors, civil society and other stakeholders will collectively work together to create a clean and healthy government—free from corruption, collusion and nepotism.[128] In the meantime, the KPK will go after grand corruption cases where national interests are at stake. The issue is not only the financial losses suffered by the state in terms of money but also the sustainability of the state, since all these sectors significantly affect the livelihood of the state and the people at large.

Some corruption cases pursued by the KPK between 2010 and 2020 seem to reflect a strategy of pursuing oligarchs through strategic non-political corruption cases, both in Jakarta and the regions.[129] The case of Gayus Tambunan, of the Directorate General of Tax in the Department of Finance, is an example. Tambunan was not a particularly high-ranking official, but he was in charge of checking and examining tax returns of many big companies and conglomerates. In this role, he assisted companies and conglomerates in evading taxes.[130] One major conglomerate assisted by Tambunan was Bakri Group, from which case Tambunan allegedly received Rp 100 million.[131] Tax evasion can involve large sums of money, and it was ironic that the trial of Tambunan related only to a small tax evasion case while grand tax evasion cases seemed to be forgotten.[132]

Another case involved the former President of Partai Keadilan Sejahtera (Justice Welfare Party), Luthfi Hasan Ishaaq. His party is known as a progressive Islamic party that opposes corruption and, interestingly, is also a member of the government coalition. The case related to the corrupt issuance of import permits for beef to a number of companies.[133] This is a traditional rent-seeking mode of corruption, which enables a cartel of several companies to control the beef trade. It is no accident that for some time beef prices in Indonesia have been the highest in the world.[134]

A third case involved Rudi Rubiandini, the head of SKK Migas, an agency responsible for oil and gas upstream business. Rubiandini allegedly received approximately US$700 000 as a bribe from an oil trading company.[135] The status of this case is unclear, but may concern competition within oil trading companies that control the import and export of oil. This is not new for Indonesia. Monopolies in oil trading have existed since the New Order under Soeharto, and seem to be a highly lucrative business for traders and for their political protectors. On paper, everything may appear to be legal, but in reality the state surrenders its authority to oil traders, earmarking portions of the state budget to import oil, given that the actual oil price has been lower than the price fixed by the state. In this case, marking up US$1 per barrel was exorbitantly high, given the huge amount of oil imported since the New Order of Soeharto. This is what is called a state capture in a simple sense. Given the extent of financial loss likely suffered each year by the state (and by extension the people), this has been the worse incidence of corruption. In addition, oil traders have been able to block any plan by the government to build oil refineries onshore in Indonesia, instead of importing.[136] Indonesia, a net oil importer, consumes 1.45 million barrels per day, yet domestic production is roughly 700 000 barrels per day. To meet demand, Indonesia relies on importing 700 000 barrels per day. Oil importing companies, with no competition from local refineries, can obtain significant profit margins, marking up oil by US$1 per barrel.[137]

The fourth case is an infrastructure-related case, involving the Wisma Atlet (Jaka Baring) and Hambalang sports facility projects.[138] Each was engineered and marked up in such a way that the total value of the project was substantially increased, with the true value of the projects being much lower. Court proceedings and testimonies of witnesses indicated that various parties benefited from the projects. A substantial amount of the money was used to secure votes in the congress of the ruling party, Partai Demokrat. That explains why the chairman of the party, Anas Urbaningrum, was named the chief suspect and eventually jailed.

The fifth case is Chief Justice Akil Mochtar, who was also a senior politician in the Golkar Party. Election results can be annulled by the Constitutional Court and a new election held. Mochtar abused his power in almost every local election dispute he heard, for substantial bribes, using a particular middleman to collect bribes; the Constitutional Court became a black market for justice. It takes two to tango, and often the advocates took the initiative to approach the Chief Justice. In some instances, the interested parties directly approached the Chief Justice in person. The Chief Justice was sentenced to life imprisonment.[139]

The last case involved a senior politician, also from the Golkar Party, a businessman and a Speaker of Parliament, Setya Novanto. He was the mastermind of the electronic identification card (E-KTP) scam that caused an incredible state loss of more than Rp 2 trillion. The total value of E-KTP's project was more than Rp 5 trillion, and Novanto managed to embezzle an extraordinary amount from that, which he shared with his fellow members of parliament, high-ranking officials and businessmen. Novanto shocked the public and not only lost his high position and money but also destroyed his own political and business future.[140]

Many corruption cases are handled by the KPK, and not all can be mentioned. However, these six cases are good examples of grand political corruption. The question here is whether these corruption cases were the result of state capture, as is normally the practice within a criminalised state.[141] Have the legislature, executive and judiciary been hijacked by corrupt officials or politicians to pass legislation, executive orders or judicial decisions? Have the corrupt actions in these cases been facilitated by the abuse of power for the benefit of corrupt individuals, political parties or cronies? All these cases indicate that there seems to be a strong correlation between corruption and political parties, an issue I return to later.[142]

Chapter 2

Historical perspective

How were these serious shortcomings to be explained? How could they be squared with the fact that this was now the period of independence of which so much had been expected? Many found consolation in the expressed idea that 'we are still a young state', that 'these are children's diseases', and that 'this is still the period of transition'.

Herbert Feith, *The Decline of Constitutional Democracy in Indonesia*

The late first Vice President of Indonesia, Muhammad Hatta, once said that corruption has become a culture, and since then, that statement has been quoted over and over in almost every debate on corruption.[1] Laode Muhammad Syarif, former Vice Chairman of the KPK, has even said that he does not want to be condemned by Hatta's words.[2] Hatta was right, however. Corruption became the norm in Indonesia, and was hardly perceived to be a bad thing, much less an offence. It became tacitly accepted and practised.

Corruption has a long history in Indonesia. In the past, it was not called 'corruption', but predatory behaviour is certainly not new; it is deeply entrenched within society.[3] The ruler forced his people to hand over gifts regularly as a sign of obedience, whether the ruler was an older person, a village 'head', a wealthy trader or a gang leader. People had to work hard to meet the ruler's demands, or otherwise face significant hardship, often in the form of violence. The authoritarian nature of the ruler is manifest in various forms, but rulers were usually perceived to hold some sort of divine power, justifying their oppression of their own people. The concept of serving the people was absent; instead the concept applied was that the people subordinated their position to the ruler, and served him or her at all costs. The people were thus always at the mercy of their rulers. Accountability was something alien to both the ruler and the ruled.

This has to do with the degree of power possessed. Power justified and legalised the ruler's predatory behaviour over the weak, the marginalised and the poor. Within society at large, the powerful oppress the powerless, and this practice has been oft-repeated, becoming widespread. Social structures seemed to have eternally facilitated the existence of predatory behaviour to different degrees. Over time, this transformed the pattern of relations within society into patron–client relationships in the sense that the patron had the right over the client, although some sort of obligation was also attached to the patron in the sense that the client must be protected. This is not to deny that there had been patrons who were generous and kind to the clients, and seen as benevolent, a term that would at a later time be used to refer to the less rapacious among despots or dictators.[4]

Giving gifts to rulers is often considered an expression of gratitude, and should not necessarily be viewed as bribery or corruption, toxic and dangerous to state and society. The same applies to collusion and nepotism where people must work together, especially with close family relations.[5] It has been said that in the past, loyalties to the family are much stronger than loyalties to the state.[6] In this context, the notion of corruption was not understood, even if modern political, economic and legal thought regarded bribery, collusion and nepotism as corruption.[7] If corruption eradication faces enormous challenges in society, it is mainly owing to the cultural notion that corruption has always been interpreted as a manifestation of appreciation and subordination.

Moreover, a gift differs from corruption because, if it were not given in secrecy, it was not a violation of duty or the rights of the public and it was not a form of state revenue.[8] Perhaps it is not wrong to argue that corruption has been embedded in some sectors for long periods. Traditionally, the giving of gifts was partly obligatory and, in many circumstances, was embedded in elaborate networks of social alliances and class differences.[9]

Dhakidae argues that, in the past, corruption as a concept did not exist.[10] The kingdom belonged to the king or queen and was inherited by their children unendingly. Everything belonged to the king, queen and their family. There was no public or personal property. Therefore, if the king and the queen received gifts from their people, it could not have been interpreted as bribery or corruption because the king and queen only took and received their own property. Dhakidae argues that corruption is actually an invented crime, to respond to the emergence of the notion of citizenship and public property along with the rise of the modern state. It is in such circumstances that citizens become 'the public' with all the rights vested in them. Only then can a violation of their rights—including stealing their property—become an offence. Thus, stealing public property must have been interpreted as corruption, although the term 'corruption' was not mentioned.

In any case, the emergence of the modern state has radically changed relationships between people as well as their relationships with property. A new regime of law came into being, along with definitions of what is right and wrong. Those who committed wrongdoings—including corruption—must be punished. Corruption has evolved from initially being an unethical use of authority to an illegal act and abuse of governmental authority for personal gain. Evolution of this regime of law took the world to an entirely different reality, where law enforcement became an instrument of the state.

Corruption certainly occurred in colonial times when the Dutch occupied Indonesia, then called the Netherlands East Indies. In fact, the Dutch corrupted Indonesia's wealth for 350 years, fantastically enriching themselves to the point that the Dutch state no longer had to worry about the prosperity of its people. Without delving deeply into this, I will mention one case involving a respected politician from North Sulawesi, Sam Ratulangi, who was accused of corruption in 1937. Ratulangi was a member of the nominal colonial parliament representing indigenous people, the Volksraad,[11] who unlawfully abused his power, corrupting state funds to the amount of one hundred gulden and was sentenced to four months imprisonment in addition to forced dismissal. This is significant not because of the theft of so-called state or public money, but because his conduct was seen as degrading the good name of parliament. Dhakidae sees this early case of corruption as 'proto-corruption'.[12]

Bad apples

Indonesia proclaimed its independence in 1945, but this did not mean that it was independent or free from corruption. As mentioned, the prevailing cultural notion adhered to by many people in Indonesia is that giving gifts does not constitute a breach of ethics and law. Gift-giving as a sign of appreciation is still seen as an accepted custom, and in a new nation where a new and inexperienced bureaucracy is unfamiliar with best practices for good governance, this practice was, in many cases, seen as permissible. In these circumstances, corruption gradually grew in society and, in particular, in the bureaucracy.

Despite the prevailing cultural notion allowing the practice of gift-giving as a token of appreciation, the prohibition of corruption was actually enshrined in the Criminal Code inherited from colonial times, and re-enacted in 1946, which remains the substantive criminal law of Indonesia. In fact, there are two categories of corruption in the Code: active corruption and passive corruption, as stipulated in Articles 418 and 419 of the Criminal Code respectively.[13] Article 418 provides that:

> An official who accepts gifts or promises that is known or should reasonably be suspected of having been given,

because of the power or authority related to his position, or in the mind of the person giving the gift or promise to be related to his position, shall be subject to the maximum criminal penalty of six months' imprisonment or the maximum fine of three hundred rupiah.

Passive corruption is stipulated in Article 419 of Criminal Code as follows:[13]

An official shall be subject to the maximum prison penalty of five years who:
(1) Accepts gifts or promises, being aware, that it was given so that he would do or omit to do something in office that is contrary to his obligations;
(2) Accepts gifts, being aware that it was given as a consequence of or because he has done something in office that is contrary to his obligations.

Further prohibitions of corruption can also be found in various articles within the Criminal Code, even though there is no specific mention of corruption. Article 362 of the Criminal Code, for instance, stipulates that the unlawful act of stealing another's property is a punishable offence.[14] Other articles prohibit public officials from taking or receiving something without having any right to said property.[15] These provisions reflect the tension between prevailing cultural notions and existing laws, particularly the Criminal Code.

Concerns about corruption were openly voiced by many politicians and intellectuals in the years following independence. Sutan Takdir Alisyahbana, a well-known and influential novelist and intellectual, wrote in 1957:

Thus, financial corruption goes hand in hand with large-scale political corruption, and the interests of people and the State are lost from sight. The high point of political and financial corruption was reached some time before the general elections, when the parties were in great need of money for the elections, success in which was to mean four years of power and spoils.[16]

In an address to a bank employees conference in 1964, the prominent politician D.N. Aidit of the Indonesian Communist Party (PKI)[17] also directly complained about corruption, stating: 'For quite a long time now we have all felt that whenever we begin to analyze economic problems we have always to deal with the same things, the same unchanging problems—there are mismanagement, corruption, confusion, stifling bureaucracy, and over and above all this mess are the bureaucratic capitalists, who always seem able to profit abundantly from it.'[18]

As these two statements suggest, many intellectuals, journalists, writers and politicians understood that something was already wrong with the country, as early as a decade after Independence. In 1955, one corruption case that was widely reported in the media involved the then Minister of Justice Djody Gondokusumo, who was forced to resign from his position immediately.[19] Gondokusumo was charged by respected Attorney General Soeprapto for receiving a bribe of Rp 40 000 in return for issuing a visa for an ethnic Chinese.[20] He was sentenced to a term of imprisonment of one year, but was pardoned by President Soekarno.[21]

The Minister of Economy Iskaq Tjokroadisurjo was also on the list to be arrested, but when the arrest was about to take place in 1955, he left Jakarta for the Netherlands together with his son, who was to be placed in a school for disabled children.[22] It was not clear what violation of the law Tjokroadisurjo had committed, aside from the fact that, as Minister of Economy, he was tasked with empowering local businessmen by granting business licences.[23] The government at that time wished to groom a group of native Indonesians to become pioneers in business to deal with foreign companies. The idea was to avoid the rise of non-Indonesian businessmen controlling the economy. The name of 'benteng' was chosen because 'benteng' or 'bull' represents strength and resilience. The idea was to facilitate and assist local businessmen to be able to compete with foreign enterprises, including, but not limited to, better organised Chinese businessmen. It has been assumed that the minister benefited from his ministerial position, which was mandated to build a new class of indigenous businessmen; however, it is not clear how much benefit or illegal facilitation payment he had received, if any. What was clear is that he was tried in 1959 and again in 1960 on charges related to his position as Minister of Economy from 1953 to 1954.[24]

Several employees of the Central Import Office and the vice consul in Singapore were also arrested for corruption, as well as a number of individuals employed by the Minister of Justice.[25] Another person arrested for alleged corruption was Foreign Affairs Minister Roeslan Abdulgani, in 1956,[26] accused of receiving a house and a car from Chinese businessman Lie Hok Thay. He also carried dollars overseas in violation of foreign exchange regulations. Interestingly, a committee led by Deputy Prime Minister Muhammad Roem issued a fact-finding report dismissing the allegations. It saved Abdulgani, but then a senior *Indonesia Raya* journalist, Mochtar Lubis, in 1956 published all the evidence of transactions between Roeslan Abdulgani and businessman Lie Hok Thay. This evidence convincingly refuted the report of the Roem Committee, and in 1957 Abdulgani was subsequently prosecuted by the Supreme Court.[27] Abdulgani was charged with violating foreign exchange regulations, found guilty and fined Rp 5000.

A further corruption case involved a former Minister of Finance, Jusuf Wibisono, who was arrested in 1957 and accused of extending illegal credit to a businessman who happened to be his crony.[28] Later, another former Minister of Finance, Soemitro Djoyohadikusumo, was pursued for illegally raising funds for his political party, Partai Sosialis Indonesia. Djoyohadikusumo was interrogated, but managed to flee the country before an arrest was made.[29]

These cases of high-ranking politicians, publicised in the media, were only the tip of the iceberg. Although statistics are not available, it is believed the number of corruption cases investigated and brought to court was certainly increasing in the 1950s. Corruption then seemed to be a mixture of financial and political corruption, and there were no reports of large-scale corruption, although it is not possible to conclude that it did not exist.[30] However, most of it was the sort of corruption committed by individuals violating the law and social norms; what Legvold calls 'bad apple' corruption.[31]

During the Soekarno period, law enforcement agencies encountered significant difficulty in pursuing corruptors, primarily because the existing laws were not fully equipped to deal with corruption cases in terms of procedure and evidence. Often, evidence was destroyed and many challenges were encountered when arresting the alleged corruptors. Simultaneously, the suspicious wealth of high-ranking officials became conspicuous and known to the public at large. This was problematic given that high-ranking officials cannot accumulate extreme wealth or become wealthy on their remuneration as office-holder alone. It is for this reason that in 1955 the government planned to introduce a type of emergency anti-corruption law. President Soekarno refused to sign it, however, and the initiative was therefore immediately brought to an end.[32] Subsequently, the government decided to introduce a draft bill on anti-corruption to the national legislature, and public consultations were held. Regrettably, the draft bill was never actually submitted to the legislature.[33] If the draft bill had become law, it would have been the first anti-corruption law of the young republic. This might have also led to the establishment of the first anti-corruption court responsible for deciding corruption cases.[34]

Power corrupts

Sebastian Pompe made an observation that, while true, is very disturbing to many Indonesians, particularly those in the legal community. He wrote: 'It is a brutal historical fact that within twenty years of Indonesian independence, the nation's judiciary officially ceased to exist as a separate and independent function of government.'[35]

The question is, how can corruption cases be eradicated if the judiciary lacks independence? Pompe perhaps understates the capability of the Indonesian judiciary, but it must be admitted that while the judiciary was never dissolved, it was severely weakened under President Soekarno's Guided Democracy. After he unilaterally declared a return to the 1945 Constitution in 1959, replacing the Provisional Constitution of 1950, a near complete collapse of the Supreme Court was triggered. President Soekarno refused to adhere to the notion of separation of powers, and the judiciary was placed under the executive branch of government. The concentration of power in the hands of Soekarno as head of the executive branch was a hallmark of this period, during which corruption eradication efforts quickly became much weaker.[36] President Soekarno, who had long been obsessed with revolution, applied revolutionary law, meaning that he had the supreme authority to exercise power in every path of revolution; that is, in every governmental body, including, but not limited to, the legislature and the judiciary.[37] Power rapidly became concentrated in the hands of the president.

It is heartening that the Indonesian Judges' Association (Ikatan Hakim Indonesia or IKAHI) ardently refused to surrender its independence. The judiciary fought to retain its independence, but the political circumstances at that time made it impossible. According to Pompe, 'The struggles accelerated the erosion of the status of the judiciary during the third phase, Guided Democracy (1959–1965). This diminishment in status was an important factor that permitted more direct interference in the substance of court operations. In this period of revolutionary politics, judges lost not merely their status but also their power and autonomy from executive interference.'[38]

Before Guided Democracy, indications of weakening corruption eradication efforts appeared publicly. However, it would be wrong to conclude that corruption eradication ceased entirely. The spirit to combat corruption had never died, but the supreme leader of the country, in the name of revolution, had crushed it. Uneven development and tensions between Java and non-Java were coming to the surface, forcing the central government in Jakarta to mobilise its resources to counter rebellion and resistance in the islands beyond

Java, in order to protect the unity of the republic. Corruption eradication was sidelined.

In 1957, with the military's support, President Soekarno declared a state of emergency in response to regional rebellions in West Java, North Sumatra, West Sumatra and North Sulawesi. It was not a secret that the military lacked sufficient logistics to support their operations and therefore the military used the state of emergency to collect funds by involving themselves in smuggling. There were widespread suspicions that members of the military abused their power in doing so and, in some cases, enriched themselves, and these leaked to the media and news outlets. The army chief, Nasution, was extremely upset and ordered an investigation into the alleged corruption, including, among others, that of a Colonel Ibnu Sutowo, who himself was allegedly involved in rubber smuggling.[39] Tensions between the military and political parties forced the military to make concessions to win the inner power struggle. These accusations of corruption within the military undoubtedly weakened its overall political position.[40]

For a while, it seemed that no action would be taken against Colonel Ibnu Sutowo until 1959, when acting Attorney General Gatot Tanumihardja reopened the case. This prompted the military, led by Nasution, to retaliate by arresting Tanumihardja for his alleged involvement in illegal textile trading in Tanjung Priok. President Soekarno intervened by discharging Tanumihardja while also replacing allegedly corrupt high-ranking military officers.[41] However, this did not mean that reconciliation had been reached. Rather, political tensions between the military and political parties and President Soekarno continued.[42]

Although the term 'corruption' was not used at this time, efforts were made to combat it, including by establishing new institutions. For example, President Soekarno set up an agency called Badan Pengawasan Kegiatan Aparatur Negara (Bapekan, or State Apparatus Supervisory Agency), headed by the former Minister of Defence, Sultan Hamengkubuwono IX. Surprisingly, this new agency quickly received approximately 912 reports of corruption within the customs office.[43] As the establishment of Bapekan irritated the military, Nasution established an opposing agency, called Panitia Retooling Aparatur Negara (Paran; Committee for Retooling the State Apparatus). While Nasution initially established Paran to improve governance, it also engaged in combating corruption. Both agencies managed to investigate a number of corruption cases and claimed that they succeeded in preventing more state losses, for example in the Asian Games project. The activities of Paran, under a task force operation called Operasi Budhi (Operation Budhi), touched upon alleged manipulation and corruption within state-owned enterprises, making corrupt high-ranking officials, including political parties, nervous. It is in this context that pressure to dissolve Paran was directed at President Soekarno, who himself was not pleased with investigations by Operasi Budhi that were eventually coming close to some in his inner circle. He dissolved Paran and set up another agency that he himself led; namely, Komando Tertinggi Retooling Alat Revolusi (Kotra; Supreme Command for Retooling the Revolutionary Apparatus).[44]

In 1956, the Minister of Justice, Moeljatno, failed in efforts to introduce a draft bill on corruption eradication to parliament, for the obvious reason that the political parties did not like the idea of having such a law. Therefore eradication of corruption had to be based on the Criminal Code,[45] inherited from colonial times. However, its provisions on corruption are unclear, and not far-reaching enough to deal with the complexities of contemporary corruption, so that prosecutors and judges seemed unable to use the Criminal Code as a basis for convicting corruptors. For this reason, the government promulgated Peperpu (Peraturan Penguasa Perang Pusat, Regulation of Central War Commander) No. 113 of 1958 to deal with corruption cases,[46] followed by Peperpu No. PLP/1/17 on 17 April 1958, one day later.[47]

These two regulations were perceived as ineffective for pursuing corruptors, prompting the government to issue yet another new regulation, Peperpu No. 24 of 1964 on Investigation, Prosecution and Adjudication of Corruption Offences. This law was much more extensive, but it still failed to deliver change. Corruption had become widespread, and abuse of power by government employees was now occurring at both the local and national levels. Perhaps the absence of checks and balances and a weak judiciary's lack of control of the government had opened the avenues for corruption. And if one believes that power tends to corrupt, then it is understandable that in a new state, under the effective dictatorship of one man, corruption grew rapidly.

From 1960 onwards, the judiciary seemed to have been almost completely co-opted by the President, as the Chief Justice was also a member of cabinet, thereby doing away with the separation of powers of the executive, legislative and judiciary. In the past, the judiciary was an independent arm of government, but this was no longer the case by 1960. In order to formalise this, Law No. 13 of 1965 regarding Adjudication within the General Courts and the Supreme Court was promulgated. The elucidation (i.e. explanatory memorandum) to it states:

> This law with all its power aims at throwing out the spirit of liberalism, individualism, feudalism, and colonialism, in accordance with modern Indonesian law. It realizes the idea that the separation of powers doctrine (*Trias Politika*) no longer applies in Indonesian society. The concept that judges shall be impartial, independent from any external interference, can no longer be upheld and has been buried.[48]

This led to the transformation of the legislature and the judiciary into instruments of revolutionary law. This is what Lindsey identified as the fundamental legal principle of 'Guided Democracy'.[49] In other words, the constitutional idea of the state being based on law (*negara hukum* or *rechtsstaat*) was abolished and replaced by a state that lacked appropriate checks and balances on the exercise of power by the executive—arguably, an authoritarian state. According to Lindsey,

> ... legislative process was effectively replaced by executive instruction and the legal legitimacy lay in the ideology as defined by the President rather than in written statute or a formal jurisprudence. This, combined with executive intervention in the judicial process and a culture of contempt for the rule of law, led to widespread legal uncertainty and the collapse of the legal process. The result was a system in which the citizen was vulnerable to, and defenceless against, the instrumentalities of state, where policy was the supreme source of legitimacy ...[50]

Discussing the collapse of the judiciary and 'state based on law' around this time, Pompe adds that even

> ... the distinctive official attire of judges, their black gowns, was abolished in March 1963 and replaced by a military-style uniform which all civil servants were wearing at the time—in green camouflage colors with shoulder boards embossed with the *pengayoman* symbol. The new uniform reduced the symbolic separation between judges and other civil servants or, as the relevant statute phrases it, made judges 'more aware of their responsibilities as instruments of the state and revolution' ...[51]

In summary, corruption eradication had also been rendered completely ineffective under Guided Democracy. In fact, corruption had found fertile ground in which to thrive and, in some cases, was even legitimised in the name of *revolusi* (revolution). Marking up prices of fertiliser and copra by state-owned enterprises has been done in order to anticipate the needs of revolution, although in practice, the 'profit' was used to line the pockets of the bureaucrats.[52] In other words, we are not talking here merely about 'bad apples' but perhaps also the emergence of the 'criminal state' as conceptualised by Legvold. Nevertheless, it is perhaps naïve to conclude that Indonesia became a criminal state simply because of the policies of

Guided Democracy. The better view is that Indonesia could be seen as a 'criminalised state' insofar as the process of achieving that objective was distorted by abuse of power and widespread corruption.[53]

Integralistic state

The 'integralistic state' is an Indonesian concept, initiated by Soepomo. Although multicultural and multiethnic, the nation remains integral (united), in which it is believed that the government (executive) is the embodiment of the nation as a whole. The concept has loopholes, as the government tends to abuse the power it has. Although never formally adopted, the concept was reflected during Soeharto's era.

The abortive coup in 1965, the so-called G30S,[54] marked the beginning of the end of Guided Democracy and the gradual emergence of the 'New Order' (*Orde Baru*) government under President Soeharto. A new chapter had begun in which radical change was initiated in the political landscape that directly and indirectly affected the law and the judiciary. While under Guided Democracy, or the Old Order, so-called revolutionary law was enforced as the supreme principle binding upon every act, the New Order relied on the notion of the integralistic state,[55] where the principle of rule by law prevailed over the rule of law. Soeharto relied on the wording or text of laws to extinguish the spirit of the law, which should have ensured fairness and equality, rather than the discrimination and domination it delivered under the New Order. Soeharto later argued that under his administration he had always complied with the law, which is to a large extent true, but hardly an excuse for his behaviour since he came to exert total control over the process by which laws were made. This highlights the crux of the problem: the proper nature and characteristics of law.

To be fair, in the early years of the New Order, there were high hopes that corruption eradication would gain new momentum. In 1968, Soeharto established an *ad hoc* team consisting of lecturers and students from the University of Indonesia to conduct investigations into allegations of corruption in governmental agencies. A number of student activists were also appointed as members of the legislature to provide support for Soeharto's agenda.[56] This was the honeymoon period of Soeharto's rule, particularly as it related to students, and it reflected his promise to eradicate widespread corruption and bring corruptors before the courts. At that time, the government had arrested fifteen of Soekarno's ministers who were accused of corruption and being involved in the aborted coup of 1965,[57] including Chairul Saleh and Jusuf Muda Dalam, members of Soekarno's inner circle, both known to be outrageously corrupt.

The trial of Jusuf Muda Dalam exposed incompetence and brutal abuse of power associated with stealing from the state. Specifically, he was accused of marking up funds for procurement of ammunition and weapons while stealing Rp 97 billion from what was called the 'revolutionary fund'. At the time, this was an enormous amount and must have been regarded as mega-corruption.[58] In the meantime, Soeharto appointed a military general, Suryo, to lead a team called Pengawasan Keuangan Negara (Pekuneg or State Finance Supervision) to conduct monitoring and prevent corruption within the government. Pekuneg received countless reports, and at one point claimed to have prevented state losses of an amount equivalent to US$1.1 million and 58 million Japanese yen.[59] It was the investigations by this team that finally brought Jusuf Muda Dalam to court.

Despite these initially impressive corruption eradication measures, the legal apparatus—the police, the prosecutors and judges—seemed overwhelmed by the inadequacy of existing laws in dealing with corruption. Corruption had become rampant and widespread but was mostly untouched. President Soeharto responded to public outcry by setting up a Tim Pemberantasan Korupsi (Corruption Eradication Team) in 1967, which Attorney General Sugih Arto, a senior army officer, was tasked to lead, coordinating and supervising all law enforcement agencies in corruption investigations.[60] President Soeharto also formed what was known as Komisi Empat (Commission of Four) in early 1970, chaired by a highly respected former prime minister Wilopo, and joined by former founding vice president Muhammad Hatta, making the Komisi Empat strong and influential in the eyes of the public.[61]

However, the Komisi Empat did not have much power: it was legally limited to collecting and analysing data and reports in order to be able to issue recommendations. Komisi Empat repeatedly requested support and intervention from President Soeharto because its members came across huge and systemic corruption within governmental agencies that were, unfortunately, run by close confidantes of President Soeharto. These included Pertamina, Bulog and Perhutani, respectively the state-owned oil enterprise, the national logistics agency and a major forestry company.[62] Komisi Empat did not last long, but interestingly, towards the end of 1970, it managed to issue a report on alleged corruption within the Attorney General's Office. These were all substantial corruption cases or, as anti-corruption activists say, 'grand corruption'.[63]

Komisi Empat gave rise to high hopes that corruption eradication might be seriously tackled, but a recommendation is only a recommendation. It does not oblige the President to implement it, even if in the eyes of the public the reports and recommendations were very comprehensive. The President's inaction sparked widespread frustration, especially among students, which quickly soured the relationship between President Soeharto and students who had previously been instrumental in his rise to power. The honeymoon seemed to be over. The impatience of the students became obvious when, also in 1970, they established what they called the Komite Anti Korupsi (KAK, or the Anti-Corruption Committee).[64] KAK, being an initiative of students, did not have any legal basis and acted more as a moral force, but it received support from the public at large and became surprisingly popular, much to Soeharto's irritation.

In 1970, the Soeharto government's departure from its public goals of upholding democracy and rule of law and its commitment to fight corruption became obvious. Discontent among the people, especially students, led them to voice their concern about alleged corruption within the President's inner circle, including, but not limited to, his family and relatives.⁶⁵ In 1971, Madame Soeharto initiated a mega-project called Taman Miniatur Indonesia Indah (Taman Mini), a large theme park where every province was represented, with each major ethnic group's traditional house filled with local ornaments, traditional customs and handicrafts. The idea is simple: one does not need to travel to all provinces but simply visit 'Mini-Indonesia', a microcosm of the archipelago's immense diversity. It was a culturally grandiose idea, ridiculously and outrageously costly.

Students believed that the country did not have enough funds to finance the project and that other necessary and important projects, such as schools, bridges, roads and other essential infrastructure, should be prioritised. There were also suspicions that the project would be financed by the government from the state budget, while it had never been earmarked when the state budget was approved. In addition, Madame Soeharto asked provincial governments as well as the private sector to contribute to the financing of the project. I was one of the leaders of a demonstration against Taman Mini organised by student activists and was arrested and interrogated by the police a number of times. I took part in demonstrations because I believed a government mega-project such as Taman Mini created opportunities for corruption because there was no audit system then in place. Avenues for corruption were wide open.⁶⁶

In the early 1970s, tensions between the government and students seemed to intensify, leading to a series of large demonstrations in many big cities criticising Soeharto's government for being surrounded by cronies, close confidantes and power brokers who corrupted the wealth of the nation. By then, Madame Tien Soeharto was known among businessmen and student activists as 'Madame Ten Percent' because she was believed to ask for 10 per cent of the total value of projects funded by the government as commission.⁶⁷ In the meantime, state-owned enterprises seemed to be tasked to collect money for President Soeharto. Later, the children of Soeharto entered into business and in many cases managed to secure highly lucrative projects facilitated by the government.⁶⁸

The tensions erupted in 1974, when students demonstrated *en masse* in Jakarta and a few other big cities. These demonstrations became known as the Malari incident or the 15 January Calamity. They began as protests towards government policy on foreign investment that seemed too friendly to Japanese businesses, but beneath them was rising anger and frustration concerning widespread corruption throughout the country. These were the biggest student demonstrations since Soeharto had come to power in 1965, and I took part as one of the student leaders. I witnessed hundreds of cars burned and destroyed in Jakarta and many intellectuals, students and others being detained by the government. At the same time, national newspapers were closed arbitrarily. Many intellectuals, journalists and student activists were arrested, and some were prosecuted.[69]

As President Soeharto became more and more authoritarian, opposition and criticism seemed to have been given no room. Corruption found fertile ground. It is under these circumstances that mega-corruption in state-owned enterprises such as Pertamina and Bulog got out of control.[70] Pertamina, in particular, appeared to be President Soeharto's 'cash cow'. At the same time, President Soeharto established a number of foundations (*yayasan*) as his vehicles to collect money from state-owned enterprises and big conglomerates to finance his political operations. He introduced what was called *dana taktis* (tactical fund) and *dana non-budgeteer* (off-budget fund).[71] Use of both *dana taktis* and *dana non-budgeteer* involved no accountability because they were intended to fund activities undertaken to silence critics and anticipate political attacks. In practice, these funds were used primarily to enrich the holders of the funds, who were mostly high-ranking officials. In other words, these funds became sources of rewards, a legalised form of corruption beyond the reach of law enforcement agencies.

Corruption had become endemic and widespread, and President Soeharto was very much aware of that—indeed he had played a major part in it. Yes, there had been attempts to fight corruption, including the Komisi Empat, but it had no legal power other than to issue recommendations. Various other teams were set up to tackle corruption, but all seemed to be *ad hoc* and ineffective. The final attempt by the government to launch an anti-corruption program was Operasi Tertib (Opstib or Operation Order) in 1977. This was an operation intended to secure order and discipline under the leadership of J.B. Sumarlin and Soedomo, Minister of Empowerment of the State Apparatus and Commander for Restoration and Order (Panglima Komando Pemulihan Keamanan dan Ketertiban, Pangkopkamtib), respectively. Operasi Tertib succceded in pursuing 263 corrupt officials in the offices of customs, tax and the police, including the deputy chief of the National Police, Siswaji. However, it did not seem to extend to the big fish; despite public outcry and widespread allegations of corruption within the inner circle and family of President Soeharto, they remained untouched. Opstib proved to have been little more than a symbolic attempt to demonstrate corruption eradication by the government; it was effectively a populist strategy.[72]

In 1971, a new law on corruption eradication was promulgated, Law No. 3 of 1971. This was considered an important piece of legislation,[73] and although it was not as comprehensive as was hoped, it did open avenues for the pursuit of corruption in a country now riddled with it. To do so successfully assumed, however, that law institutions properly performed investigations and prosecutions, without intervention from higher authorities. That is, any investigation and subsequent prosecution must be seen as credible and not undermined by perceived (or actual) discrimination as the law must apply equally to all.

However, no corruption eradication strategy, legislative or otherwise, ever held the inner circle and family of President Soeharto accountable for their corrupt acts, even though the media still sometimes reported alleged instances of corruption, collusion and nepotism as well as government privileges provided to the Soeharto clan (especially the children and close relatives of President Soeharto).[74] The failure of the New Order government ever to fight corruption adequately is the result not only of the Soeharto family's immense personal power but also of the largely symbolic populist nature of corruption eradication initiatives such as Opstib, and the weakened state of separation of powers, particularly in the context of the judiciary.[75] In a country where the notion of an integralistic state was applied, it is logical that no independent judiciary could exist because the judiciary is subordinated to the executive; in this case, the President.[76] Any challenge to corruption is therefore doomed to fail. However, borrowing Legvold's categorisation, it is still perhaps not appropriate to categorise the state under President Soeharto's administration as a criminal one. Rather, Indonesia still belonged to the category of 'criminalised state', despite the undoubted potential it had by then to become a 'criminal state'.[77]

Aftermath of Soeharto

The Asian economic crisis forced President Soeharto to resign in May 1998. The movement that demanded his displacement was primarily motivated by the state of corruption, collusion and nepotism (KKN) that thrived under the New Order. Indeed, Soeharto was seen as the personification of KKN. Despite the limited available data, there can be little doubt that corruption touched almost everyone, not least because of the widening gap between classes, exacerbated by a small number of people who had become outrageously rich because of KKN. Soeharto and his family were, for example, the object of a journalistic investigation by *Time* in 1999 that identified them as one of the richest families in Indonesia, having accumulated wealth of approximately US$15 billion.[78] Transparency International reported that this amount was in reality an exorbitant US$35 billion,[79] all obtained through KKN.

The accuracy of these approximations could not be confirmed, and Soeharto himself claimed he had nothing in the bank.[80] He sued *Time* for defamation. Soeharto demanded that *Time* publicly apologise and pay damages of US$27 billion, with US$1 billion to be distributed to each of the twenty-seven provincial governments in Indonesia at that time. Soeharto was not asking for money personally (because he did not need any) but rather wanted to punish *Time*. I represented *Time* at the Jakarta District Court in this case.[81] The panel of judges unanimously opined that what was published by *Time* regarding the corruption of Soeharto's family had been in compliance with journalistic best practices in line with the press ethical code and therefore no defamation had been committed. Soeharto's claim was rejected.[82]

Soeharto appealed to the Jakarta High Court, which affirmed the decision of Jakarta District Court.[83] But at the Supreme Court, the lower court decision was overturned, and the panel of judges ruled that *Time* committed an unlawful act, ordering it to make a public apology in national and international media and to pay damages of Rp 1 trillion.[84] This decision not only threatened the freedom of the press but, more than that, threatened the corruption eradication movement. It had a chilling effect on the press in investigating and publicising corruption cases. *Time* filed a case review or *peninjauan kembali* to the Supreme Court arguing that the Supreme Court had made a fatal mistake in applying the law. According to a Supreme Court Circular Letter (Surat Edaran) sent to every District and High Court in Indonesia, such cases should be handled under the Press Law (Law No. 40 of 1999), but the Supreme Court failed to do so itself.[85] According to the Press Law, a person has a right to reply if he or she objects to a media report. He or she must exercise this right of reply before he or she can file a complaint with the Press Council. A civil claim can be filed at the court only after the Press Council has considered the complaint. Even then, the court can only apply the Press Law.

Time had to wait eight years before judgment in the case review was rendered by the Supreme Court, completely overturning the earlier Supreme Court decision.[86] The Court held that the judges in the earlier Supreme Court decision had committed a grave mistake by not applying the Press Law. *Time* won its legal battle, and press freedom to publish details of alleged corruption in the public interest was confirmed. As a result, the corruption eradication movement again found new energy.

As more and more corruption cases were exposed in the wake of Soeharto's fall, the media would send their reporters to investigate. At the same time, anti-corruption organisations emerged in many cities, making the anti-corruption campaign more visible than ever before, and corruption eradication was now being discussed within and outside the government. The former vice president, B.J. Habibie, had replaced his mentor, being sworn in within minutes of Soeharto reading out his resignation on national television in May 1998. Habibie commenced his administration by ushering in huge changes, reforming the electoral system, allowing new parties to be formed, and restoring freedom of the press.[87] In response to public outcry, he instructed the Attorney General's Office to investigate Soeharto's alleged corruption, which was believed to involve seven *yayasan* and amount to approximately Rp 4.1 trillion. An investigation was also conducted into the national car program and other undertakings of Soeharto and his family, which were suspected of being corrupt.[88] Although potentially uncomfortable investigating his predecessor, Habibie was required to undertake the inquiry by a decree of the People's Consultative Assembly (Majelis Permusyawaratan Rakyat Republik Indonesia or MPR), which was then the sovereign body in Indonesia. The decree provided that the incumbent president's '[a]ttempt to eradicate corruption, collusion and nepotism must firmly be conducted toward anyone be it state official, former state official, families and cronies including but not limited to private sector/conglomerates and former President Soeharto'.[89]

Due to Soeharto's illness, conducting the investigation was often difficult. There was speculation that Habibie, as Soeharto's former protégé, was so uncomfortable that he referred the matter to prosecutors to decide, putting himself at arm's length. When acting Attorney General Ismudjoko issued an order to cease investigation of Soeharto owing to the lack of evidence, Habibie did not question the decision.[90] But another case of corruption known as the Bank Bali Case was also being investigated in which Habibie's campaign team was allegedly involved.[91] The media widely reported this case, but the formal investigation made little progress. The impression was that Habibie did not really want the investigation to be completed as it would come too close to him and Golkar, the party he had inherited from Soeharto.

Although it was Habibie who promulgated and announced the groundbreaking new Law on Corruption Eradication, No. 31 of 1999,[92] his half-hearted investigations contributed to his unsuccessful bid for re-election. The presidential 'election' of 1999 was conducted by the People's Consultative Assembly, which had the exclusive power to appoint any person it chose as president. In 1999, this body rejected the formal 'accountability report' that Habibie as President was legally required to submit to it. There was therefore no way the Assembly would elect Habibie, forcing him to withdraw his candidacy.

The General Election (to choose members of legislative bodies) held in 1999 is generally considered to have been subject to less manipulation and intimidation than previous elections. International observers from many countries monitored the election in many locations throughout Indonesia and concluded that it was free and fair, democratically held, and offered legitimacy to the winners. I was Deputy Chair of the National Election Supervisory Body (Panitia Pengawas Pemilu or Panwaslu), and, together with international observers, examined all findings and reports. We unanimously decided that the election was reasonably democratic.

Abdurrahman Wahid (known as 'Gus Dur') was chosen by the MPR as Indonesia's fourth president in spite of the fact that his political party did not win the majority of votes.[93] He was a consensus candidate who was supported by various parties, including Islamists and nationalists. He outmanoeuvred Megawati Soekarnoputri, a former leader of opposition to Soeharto, even though her party, the Democratic Party of Struggle (Partai Demokrasi Indonesia—Perjuangan, or PDI-P), actually won the largest number of seats in the election. Megawati had to settle instead for the vice presidency. However, the nature of his victory meant that Wahid was seen as captured by political parties and lacking personal legitimacy. That made him appear a weak president, compromised to the benefit of the prevailing interests of other parties and the military. Inevitably, this made him ineffective, although he did his best to fulfil his commitments, complying with the demands of the people at large.[94] Critical civil society groups and intellectuals extended their support to Wahid, but he remained vulnerable to elite pressure.

A few major corruption cases were investigated under Wahid, but intervention from the various parties on which he relied to exercise power rendered these investigations ineffective. For example, Marimutu Sinivasan, owner of a major conglomerate, Texmaco, allegedly misappropriated loan facilities received from a state-owned bank. Sinivasan managed to prove that no losses had been suffered by the state.[95] The case of Soeharto was also reopened, and Wahid ordered an investigation as part of which Soeharto was questioned. Despite intense political pressure, the case was eventually litigated; however, it was dismissed because Soeharto's claimed illnesses prevented him from attending.[96] Additionally, alleged corruption within the military was reported by the media, but these allegations were never investigated, most likely owing to conflict within the military itself.[97]

It is not entirely accurate, however, to regard Wahid as a failed president as regards fighting corruption. Two cases demonstrate this: Hutomo Mandala Putra, better known as Tommy Soeharto, and Muhammad 'Bob' Hasan. Tommy Soeharto was accused of corruption regarding a land swap that caused state losses of Rp 96.6 billion. He was sentenced to eighteen months imprisonment and fined Rp 10 million. Tommy Soeharto could not accept he was sentenced by the court, and in revenge he orchestrated the killing of a Supreme Court justice, Syaifudin Kartasasmita.[98] Bob Hasan was accused of stealing US$75 billion from the national forestry fund. He was sentenced to six years imprisonment and fined US$24 billion.[99]

Additionally, Wahid established Tim Gabungan Pemberantasan Tindak Pidana Korupsi (TGPTK; the Combined Team for Corruption Eradication), consisting of lawyers from various law enforcement agencies. This was motivated by Wahid's frustration with the inadequacies of law enforcement agencies that, according to Wahid, were corrupt and unresponsive to the demands of the public to eradicate KKN. The TGPTK investigated a number of alleged corruption cases, including a justice of the Supreme Court, Yahya Harahap, who was accused of receiving a bribe from an advocate.[100] The TGPTK thus created great unease among corrupt law enforcers, which prompted the Supreme Court to declare that the team lacked a legal basis for its foundation, reviewing Government Regulation No. 19 of 2000, which had established the TGPTK.[101] Dissolution of the team temporarily halted the fight against corruption.

Before long, the political enemies of Wahid mobilised their resources to oust him from office. These efforts mainly targeted his increasingly erratic and unpredictable policies, particularly his threat to dissolve the national legislature, the DPR, which, controlled by Megawati's party, PDI-P, had become a source of opposition to Wahid's policies. Wahid, no longer a consensus choice, increasingly appeared an isolated president in his palace, like Soekarno in his last weeks in power in early 1966. His position was weakened still further by media reports alleging Wahid's involvement in what were called as 'Bulogate', in which he allegedly received money to promote someone to become Deputy Head of the National Logistics Agency (Bulog), and 'Bruneigate', where he allegedly received money to be distributed to civil society but did not do so.[102] Nothing was proven, but Wahid was soon impeached despite the absence of clear impeachment procedures in the Constitution. He was removed from office after little more than eighteen months.

Megawati came to power in July 2001 (in what would have been the second year of Wahid's presidency) and ruled until October 2004. In her three years of running the country, Megawati arguably did little to fight corruption, but under her presidency, the fourth and final amendment of the Constitution was concluded. The four years of constitutional amendments that culminated in 2002 must be regarded as a significant achievement, as they effectively changed the architecture of the state.[103] Additionally, it was under Megawati's administration that Law No. 30 of 2002 was promulgated, establishing the KPK (as discussed above).[104] Legally, a new era of corruption eradication began with the creation of the KPK.

During Megawati's presidency, a few important corruption cases were prosecuted. One that received considerable media attention was a purchase from Russia of four Sukhoi jets for the military for US$26 million. The jets were meant to be paid for with commodities, but the Minister of Finance, Budiono, required them to be paid for in cash. Budiono's refusal to make the payment motivated parliament to investigate the circumstances surrounding the transaction. However, the investigation was not conducted seriously, and allegations of corruption went nowhere.[105]

One of the very few corruption cases that did reach the court during Megawati's presidency related to the misuse of off-budget funds amounting to Rp 40 billion by Akbar Tanjung, when he was Minister of the State Secretariat. At the court of first instance, Tanjung was declared guilty and sentenced to three years imprisonment.[106] The High Court reaffirmed this decision, but the Supreme Court overruled it, annulled the previous judgments and acquitted him.

There were many other allegations of corruption, but none were prosecuted. Nevertheless, it is important to mention the existence of the Badan Penyehatan Perbankan Nasional (BPPN or National Banking Restructuring Agency, commonly known as IBRA). This agency had been under public scrutiny because it held Rp 533 trillion and shares in 200 companies related to Indonesian banks that collapsed in the aftermath of the Asian financial crisis that began in 1997. At the time, the government had bailed out the banks in return for all their assets, thus making the agency the most powerful and resource-rich agency in the country. Suspicions of mishandling funds—not to mention outright corruption—have always dogged BPPN.[107] The issuance of releases and discharges to debtors was later questioned and prosecuted.[108] All this tainted Megawati's reputation and her work combating corruption, which can be considered the weakest of all the post-Soeharto presidencies.[109]

In fact, Megawati lost the presidential election in 2004 partly because of her poor record in corruption eradication, despite the fact that it was she who officially inaugurated the leadership of KPK in December 2003.[110] However, the KPK was still in its infancy and unable to properly pursue alleged corruptors. For its first two years, it seemed preoccupied with drafting action programs, codes of ethics and the recruiting of staff, investigators and prosecutors. With great power vested in the KPK, it was important to ensure that all its actions and programs aligned with the KPK Law. No abuse of power could be tolerated; it could not afford to make mistakes because one mistake could cause enormous damage to its reputation. In other words, the KPK had to appear fair, objective and professional, and be accepted by the public as such. There could be no collusion between investigators and those questioned or called to testify. Naming someone as a defendant had to be supported by conclusive evidence. This was a new era of corruption eradication.

In Indonesia's first-ever direct popular election of a president, Susilo Bambang Yudhoyono came to power in 2004, with a commitment to fight corruption, empowering the KPK as the leading institution to do so. Yudhoyono ensured that the KPK had all the resources and support needed to pursue the big corruption cases that would otherwise be left untouched. However, the KPK was still strengthening its investigation, prosecution and prevention capacities, and was therefore unable immediately to take on big cases. For this reason, Yudhoyono formed Tim Pemberantasan Tindak Pidana Korupsi (Timtas Tipikor; Team to Eradicate Corruption), consisting of prosecutors, investigators and auditors headed by the Junior Attorney General for Special Crime, Hendarman Supandji.[111] This team immediately investigated former Minister of Religion Said Agil Munawar, for stealing US$71 million in funds for the Haj pilgrimage. Munawar was sentenced to five years imprisonment and fined US$250 000.[112] Another case investigated by the team involved the President Director of the state-owned insurance company providing insurance to workers, PT Jamsostek, Achmad Junaedi. It has been estimated that owing to his actions, the state suffered losses of up to US$31 million. Junaedi was found guilty, sentenced to eight years imprisonment and fined US$6.5 million.[113]

National Police Chief Sutanto played his part by investigating three-star police general Suyitno Landung, who served as head of the Police Investigation Unit. Landung was found guilty of mishandling fictitious bonds of BNI (Bank Negara Indonesia, a state-owned bank), causing state losses of Rp 1.7 trillion. Landung was sentenced to eighteen months imprisonment. This was the first conviction of a three-star general for corruption.[114] In 2004, the KPK decided to enter the fight against corruption by detaining Abdullah Puteh, Governor of Aceh, for alleged corruption in helicopter procurement. Puteh was accused of marking up helicopter prices to US$1.2 million, causing state losses of Rp 4 billion, according to the KPK. This was the first corruption case handled by the KPK, and it immediately faced pressure, intimidation and threats. The case of Puteh alerted the status quo elite to the KPK's intentions, and they tried everything they could to sabotage the investigation. The KPK resisted with all the legal power it could muster and, in the end, secured a ten-year jail sentence, with a fine of US$50 000.[115] The case of Puteh was the first corruption case against a sitting governor. It was unprecedented and signalled a new era in the fight against corruption by a new agency.

After Puteh, a series of major corruption cases were handled by the KPK. A commissioner of the Komisi Pemilihan Umum (KPU or Election Commission), Mulyana W. Kusumah, was caught red-handed receiving a bribe of Rp 300 million in a hotel. He was sentenced to three years imprisonment and fined Rp 60 million.[116] Meanwhile the chair of the KPU, Nazaruddin Syamsuddin, admitted receiving US$125 000 from a vendor and received six years imprisonment and a fine of Rp 300 million. He also had to pay compensation (*uang pengganti*) to the state amounting to Rp 1068 billion.[117] The KPK also managed to secure convictions for corruption committed by former Minister of Marine and Fishery Rokhmin Dahuri and the chair of the Investment Coordinating Board (BKPM), Theo Toemion. In addition, a number of governors and regents were investigated and successfully prosecuted by the KPK.[118]

However, the KPK's momentum seemed to evaporate when a new leadership team was appointed. Many—particularly anti-corruption activists—were disheartened because the newly appointed KPK leadership were chosen by the DPR and were arguably not the best candidates among those who took part in the selection processes. For example, Antasari Azhar, the new chairman of the KPK, was perceived as a controversial choice.[119] As a prosecutor with a questionable track record, he needed to establish credibility and prove his capacity to lead anti-corruption efforts. It has been reported in the media that the selection process of Antasari Azhar did not properly investigate his background and negative reports about him.[120]

Despite these concerns, Azhar acted quickly, launching an intensive investigation into allegations of corruption involving the former National Police Chief, Rusdihardjo, who was suspected of receiving bribes amounting to Rp 2.2 billion while he was Indonesia's ambassador to Malaysia. Rusdihardjo was ultimately sentenced to two years imprisonment and fined Rp 200 million.[121] The KPK also investigated corruption involving the Governor of Bank Indonesia (the central bank), Burhanuddin Abdullah. He was accused of abusing his power by pocketing Rp 100 billion belonging to Yayasan Lembaga Pengembangan Perbankan Indonesia (Indonesian Banking Development Institute Foundation), a foundation set up by the Bank Indonesia. He was sentenced to five years imprisonment and fined Rp 250 million.[122] The new leadership of the KPK most impressed its sceptics when the KPK arrested Aulia Pohan, Deputy Governor of Bank Indonesia, who happened to be an in-law of President Yudhoyono and in the pre-KPK era could therefore have expected to enjoy impunity. The Supreme Court sentenced Pohan to three years imprisonment and fined him Rp 200 million, and the president publicly declared he would not intervene.[123]

The impressive—even heroic—work of the KPK compelled the Attorney General and the police to slow the progress of their anti-corruption drive. As well as the threat the KPK posed to elite corruptors, there was institutional jealousy over the growing role and popularity of the KPK in the anti-corruption fight. Wide-ranging authority and a substantial budget allocated for the KPK's corruption eradication negated the trust of the people towards the Attorney General and the police, which they had enjoyed in the past, to some extent at least. Although it is unclear whether this motivated the investigation of Antasari Azhar, the KPK chairman, it was subsequently publicised that Azhar had an affair with a female caddy at a golf course he frequented. Azhar was then charged with masterminding the murder of a high-ranking executive of a state-owned enterprise, Nazaruddin Zulkarnain,[124] who was supposedly linked to the caddy. Azhar was arrested by police, tried and eventually sentenced to eighteen years imprisonment, despite some significant problems with the prosecution's evidence.[125] The fall of the KPK chairman looked like the beginning of a major attempt to undermine the KPK.

After Antasari Azhar's fall, two commissioners of the KPK, Chandra Hamzah and Bibit Samad Riyanto, were named suspects for alleged abuse of power for issuing travel bans against two corruption suspects who happened to be fugitives, Anggoro Widjoyo and Joko Tjandra.[126] Both Anggoro Widjoyo and Joko Tjandra had allegedly been involved in big corruption cases related to forestry and unlawful land acquisition respectively. It has never been made clear exactly what abuse of power was said to have been committed by the two KPK commissioners, but it was clear that police anger towards the KPK was growing. In fact, the police force then mobilised a campaign to weaken the KPK, presumably intending to take over the handling of corruption cases. It looked as though the KPK was about to be closed, but the public rallied behind Hamzah and Riyanto, condemning the undermining of the KPK and demanding their rehabilitation of the two commissioners. Tensions were very high and demonstrations were held in many cities, both in support of the KPK and against it.

President Yudhoyono, who campaigned for 'clean government' and 'zero tolerance of corruption', stepped in and established what was called Tim Delapan (Team of Eight), consisting of eight prominent lawyers and anti-corruption activists. I was one of them. Our task was to conduct a fact-finding investigation and mediate the conflict to find an acceptable solution that would enable the KPK to continue its corruption eradication operation.[127] Tim Delapan gathered evidence and interviewed almost everyone directly or indirectly related to the dispute between the police and KPK. The team concluded that there was no convincing evidence supporting the police decision to name the two KPK commissioners criminal suspects. Tim Delapan was under huge pressure from various people to help weaken the KPK, but it managed to resist it, issuing recommendations to President Yudhoyono for the rehabilitation of the two KPK commissioners, supporting the fight against corruption.[128] It was clear that the accusations made against them had no legal basis.

President Yudhoyono's determination to combat corruption won the hearts and minds of the public, leading to his re-election for a second term. It seemed that he was off to a good start; however, a series of corruption cases involving trusted aides of Yudhoyono ruined his relationship with the KPK. They undoubtedly caused a lot of headache and embarrassment because the alleged corruptors were either members of cabinet, legislators or leaders of Yudhoyono's own political party, Partai Demokrat, the largest at that time.[129] These cases undeniably tarnished the reputation and public perception of Yudhoyono's leadership and Partai Demokrat. Those who went to jail were, among others, Nazaruddin, Angelina Sondakh, Andi Malarangeng and Anas Urbaningrum, who were at that time major political figures appearing in the media and on national television almost daily. Perhaps it is necessary also to mention other big names from Yudhoyono's party, such as Jero Wacik, Hartati Murdaya, Sutan Batoegana and Agusrin Najamuddin, respectively Minister of Tourism, a leading businesswoman, a legislator and the Governor of Bengkulu Province.[130] The list can be expanded given that many local parliamentarians, regents and mayors with links to his party have also been convicted of corruption.

To be fair, it is important to note that corruption took place across party lines, and no one party could claim to be free from corruption. Legislators from a number of political parties were arrested by the KPK for receiving bribes to endorse the election of a noted economist, Miranda Gultom, who stood to become Senior Deputy Governor of the central bank.[131] Senior politicians from Partai Keadilan Sejahtera (PKS or Prosperous Justice Party), which was an Islamic party, were prosecuted by the KPK and subsequently convicted in relation to a beef importation scandal. Luthfi Hasan Ishaaq, the chair of PKS, together with his assistant, Ahmad Fattanah, allegedly received bribes amounting to Rp 1 billion. This amount was only a portion of the total number of bribes received, which apparently exceeded Rp 1 billion.[132] Another senior politician of PKS, Nur Mahmudi, was also sent to jail for corruption.[133] Nur Mahmudi was a former Minister of Forestry and mayor of Depok.

Additionally, those arrested for corruption included former top officials such as the former Minister of Social Affairs, Bachtiar Chamsyah, and the former Minister of Home Affairs, Hari Sabarno. Public procurement was greatly abused by high-ranking officials, including both Sabarno and Chamsyah.[134] The fact that so many people were involved in so many corruption scandals shows how deeply embedded corruption had become within executive power.[135] This tension is perhaps most clearly exhibited by the conduct of the former Chief Justice of the Constitutional Court, Akil Mochtar, who delivered judgments in local election disputes in favour of those who paid him. Mochtar maintained that he was being framed and therefore refused to admit that he was corrupt.[136] This case was deeply humiliating for Indonesia's democratic reputation, given that the Constitutional Court was born out of Reformasi, and had been considered one of the success stories of Indonesia's post-Soeharto transition to democracy.[137]

The humiliation did not stop there. Not long after the imprisonment of Chief Justice Mochtar, another justice of the Constitutional Court, Patrialis Akbar, was arrested and later sentenced to eight years in prison.[138] This case cemented the public's fear that the fight against corruption could not be won. It seemed there was no hope at all. If there were any ray of hope, it was because at the Supreme Court, the senior justice who headed the criminal chamber, Artidjo Alkostar, consistently increased the sentence for every person found guilty of corruption by the lower courts. He positioned himself as a formidable foe of the corrupt.[139]

It is no exaggeration to say that the state was captured by corruption and that many people abused their power for their own and their party's enrichment, maintaining the status quo by co-opting the media and critics. It is in these circumstances that Yudhoyono completed his maximum two terms in office. In 2014 Joko Widodo or 'Jokowi', as he prefers to be known, won the presidential election. He promised to 'clean up' the country, rid it of systemic, endemic and widespread corruption, and thereby rehabilitate the state to become one based on the rule of law.[140]

According to Indonesian Corruption Watch (ICW), a leading anti-corruption non-government organisation, in 2014, there were approximately 629 corruption cases, which together caused the state to suffer losses amounting to approximately Rp 5.29 trillion.[141] These cases were investigated and prosecuted by both the KPK and the prosecutor's offices, but not all were brought before the courts. Some that were involved Minister of Religion Suryadharma Ali, Minister of Tourism Jero Wacik, legislator Sutan Bhatoegana and Chairman of the State Audit Agency Hadi Purnomo.[142] Interestingly, at the regional level, corruption involving governors, regents and mayors as well as local parliamentarians was also significant, with forty-three cases involving governors, regents and mayors, in addition to eighty-one local parliamentarians who had been investigated for suspected corruption.[143]

In 2015, the number of corruption cases increased, especially in the regions. They involved, among others, the Governor of North Sumatra Province, Gatot Pudjo Nugroho, the Governor of Banten Province, Ratu Atut, and the Governor of Riau Province, Anas Maamun.[144] In North Sumatra Province, two governors were found guilty of corruption, while in Riau Province, three governors were jailed for their part in corruption.[145] This served as a reminder, if one were needed, that corruption in the post-Soeharto era had become decentralised and was rife in local administrations, with governors, regents, mayors and local parliamentarians jointly and separately engaged in corruption in a way never possible under the highly centralised New Order.[146]

According to Indonesian Corruption Watch, approximately 71 per cent of corruption cases resulted in convictions, reinforcing public concern about widespread, systemic and endemic corruption.[147] Most of those involved in corruption were associated with political parties, although one may also find civil servants and businessmen who are without political affiliation among those convicted. In fact, as a matter of practice, corruption in most cases, including those in which politicians were prominent, involved other individuals, be it government employees or people from the business community.

In 2016, the KPK conducted seventeen of what it called Operasi Tangkap Tangan (OTT or Operation Red-handed), directly intercepting illegal transactions or deliveries of bribe money.[148] No fewer than ten heads of municipalities were tried for corruption, in addition to legislators, civil servants and businessmen.[149] Again, those imprisoned for corruption were mostly associated with political parties such as Governor Nur Alam, a Partai Amanat Nasional (PAN) cadre; Damayanti, a PDI-P cadre; Mohammad Sanusi, a Gerindra party cadre; and I Putu Sudiartana, a Partai Demokrat cadre.[150] One senior politician who regarded himself as not being a member of a political party, Irman Gusman, former chairman of Dewan Perwakilan Daerah (DPD or Regional Representative or Senate), was also imprisoned for corruption.[151] It follows that corruption is not unusual for politicians; in fact it is standard practice. Arguably, politicians have always lived with corruption, and the problem is that their powers, by their own nature, are inherently corrupting. Politics is obviously expensive, and those in politics need substantial amounts of money to fund their campaigns and other activities. The fact that their remuneration is far from enough, together with weak legal and institutional checks and balances, have enabled politicians to abuse their power in order to accumulate the funds they need to stay in power.

In 2017, the KPK investigated seventy-two corruption cases and conducted nineteen OTTs throughout the country,[152] an increase from 2016. Again, many prominent people were named as suspects, including, as mentioned, Justice Patrialis Akbar of the Constitutional Court,[153] and Governor Ridwan Mukti of Bengkulu Province.[154] As in 2016, a reasonably high number of municipal heads were arrested by the KPK, mostly for receiving bribes for various procurements and issuing business permits such as mining and plantation rights.[155] Interestingly, in 2017, a number of law enforcement officials, prosecutors, judges and advocates were also arrested by the KPK through OTT.[156] Parlin Purba and Rudy Indra Prasetya, prosecutors from Bengkulu and Pamekasan respectively, were alleged to have accepted bribes. Two judges, Sudiwardono and Dewi Suryana, of the High Court of North Sulawesi and Bengkulu, were also alleged to have accepted bribes. Additionally, court clerks and advocates were also named as suspects.[157]

In 2018, there were more municipal heads, national and local parliamentarians investigated, prosecuted, tried and imprisoned for corruption, mostly for accepting bribes.[158] Among those named suspects were two governors, the governor of Jambi Province, Zumi Zola, and the governor of Aceh Province, Irwandi Yusuf.[159] In total, there were twenty-nine heads of municipalities. Together with those municipal heads, a significant number of local parliamentarians who worked in concert with governors, regents or mayors were also involved in the corruption cases. A member of cabinet, Minister of Social Affairs Idrus Marham, was also named as a suspect for accepting bribes through his assistant, Eni Maulani Saragih, who happened to be a member of the DPR. (Marham was later convicted.) This corruption related to a power plant project in Riau Province.[160]

In 2019, the number of corruption cases seemed to decrease. The KPK and civil society had been cornered by politicians who accused the KPK of focusing more on sending perpetrators of corruption to prison than building up governance that minimised corruption. Law No. 30 of 2002, which granted the KPK vast power to go after corruption perpetrators, was perceived by most politicians as the source of the problem. Therefore revision was badly needed, they argued, and in their proposal to revise Law No. 30 of 2002, most of the KPK's authority was curtailed. The attempt to revise the said law forced the KPK to focus its efforts on countering it, but this came at a cost for corruption eradication. Hence the KPK prosecuted substantially fewer corruption cases in 2019. Among others were cases involving the Minister of Sports and Youth Imam Nahrowi, the Governor of Riau Islands, Nurdon Basirun, and a few heads of regencies and legislators, regional as well as national.[161] Laode Syarif, Deputy Chair of the KPK, admitted that the KPK prioritised revising Law No. 30 of 2002 because its leaders knew it could not be effective if the law as drafted was passed.[162] Eventually, the revision of Law No. 30 of 2002 was passed; the KPK and civil society were not able to block or delay the revision.

It is not an exaggeration to say that the state has been captured by a network of corrupt officials both at regional and national levels. As seen, corruption is still endemic and systemic, but perhaps it is not warranted to conclude that the state has become a 'criminal state'.[163] When petty corruption and grand corruption cases are combined, whether investigated by the police, prosecutors and/or the KPK, it is difficult to avoid the conclusion that corruption remains widespread and pervasive such that the thousands of corruption cases handled and the hundreds of corrupt individuals imprisoned have had little or no deterrent effect. Those arrested by law enforcement officials feel that they were caught due to bad luck. They believe that the numbers involved in corruption and untouched by law far outnumber those arrested and imprisoned.

This is ironic, and it has happened despite the fact that in the history of Indonesia, there have never been so many corrupt people—thousands in fact—investigated, prosecuted, tried and jailed, including many from the centre of power, such as ministers, governors, regents, mayors, parliamentarians, prosecutors and judges, most of whom worked together with business people to steal the wealth of society.

A new political will

As explained earlier, when Reformasi began in 1998, corruption in Indonesia was among the worst in the world.[164] Undoubtedly corruption has been the number 1 challenge of all governments that followed the collapse of the New Order regime. Many packages of legislation dealing with corruption eradication, state audit systems, the ombudsman, money-laundering, whistleblowers and others have been promulgated by different governments, but by far the most important law—a milestone—was that establishing the KPK. This new state auxiliary agency was a child of Habibie's Reformasi. Distrust of existing legal agencies such as prosecutors and police meant that the public wanted a more powerful anti-corruption agency, and the experiences of other countries, particularly the Independent Commission Against Corruption (ICAC) in Hong Kong, inspired the creation of the KPK.[165]

Since its inception, the KPK has imprisoned a great number of politicians, bureaucrats and businesspeople for corruption. Every day, it seems, the media publish reports on corruption and OTTs conducted by the KPK. While the total number of corruption cases far exceeds the number handled by the KPK, it is undeniable that the KPK's achievements have been outstanding.

Of course, the KPK has not been able to stop corruption—in fact, it remains a cancer in the body of the Indonesian state. However, confidence has been growing that the cancer might one day be cured, as Transparency International's Corruption Perceptions Index of Indonesia suggests. Since 2009, Indonesia's index on corruption has been steadily improving from 2.8 (out of 10) to 37 (out of 100) in 2020. However, Indonesia's score on the Corruption Perceptions Index certainly needs to improve, but to reform its governance system, law enforcement and culture of permissiveness will take some time. Therefore the KPK's work is definitely a step in the right direction.

Chapter 3

KPK: a superbody?

> ... *government agencies that have handled corruption cases have not been functioning effectively and efficiently in eradicating corruption.*
> Law No. 30 of 2002 on Corruption Eradication Commission

Law No. 30 of 2002 on the Corruption Eradication Commission (the KPK Law), states in its preamble that corruption has become pervasive and prevalent, endemic, systemic and widespread. As a legal expert from the University of Sydney, Simon Butt, says:

> By any standard, Indonesia's corruption levels are high. Corruption has been prevalent in government throughout most of Indonesia's modern history, including under Soekarno's Old Order (Orde Lama) (1947–1966) and even during Dutch colonialism. By most accounts, however, corruption increased significantly and became deeply entrenched in government institutions during Soeharto's reign. There are indications, albeit anecdotal, that since Soeharto's fall, overall corruption has in fact increased. Regional autonomy is commonly blamed for this because it disperses power to regional officials, many of whom are thought to exploit their office for private gain.[1]

A historic turning point for the nation occurred in 1998, when evidence of widespread and systemic corruption, increasing poverty and widening class disparity were widely publicised. Reformasi triggered popular demands to combat KKN.[2] The need to eradicate KKN became the common denominator and the most significant motivator of every mass demonstration throughout the nation, and naming people accused of corruption became a manifestation of the public's deep anger, which had remained unspoken in the past. This led Habibie's government to promulgate a new law on corruption eradication, namely Law No. 31 of 1999 on the Eradication of Criminal Acts of Corruption.[3] The preamble to the law stipulates (among other things):

> b. that the result of criminal acts of corruption so far creates loss to state finances or the state economy, it can also hinder the growth of national development, which demands a high level of efficiency;
> c. that the Law No. 3 of 1971 on the Eradication of Criminal Acts of Corruption is no longer in line with the legal needs in society. For that reason, it is deemed necessary to replace it with the Law on Eradication of Criminal Acts of Corruption, which is expected to be more effective in preventing and eradicating the criminal act of corruption.

Clearly, KKN was public enemy number 1. President Habibie was then perceived as the protégé of Soeharto,[4] little more than an extension of his former mentor, and most doubted he would seriously combat corruption. The new law was therefore met with suspicions that it was merely a public relations exercise, particularly when people realised that Habibie would not seriously commit his government to investigate the alleged corruption of Soeharto and his family.[5] One may doubt President Habibie's sincerity in fighting corruption, but the fact remains that Law No. 31 of 1999 was promulgated by President Habibie, and Article 43 stipulates:

> 1. Within a maximum period of 2 (two) years since this Law takes effect, a Commission for the Eradication of Corruption Criminal Act shall be set up;
> 2. The Commission referred to in paragraph (1) has the duties and authority to establish coordination and supervision, including conducting the inquiry, interrogation and prosecution in accordance with the existing legislations;
> 3. The members of the Commission referred to in paragraph (1) comprise elements of the government and the public;
> 4. Provisions on the establishment, composition or organisation, working system, accountability, duties and authority as well as the membership of the Commission as referred to paragraph (1), (2) and (3) will be determined by statute.

It is not entirely fair to view Habibie simply as an extension of his former mentor. He had embarked on a number of bold initiatives, such as revoking the permit previously needed to publish newspapers and magazines, promulgating the Law on Government Officials Free and Clean of Corruption, Collusion and Nepotism in addition to the Law on Political Parties, which opened the door for new political parties, and granting East Timor the right to a referendum for independence—all at significant political risk.[6] In circumstances where the status quo was still intact, it was difficult for Habibie to manoeuvre to open a new chapter for the nation that allowed it the possibility of being more open, democratic and free from corruption, but he did precisely this.[7] Accordingly, many Indonesians still perceive Habibie as a champion of reform, the author of a new page in the history of the nation.[8] For example, the establishment of the KPK under President Megawati was the follow-up of the idea first put forward by President Habibie. Governance reform preoccupied President Habibie's thinking, which is why legislation on corruption eradication, free press and democratisation came into being. Habibie believed that corruption eradication required a strong free press and a functioning democracy. Those who carefully read the KPK Law, including its general elucidation, can understand Habibie's reasoning.

Corruption in Indonesia has become a culture that has successfully proliferated in the community, and corrupt acts have been on the increase over the years, both in terms of the number of uncovered cases and the losses to society, as well as in terms of how corrupt acts have become more methodical and systemic, as they bore into every aspect of everyday life in Indonesia.

This rampant growth of corruption will wreak havoc not just to Indonesia's economic life but also to the viability of the nation in general. Corruption is a violation of the social and economic rights of society, and as such should no longer fall under the standard category of merely 'crime'; corruption is an extraordinary crime. Therefore, the effort to eradicate corruption must no longer be just acting against a criminal act, corruption must be prosecuted by extraordinary means.

A new Indonesia seemed to be a dream of President Habibie, and President Abdurrahman Wahid, who replaced Habibie, shared this vision. He passed Government Regulation No. 71 of 2000 concerning Procedures for People's Participation and Awards for Prevention and Eradication of Corruption. President Wahid understood that the public plays a significant role in combating corruption through reporting or whistleblowing. In this regard, the government can either issue a letter of appreciation or pay a commission to the Attorney General from the proceeds of recovered corruption money, albeit relatively insignificant in amount.[9]

President Wahid did not come from a major party, and he struggled to stay in power. In any case he was too erratic and physically unwell to achieve much. Frustrated, he finally declared political war by threatening the dissolution of the DPR, the national legislature.[10] He lost that fight, and the DPR forced Wahid to step down before his term ended.[11] In retrospect, President Wahid should have not taken on the DPR, given that his party was a minority and lacked the support of a reliable coalition. His uncompromising attitude finally brought an end to his presidency. In this situation, according to the Constitution, Megawati, as Vice President, replaced Wahid. As mentioned in chapter 2, it was under Megawati that Law No. 30 of

2002 on the Corruption Eradication Commission was promulgated, together with Law No. 20 of 2001 on the Amendment of Law No. 31 of 1999 on Eradication of Criminal Acts of Corruption, although, as mentioned, these initiatives had their origins under previous presidents.

Law No. 30 of 2002 on the Corruption Eradication Commission was enacted on 22 December 2002, and mandated the government to form the KPK. Unfortunately, President Megawati did not actually form the KPK until the DPR reminded her to do so. Many believed Megawati had no interest in expediting the process of setting up the KPK. People around her were not in favour of the KPK, but mounting pressure from various corners finally forced her hand.[12] Even then, it took Megawati a full year to establish the KPK. A Selection Team (Panitia Seleksi), of which I was a member, helped screen candidates for the five leadership positions on the commission. Thousands of candidates filed applications for positions as KPK leaders, and after long and heated debates, the Selection Team identified ten prospective candidates to be submitted to the DPR, who were then publicly interviewed by it. Five of the ten were chosen by the DPR to be commissioners of the KPK, namely Taufikurahman Ruki, Erry Riyana Hardjapamekas, Tumpak Hatorangon Panggabean, Amin Sunaryadi and M. Rasul. Taufikurachman Ruki was selected as the first chairman of KPK while the others served as deputy chairs.

The KPK was formally established in December 2003. However, it was not yet ready. As a new institution, it needed time to recruit and train investigators, prosecutors, financial analysts and other staff. It also needed time to draft its operational manual and priorities, not to mention secure an adequate operational budget. The KPK therefore went through an institutional capacity-building process in its first two years before embarking on corruption eradication.

Yudhoyono, who was sworn in as President after defeating Megawati in the 2004 elections, campaigned to fight corruption and, in his inaugural address, assigned the highest priority to combating corruption. Despite this, tangible results were slow in coming.[13] Yudhoyono maintained his rhetoric on anti-corruption while allowing the KPK to build its institutional capacity by developing its program and priorities, internal disciplinary guidelines, code of ethics and recruitment of personnel. The KPK held a series of brain-storming sessions with legal and financial experts in order to understand the complexities of corruption and its eradication. I was invited numerous times to the KPK to share my view as to why the KPK needed some time to be ready to declare war on corruption perpetrators. It was clear that the fight against corruption was a fight the KPK could not afford to lose. Public expectations were undoubtedly high, and failure would quickly erode support for the KPK.

Yudhoyono, in keeping with his campaign promises, initially formed an *ad hoc* team to fight corruption, namely, Timtas Tipikor or the Coordination Team for Corruption Eradication, which consisted of prosecutors, police and financial officers from the Attorney General's Office, the Ministry of Law and Human Rights and the National Police.[14] This team immediately investigated a number of high-profile corruption cases involving high-ranking officials, including but not limited to former cabinet members, a police general and top businessmen. Aside from Timtas Tipikor, similar initiatives were pursued by the Chief of Police and Minister of Finance. The momentum to fight corruption seemed to be on the rise, with different initiatives complementing one another.

Despite daily media reporting corruption and other malfeasance, actual prosecutions seemed slow. One reason for this is that, by law, the KPK must ensure that it has at least two pieces of legally convincing evidence before naming someone as a corruption suspect.[15] It cannot afford to be reckless about this because, until recently, the KPK could not issue a letter of investigation termination (SP3). This means that once a suspect has been named, the KPK is obliged to proceed all the way to trial.[16] This explains why the KPK needs substantial time to reach the stage where it is able to name someone as a suspect, a stage loosely equivalent to charging a person in countries with the common law system. Under normal practice, police investigators as well as prosecutors can terminate an investigation by issuing an SP3, if there is not enough evidence that supports the charges. That explains why corrupt perpetrators prefer to be investigated by either the police or prosecutors.

Status quo elites as well as some lawyers, together with the DPR and politicians, have sought to amend the KPK Law on a number of occasions, usually to no avail. Only in 2019 was the KPK Law finally amended by, among other things, revoking the provision that prohibits the KPK from issuing an SP3. Under the revised KPK Law, the KPK can now terminate an investigation, giving hope to corrupt perpetrators that they might be able to arrange discharge.[17] The revised KPK Law, Law No. 19 of 2019, marks the beginning of formal weakening of the KPK in combating corruption. Other initiatives that have since undermined the KPK will be discussed later.

By the end of 2004, the KPK's institutional and capacity building were nearly complete, and it immediately commenced pre-investigations, investigations and prosecutions in addition to working on prevention, supervision and coordination of corruption eradication.[18] Yudhoyono was thus the first president to have the opportunity for a fully-fledged fight against corruption. Corrupt officials, politicians and businessmen were summoned by the KPK, one after the other, to be investigated as witnesses or suspects. The corruption eradication machinery moved into high gear, and for the first time, corruption eradication was undertaken as aggressively as expected by the public, something unprecedented. Those previously perceived as legally untouchable were now subject to questioning by the KPK, and hopes of corruption reducing seemed to run high.

Transparency and accountability were mentioned in every speech by government officials, but it was not long before corruption eradication was confronted by mounting criticism and resistance aimed at dissolving the KPK, or at least undermining it. Yudhoyono defended the KPK and assisted by requiring all governmental agencies to work on strengthening governance and making the system cleaner and more efficient.[19] But attempts to dissolve and undermine the KPK continued by various means, be it through review by the Constitutional Court of the KPK Law, or the police and prosecutors threatening to withdraw investigators and prosecutors from the KPK.

This was possible because, as a new anti-corruption body, the KPK had no trained investigators and prosecutors of its own. It had to rely on the police force and the prosecutor's office, and that is the way it should be. Corruption eradication has always been the task of the government, especially law enforcement agencies. Later, the KPK also recruited its own investigators independently. At one point, there was open conflict between the KPK and the police that almost threatened the KPK's survival, but the support of Yudhoyono saved the KPK from the most serious attacks.

Tension between the KPK and the police arose on the first day the KPK was established. The police felt cornered and discriminated against, because a great deal of police power was taken over by the KPK; however, the police managed to control its disappointment and anger, and they did not initially surface. This did not last long. Inevitably conflict came to the surface. It started when the former chair of the KPK, Antasari Azhar, who himself was in police detention, accused KPK Commissioners Chandra Hamzah and Bibit Samad Rianto of abusing their power and allegedly receiving envelopes with money. According to the police, the envelopes were received in the parking lot of an office building in Jakarta.[20] The two KPK commissioners were named suspects and later detained at the police detention facility. By detaining Hamzah and Rianto, the KPK seemed to lose its authority and was unstable because the remaining commissioners, Muhammad Yasin and Haryono Umar, were overwhelmed by their tasks. The KPK appeared to be losing its grasp.

President Yudhoyono commissioned five senior and reputable persons, known as Tim Lima (Team of Five), to investigate the conflict and select interim commissioners to lead the KPK. Tim Lima was headed by Coordination Minister of Politics, Law and Security Admiral A.S. Widodo, with Minister of Law and Human Rights Andi Matalata, former chair of KPK Taufikurachman Ruki, Presidential Adviser Adnan Buyung Nasution and myself as members. The Tim Lima was given two weeks to finish its assignment, and, after interviewing reputable people from the legal and business communities, it selected three candidates to be interim KPK commissioners: Tumpak Hatorangan Panggabean, former Commissioner of the KPK, a senior prosecutor; Mas Achmad Santosa, public interest lawyer; and Waluyo, at that time director of state-owned oil company Pertamina.[21] President Yudhoyono accepted Tim Lima's recommendations and immediately instructed his Secretary of State Minister, Hatta Rajasa, to prepare the inauguration of the interim commissioners of the KPK. Owing to his experience and seniority, Tumpak Hatorangan Panggabean was chosen as interim chair of the KPK. The addition of new blood made the KPK able to function again, despite all the problems lingering between it and the police. I remember clearly the huge relief I felt at the time, and my conviction that Indonesia could not afford to lose the KPK.

However, it was only a matter of time before the conflict between the KPK and the police resurfaced. The head of the police Investigation Division, General Susno Duaji, launched a public attack by labelling the KPK a 'lizard' (*cicak*) that should not dare fight the police, whom he called a 'crocodile' (*buaya*). This comment was perhaps a manifestation of Duaji's anger at the criminal investigation of the Bank Century case, in which his name had been mentioned. Thus, naming Chandra Hamzah and Bibit Samad Rianto suspects followed by detention seemed to be a type of retaliation. But Duaji underestimated the popular support of the public for the KPK, which soon named the conflict between the police and the KPK 'Cicak vs Buaya', wearing badges that read 'Aku Cinta Cicak' (I Love the Lizard).[22]

The conflict was very damaging both to the KPK and the police, making many people, including President Yudhoyono, worried. Attempts to mediate did not succeed, and finally the President was forced to set up another team known as Tim Delapan (Team of Eight) to do fact-finding and present recommendations. Tim Delapan was asked by the President to find ways to resolve the conflict in accordance with the prevailing law to strengthen the momentum of corruption eradication by holding the culprits accountable before the courts. Tim Delapan was also asked to suggest how the institutions of the KPK and the police could be 'saved' and reformed accordingly.²³

Tim Delapan first demanded the police to suspend the detention of the two KPK commissioners, Chandra Hamzah and Bibit Samad Rianto, as a prerequisite to resolving the conflict. In a gesture of good faith, the police temporarily suspended their detention so Tim Delapan could conduct its fact-finding in a way that would cool the tensions. Tim Delapan did so by gathering available information, and verified it by cross-examining all parties directly or indirectly related to the conflict. Tim Delapan also consulted experts for their professional opinions and recommendations. Among others cross-examined were General Susno Duaji, Chandra Hamzah, Bibit Samad Rianto, investigators from both KPK and the police, and other people identified as involved in the conflict.²⁴

Tim Delapan finished its fact-finding and submitted its report and recommendations to President Yudhoyono. In essence, the report described the background and causes of the tension between KPK and the police, which was mainly triggered by the police feeling left behind in the fight against corruption, feeling distrusted in handling corruption cases and, ironically, indirectly losing opportunities to earn corrupt fortunes. Tim Delapan recommended that Hamzah and Rianto be rehabilitated and those involved in attempting to criminalise them be prosecuted.

President Yudhoyono commended Tim Delapan at the palace and reiterated his commitment to continue fighting corruption. He even mentioned that he wanted to have the Indonesian Corruption Perceptions Index gradually improved, hoping that it would make Indonesia 'investment grade' and that foreign investment would eventually feel more secure in conducting business in Indonesia. At the time, I chaired Transparency International Indonesia and was thrilled to see the generally positive reaction of appreciation of what had been done by Tim Delapan. The President's hope that the Indonesian Corruption Perceptions Index would improve over time was encouraging for me because the Corruption Perceptions Index has been a core project of Transparency International, and is used as reference by almost every state in the world.

Formally, the conflict between the KPK and the police had ended. Hamzah and Rianto regained their positions as vice chairs of the KPK, and corruption eradication resumed. This is not to say that the police wholeheartedly accepted the resolution of the conflict, but for the sake of the nation, everyone agreed to accept what was recommended and decided by President Yudhoyono on the basis of the recommendations of Tim Delapan. President Yudhoyono had done his best to find ways to keep the momentum of corruption eradication alive, and the public seemed to appreciate the political support of Yudhoyono for the KPK, enabling its survival in the face of a major threat.

Yudhoyono's successor, President Joko Widodo (or Jokowi) also campaigned to combat corruption and therefore also supported the mission of the KPK. For him, corruption is a cancer and, if necessary, the most severe punishment must be imposed. In personal conversation, Jokowi told me he has no interest in theories about corruption. It is a straightforward issue and must be tackled seriously, if necessary, by imposing the death sentence.[25]

Jokowi's commitment to fight corruption has not changed; however, he has been surrounded by political parties that have been made angry and stressed by the aggressive corruption eradication measures taken by the KPK in which many politicians have been jailed for corruption. The political parties orchestrated a series of amendments to the KPK Law that were passed under Jokowi's rule and have severely weakened it, as I explain below. By default, Jokowi had his share in this weakening process, tarnishing his reputation, especially in the eyes of people who had high hopes for the KPK as the sole champion of corruption eradication. Undoubtedly, the KPK is now much weaker, although hope is not totally depleted. A substantial number of people still maintain hope for it, and in fact the main source of the KPK's strength and support comes from the public, as it acknowledges:

As the brainchild of Reformasi and an independent body, KPK's ultimate responsibility is to the people. The public has been KPK's most reliable ally in times of crisis. It is true that maintaining public support and trust is essential to KPK's very existence, but more importantly, the public is the blood and drives the fight against corruption itself. Without public support and awareness, the fight against corruption will simply cease to be.[26]

Powerful institution

Normally, an Indonesian independent state auxiliary institution is accountable to either the president or the DPR. Generally, there is no institution, even if independent in its operation, that can escape accountability—at the minimum, it must be accountable to the higher institution that established it. However, the KPK is an exception. It was established by virtue of the KPK Law, which states in Article 3 that 'the KPK is a state agency that will perform its duties and authority independently, free from any and all influence'.[27] This independence was dismantled by Law No. 19 of 2019, by which the KPK was made part of the executive branch and accountable to the President.[28] Furthermore, Article 25 of Law No. 19 of 2019 stipulates that all KPK staff are part of the civil servant corps. This signifies the KPK's loss of independence and neutrality.

Corruption eradication in the past has been considered a failure for a number of reasons, one of them being that no institution previously set up enjoyed independence in its operations; all were subordinated to the appointing agency. Corruption eradication in most cases was therefore undertaken half-heartedly, because the overseers felt threatened. This means that all of them functioned as little more than a symbolic gesture for the international community, including foreign investors and donors.[29] When corruption eradication was finally tabled by the Habibie and Wahid governments as a priority matter, the demand from various anti-corruption and social activists was to have an institution strictly independent of all influence, including, but not limited to, the president and the DPR.[30]

That thinking directed both the government and legislators to design the KPK as an independent institution accountable to the public but not to other state institutions, as is clear from Article 20 of Law No. 30 of 2002:

(1) The KPK is responsible to the public in performing its duties. The KPK is also obliged to convey reports transparently and regularly to the President, the DPR and the State Audit Agency;
(2) Responsibility to the public as outlined in the paragraph (1) is to be expressed in these manners:
   a. Obligation to audit synergy and financial accountability in accordance with the (KPK's) work program;
   b. Publication of annual reports;
   c. Open access to information.

With this type of legal arrangement, the KPK is guaranteed independence and security in the sense that it cannot be dissolved and the commissioners cannot be discharged by either the President or the DPR.[31] But it remains to be seen whether this security is still guaranteed with the revision of the KPK Law that placed the KPK as part of the executive branch. This means that the head of the executive branch is legally authorised to impose certain restrictions and limitations such as requiring the investigators to obtain permission from the Supervisory Board (Dewan Pengawas) to wiretap conversations of alleged corruption perpetrators. This deprives the KPK of its independence and security.[32] The latest restriction imposed was forcing the investigators and prosecutors of the KPK to pass a type of allegiance test in order to continue their tenure in the KPK.[33]

Attempts to dissolve the KPK have been made several times on the basis of the argument that initially the KPK was designed as an *ad hoc* institution primarily due to public distrust of both the police and the Attorney General. Accordingly, once distrust is eliminated, corruption eradication should be given back to the police and Attorney General, as has been done in many countries.[34] During mediation between the KPK and the police that I was involved in when open conflict occurred, the police repeatedly made this point, emphasising that the KPK is an *ad hoc* institution. At one point when the police were deemed ready (or rather, reformed) to perform the function of corruption eradication professionally and independently, then the KPK must be dissolved. However, all attempts to dissolve the KPK have thus far failed for the reason that corruption is still systemic, endemic and widespread,[35] and the support of the public at large remains profoundly strong.[36] In fact, proponents of the KPK have urged the president and the DPR to declare the KPK a permanent corruption eradication institution and even to insert it in the Constitution.[37]

The KPK leadership consists of five commissioners, one of whom serves as chair while the other four serve as vice chairs. Leadership of the KPK is collective, meaning that all commissioners have equal rights and responsibilities. The chair of KPK is not above or superior to other commissioners. In practice, all decisions require collective agreement.[38] Selection of KPK leadership is done by a selection committee set up by the President.

KPK commissioners enjoy a term of office of four years with the possibility of one more term.[39] However, in the history of the KPK, no commissioner, with the exception of Alexander Marwata, has served more than four years, because none have passed the fit and proper test conducted by the DPR for a second term, for the obvious reason that the DPR dislikes them for pursuing corrupt parliamentarians.[40] It is important to remember that statistically, the number of corrupt parliamentarians arrested, investigated, prosecuted, tried and imprisoned by the KPK outnumbers every other category of corrupt individuals, be it ministers, governors, mayors or heads of regencies.[41] Between 2004 and 2019, almost 400 politicians were prosecuted by the KPK. This number is much higher if co-perpetrators are included.[42]

The KPK Law does not have any provision that allows either the President or DPR to discharge commissioners of the KPK. This helps guarantee their independence. Their tenure is fixed and guaranteed by law unless the commissioner: dies; reaches the end of his or her term of office; is convicted of a criminal offence; is unable to perform his duties for more than three months consecutively; voluntarily resigns; or violates Law No. 30 of 2002.[43] Antasari Azhar was discharged by President Yudhoyono after he was convicted of murder and sentenced to eighteen years imprisonment. Antasari Azhar seems to be the only commissioner of KPK discharged from his chairmanship for involvement in a criminal case.

The KPK therefore legally appears as a powerful institution with a broad range of powers and authorities under Article 6 of the KPK Law: coordinating and supervising relevant institutions in combating corruption; conducting pre-investigations, investigations and the prosecution of corruption cases; undertaking prevention of corruption activities; and monitoring the running of the government. Article 7 of the KPK Law further stipulates that KPK is authorised to: coordinate pre-investigations, investigations and prosecutions; decide the reporting mechanism of corruption eradication handling; request information concerning corruption eradication programs from other relevant institutions; hold hearings or meetings with relevant institutions dealing with corruption eradication; and request reports from relevant institutions concerning preventive action taken against corruption.

Articles 8 and 9 explain that supervision involves authority to take over the handling of corruption cases if there are problems that hamper the pre-investigation, investigation and prosecution stages. In practice, the KPK will take over handling corruption cases only if: (a) there are reports by a member of the general public about corruption cases being ignored; (b) there is unnecessary delay in corruption case-handling; (c) there are suspicions that such delay is aimed at protecting the corrupt; (d) there are indications of corruption in the handling of cases; (e) there is intervention by the executive, legislative or judicial branches; or (f) there are circumstances in which the police and prosecutors are practically unable to conduct the investigation and prosecution. It is clear that the KPK has a great deal of power and authority to do whatever it deems necessary to eradicate corruption.

The revised KPK Law has made KPK weaker and compromised. Articles 6 to 11 set out restrictions curtailing the original powers of the KPK, obliging it to report to the President, with the procedure for submitting the report to be determined by government regulation. The KPK must now obtain approval from the new Board of Supervisors formed under the revised KPK Law to perform some actions. Despite the fact that at the time of writing the Board of Supervisors consists of people with integrity, no one can deny that the KPK has been weakened. In particular, wire-tapping and confiscation now need approval by the Board of Supervisors, which may be rejected or withheld.[44]

Certainly, the KPK is not able to pursue and handle all corruption cases because it lacks sufficient resources, being a newer and much smaller institution than the police and the Attorney General's Office, and the number of corruption cases throughout the country is unimaginably vast.[45]

In its original form, the KPK Law placed some limits on the type of case the KPK can, on its own initiative, handle or take over. It can only deal with:
- cases that involve law enforcement officials or civil servants (whether only civil servants or civil servants acting with other people);
- cases that attract the attention of the public at large; and
- cases that cause loss to the state in the amount of at least Rp 1 billion.[46]

Petty corruption is not within the mandate granted to the KPK.[47]

This means all other corruption cases, particularly petty corruption, are handled by the police and the Attorney General's Office. However, it is important to note here that, in reality, the police and the Attorney General's Office do handle grand corruption cases too.

The revised KPK Law amended Article 11 of the KPK Law to further narrow the ambit of cases the KPK can handle to cases that (1) involve law enforcement, state officials and any person involved with the alleged corruption of the law enforcement official; and (2) cases that cause loss of at least Rp 1 billion to the state. Cases that attract public attention can no longer be taken over by the KPK, for reasons that are not clear. It is fair to guess that the exclusion of the above cases is perhaps because so many corruption cases involving politicians caught the public's attention. Amendment of Article 11 of the KPK Law is an act of self-protection by politicians.

In performing its pre-investigation, investigation and prosecution duties, the KPK Law confers a broad range of powers on the KPK, including to:

a. Tap into communication lines and record conversations;
b. Order the relevant institution to ban a person from leaving the country;
c. Request financial information of a suspect or a defendant from banks or other financial institutions;
d. Order banks or financial institutions to block accounts of a suspect or defendant;
e. Order a temporary suspension of a suspect or a defendant from his job;
f. Request financial and tax information of a suspect or a defendant;
g. Temporarily halt financial and business transactions, temporarily revoke permit, licence and concession belonging to a suspect or defendant, assuming that those are related to alleged corruption currently being investigated;
h. Request Interpol or another nation's law enforcement agencies to search, arrest an alleged suspect or confiscate any and all evidence in their jurisdictions; and,
i. Request assistance from the police and other law enforcement agencies to arrest a suspect(s) and to confiscate any and all evidence related to a current corruption case being investigated.[48]

With such wide powers, there is no reason—apart from resources—the KPK cannot function properly and effectively in going after corrupt individuals and corporations. It is regrettable that the power to tap into communication lines and record conversations has now been curtailed by the revised KPK Law, which requires the KPK to seek permission from the Board of Supervisors to conduct wiretaps.[49] What has been undermined here is not only the delay the approval process inevitably creates, because time is of the essence in corruption eradication, but also, most importantly, this requirement will leave room for leaks that might have been communicated to the suspects, providing them the opportunity to destroy evidence, hide or leave the country. This is not to say that the Board of Supervisors is not credible, but the possibility of leaking cannot be ruled out. After all, the success of corruption eradication in most cases is due to the power to intercept, tap and record telephone conversations. Most corrupt perpetrators caught by the KPK have been implicated as a result of intercepting and recording telephone conversations and prosecuted on the basis of that evidence.

The KPK has also often been supported and helped by the public at large. There have always been information and reports received by the KPK from private citizens knowledgeable about particular corruption cases. There are also whistleblowers who voluntarily come forward with all manner of proof to be reviewed by the KPK.[50] In addition, the media and civil society are behind the KPK in rallying nationwide public opinion and support in order to strengthen the KPK in performing its duties. But going after corrupt individuals is easier said than done. The status quo, rent seekers who swallow exorbitant fortunes, are still strong in all their embedded networks—they have their 'people' within the government, although their influence has been gradually diminishing. The failure to prosecute Soeharto is a good example of the impunity some still enjoy. The tensions between the KPK and the police and prosecutors on a number of occasions, discussed above, reflect the uneasy relationships between these law enforcement agencies.

Sending the corrupt to jail does not necessarily mean that people in general will be deterred from committing corruption. Look at what happened in 2016, when the KPK's clandestine operations caught twenty-nine parliamentarians, businessmen, governors, mayors, heads of regencies and judges red-handed receiving bribes for infrastructure development projects.[51] As long as there are opportunities, corruption will keep recurring. Therefore corruption eradication must also focus on prevention or on building up governance in the government as well as in the private and civil society sectors.[52] It is for this reason that the KPK Law stresses the importance of prevention in combating corruption. The KPK is, among other things, authorised to: review submissions on the income and wealth of public officials, including legislators and judges; receive reports and determine the status of gratifications paid; hold anti-corruption education at every level of education; embark on anti-corruption 'socialisation' programs; conduct anti-corruption campaigns for the public at large; and enter into both bilateral and multilateral cooperation in fighting corruption.[53]

If the prevention programs are successful, then the number of people engaging in and arrested for alleged corruption will significantly reduce. Prevention work does not attract the limelight, but it is truly the core of corruption eradication. It is perhaps regrettable that the KPK spends most of its energy in pre-investigation, investigation and prosecution of corruptors, and prevention runs second to repression. Perhaps this explains why corruption eradication has not been as successful as was hoped when the Reformasi period began in 1998. The revised KPK Law underlines the importance of 'prevention' and tasks the KPK to allocate more time and energy to prevention as a core program of corruption eradication.[54]

Another task assigned to the KPK is monitoring.[55] Monitoring means conducting thorough reviews of the management practices of government administration. The KPK is also authorised to propose changes to the government's administration management if, according to KPK, there is room for corruption. Lastly, the KPK is authorised to submit reports to the President, DPR and State Audit Agency, if its proposals for changes to the government administrative management are not implemented.[56]

In summary, the KPK was given a wide range of powers, and many rightly perceive it as the most powerful law enforcement institution ever established in Indonesia.[57] Sadly, the KPK has not been able to use its power effectively and efficiently because its capacity and independence have been gradually undermined by political contestation and resistance, both within the government and society, in ways that weaken the KPK and, perhaps inevitably, will paralyse it.[58] The revised KPK Law has weakened the KPK, making it less formidable and more vulnerable to corrupt intervention.

Inevitable rivalry

While the KPK has been weakened since the KPK Laws were amended, it generally still has vast power, even though it is no longer quite a superbody. There is no institution that will happily tolerate another institution that takes away some of its main functions, especially if those functions are a source of pride as well as fortune in the sense of additional revenue (bribery) received in performing its functions.[59] It was therefore inevitable that police and prosecutors, who traditionally had monopolies on crime investigation and prosecution respectively, would resent the KPK.

At the outset, the resentment did not seem too visible, but internally it must have been widely felt as a punishment of sorts, and slowly grew bigger and bigger until it rose it to the surface. Eventually, it exploded into open conflict, thereby wounding not only the institutions involved but also the rationale for having a new institution to further the public's dream of one day having a healthy and clean government. Alexius Jemadu wrote an interesting paper on this issue, stating: 'Ideally, the KPK and the national police would work together to build synergy for the effectiveness of the law enforcement system in eradicating corruption. Unfortunately, this is not always the case. Competition between these two powerful institutions sometimes becomes unavoidable, especially when political parties in the parliament try to intervene for their own interest.'[60]

Jemadu did not mention the Attorney General, but it goes without saying that any law enforcement agencies dealing with corruption eradication must have felt disrespected, not to mention humiliated, when an institution such as the KPK was established expressly to make up for their shortcomings.⁶¹ The KPK therefore needed be tactful in dealing with corruption cases directly or indirectly related to the interests of the police and the Attorney General's Office. It should not be seen as intentionally embarrassing by both the police and the prosecutors. It must be careful in issuing statements not to offend other institutions that have conducted corruption eradication in the past and are, to a larger extent, still engaged in prosecuting petty and medium-size corruption—and, despite the law, still run grand corruption cases as well.

Admittedly, this is a dilemma because the original intent of forming a new institution to combat corruption was precisely because of widespread distrust of the police, the Attorney General's Office and the judiciary.⁶² Interestingly, this law introduces a special court for corruption cases, although institutionally the special court for corruption is still under the auspices of the Supreme Court. In this special court, the judges consist of career judges and *ad hoc* judges where a majority of the panel of judges must be *ad hoc* judges. This suggests a distrust of ordinary court and career judges on the basis of past experiences when many corrupt officials were acquitted, allegedly because of bribery. However, if the police and the Attorney General's Office sabotage, stall or ignore assignments and instructions from the KPK, it cannot be as effective as it is expected to be. Simon Butt is correct in stating:

> The anti-corruption initiatives ... including the KPKPN (Komisi Pemeriksa Kekayaan Pejabat Negara or the State Official Asset Auditing Commission), TGPTK (Tim Gabungan Pemberantasan Tindak Pidana Korupsi or the Combined Team for Corruption Eradication) and Ombudsman, shared important features. They could coordinate, advise and offer assistance, but could take no real action themselves. Ultimately, responsibility fell to ordinary police and prosecutors to decide whether to pursue the case and to the ordinary courts to adjudicate it. Leaving corruption cases to these three (KPKPN, TGPTK and Ombudsman)

institutions has been perhaps the most significant single impediment to effective enforcement of Indonesia's corruption laws. All these are widely considered to be largely incompetent, underfunded and corrupt.[63]

Although Butt's statement only mentions KPKPN, TGPTK and the Ombudsman, it is also applicable to the police and the Attorney General's Office. In 2017, the police handled 1028 corruption cases, while the KPK handled around 114 cases.[64] In the meantime, the Attorney General's Office handled 1918 cases, far outnumbering all those handled by both the KPK and the police together.[65] To what extent both the police and the Attorney General's Office succeeded in handling all corruption cases remains disputed and/or unclear. In this respect, it is important to note that one should not be misled by the sheer number of corruption cases, if those cases are being handled by institutions perceived as among the most corrupt, tainted by so many cases involving their senior officers.

The fact that both the police and the Attorney General's Office lost some power seems to have been at the heart of their rivalry with the KPK. Law No. 2 of 2002 on Police stipulates that the main task of the police is to guard public order and uphold the law.[66] This means that the police are authorised to investigate any and all types of criminal offences, including but not limited to corruption cases, which are described as a type of special crime. In exercising investigation functions, the police are bound by the Criminal Procedure Code (KUHAP) as the basis for all criminal investigations. Furthermore, the Code of Criminal Conduct establishes police as sole investigators for all criminal offences, including corruption offences.[67] It is important to emphasise that although grand corruption cases have been taken over by the KPK, that does not necessarily mean that the police should avoid these cases.[68] The media covered almost every grand corruption case investigated by the police, which amounted to exorbitantly large amounts of money corrupted from the state. Corruption of natural resources has been widespread, and the police have seemed to go aggressively after the corrupt parties, namely governors, heads of regencies and businessmen. It is no secret that, along the way, many senior police officers have either been tempted or have been trapped and colluded with suspects.

Law No. 16 of 2014 on Prosecutors tasked prosecutors to carry out prosecution, submit dossiers to the court, represent the state in court proceedings and enforce court judgments.[69] Additionally, prosecutors are also tasked with raising the legal awareness of the people, monitoring printed materials that are in contravention of public order, and dealing with blasphemy cases.[70] However, prosecutors have also been tasked with investigating special offences such as human rights violations and corruption.[71] It is apparent that prosecutors, to some extent, still exercise their function of investigating so-called special crimes, particularly grand corruption cases.[72] Furthermore, the elucidation to the Law on Prosecution states that the prosecutor has the authority to investigate and prosecute cases related to gross human rights violation and corruption, as the crimes belong to the special crimes category.[73]

There is also a dispute over budget, especially in handling corruption cases. Both the police and the Attorney General's Office have continually complained that their budgets are far too small compared to the budget of the KPK. In absolute terms, the overall budgets of the police and the Attorney General's Office are undoubtedly higher than that of the KPK, given the fact that the KPK does not have as many personnel. The KPK is authorised to open offices in the provinces, and even if the KPK had offices in all thirty-four provinces (which it does not), the number of its staff would still be much lower than those of police and prosecutors throughout the country. In 2018, the KPK's budget was Rp 854.2 billion,[74] while for 2019, the KPK received a budget of Rp 813.4 billion.[75] The police and the Attorney General's Office for 2018 received Rp 95 trillion[76] and Rp 6.4 trillion respectively.[77] As stated earlier, the issue is not overall budgets but more the cost of handling corruption cases and the numbers actually prosecuted.

How much budget is allocated for handling corruption cases in the KPK as compared to the police and the Attorney General's

Office? Generally, the KPK spends more funds for each corruption case handled, because it wants to ensure that investigations are conducted fairly, professionally and thoroughly. Since the KPK, according to the KPK Law before it was revised, cannot cease an investigation once started, it therefore could not afford to make a single mistake.[78] This explains why the KPK allocated a reasonably significant amount of funds for investigations. The Attorney General's Office budget for a single corruption case covering pre-investigation, investigation, prosecution and enforcement of judgment is Rp 200 million, while the police spend Rp 208 million. In the meantime, the KPK spends approximately Rp 255 million for pre-investigation and investigation while prosecution and enforcement of judgments receive separate funds, and in total, the amount is very much higher than the budget received by the police and Attorney General's Office.[79] Since 2020, the annual budget of the Attorney General's Office has been increased, but interestingly the tension persists.[80]

Inevitably, rivalry cannot be overcome. It seems that both the police and prosecutors feel that they have been unfairly treated, but they ignore the whole rationale of reform in corruption eradication. Like it or not, reform is very fragile.[81] Additionally, it is important to note that, as mentioned, the revised KPK Law has granted the KPK the right to terminate investigations,[82] but the budget for case handling has not significantly changed.

With the KPK handling grand corruption cases, holding press conferences and appearing on television almost every day, the commissioners of the KPK have become media darlings and popular among the public. The commissioners receive many invitations to speak at seminars, be it in Indonesia or overseas. Commissioners of the KPK are not ministers in a presidential cabinet, not military or police generals, not film stars, but their names are widely recognised within society. How can you not be famous and respected if you are the ones that investigate, prosecute and imprison corrupt officials who often arrogantly flaunt their wealth, obtained by illegal undertakings and corruption? Since the police and the prosecutors are no longer the only institutions dealing with grand corruption, and since most high-profile corruption cases go to the KPK, the limelight shifts to the KPK. That fame enjoyed by the KPK explains why a number of KPK commissioners have been tempted to aspire to high office. For example, Abraham Samad, a commissioner and, at one point, chair of the KPK, thought about running for President or Vice President.[83] Other commissioners of the KPK have become high-ranking officials within ministerial offices or state-owned enterprises. In other words, by becoming commissioners of the KPK, they become famous and are often treated as heroes, enjoying privileges that police officers and prosecutors do not have.

In addition, it is important to mention that for the police and prosecutors, the partial loss of authority to handle grand corruption cases means the loss of 'big fish'. It has been stated earlier that in reality, the police and the prosecutors still handle grand corruption cases; however, most are handled by the KPK. For institutions perceived as corrupt institutions, the loss of high-profile grand corruption cases means that some of their access to wealth is also lost. This is not to say that all police and prosecutors are involved in illegally enriching themselves, but there are many police officers who have been caught because of their corruption. Police generals Djoko Susilo and Didik Parmono were both successfully prosecuted by the KPK for corruption,[84] and there have been other police generals, as well as senior prosecutors, who have been caught and imprisoned by the KPK. These cases reinforce the fact that the police and prosecutors are indeed still involved in corruption, the very reason the KPK was set up in the first place.[85]

Bringing police generals and senior prosecutors to court and sending them to jail inevitably increases antipathy towards the KPK in their institutions. In the name of police and prosecutor solidarity, *l'esprit de corps*, both the police and the prosecutors led by the National Police Commander and the Attorney General have struck back and tried to regain lost power and status. They have not only publicly defied the authority of the KPK in handling grand corruption cases but also were willing to resort to almost any means to strengthen their own grip and regain their power. They were even involved in weakening the KPK as an institution by withdrawing their members who had been working as investigators and prosecutors in the KPK. They tried hard to paralyse, if not even dissolve, the KPK.[86] Institutional rivalry seems unavoidable. To a certain extent, the rivalry has weakened the KPK in the sense that it is now not as effective as it was expected to be.

The corrupt fight back

Jemadu identifies two linked factors that have weakened the KPK: namely, problematic support from both the executive and legislature, and revision of the KPK Law.[87] The term 'problematic support' is not Jemadu's. It was coined to explain the ambiguity of support from the government, in the sense that in some cases, full support was extended but, in most cases, support has been half-hearted. Worse, the support was not given when the interests of the legislature and/ or the executive branches were threatened, or even when members of the legislature were caught red-handed, times when attacks on the KPK would be expected to escalate. The case of Aulia Pohan, an in-law of President Yudhoyono, is a good example.

Aulia Pohan was arrested by KPK for alleged corruption at the Indonesian central bank, Bank Indonesia. He was arrested when Yudhoyono was in office, and for Yudhoyono, the arrest was seen as a slap in the face, a blatant embarrassment. Although Yudhoyono still offered his support to the KPK, no one would have been surprised if at that time Yudhoyono had punished the KPK. Interestingly, Yudhoyono managed to reconcile his anger and the importance of corruption eradication.[88] Between the executive, the legislature and revision of the KPK Law, not-so-invisible actors have weakened the KPK, even if they have not been able to dissolve it.

Public opinion has been slowly formed, underlining the 'historical' interpretation that the KPK was set up as an *ad hoc* institution, not a permanent one.[89] From the perspective of the Constitution, the Indonesian state, like most, has only three main branches of power: namely, the executive, legislative and judicial branches. Having an institution that does not belong to the executive and judiciary but leads the fight against corruption appears an anomaly, a deviation from the normal constitutional arrangements of a modern state. Traditionally, this is not to say that it is not possible to have such an institution, but it should not be seen and treated as a permanent one. However, the contemporary development of constitutions in many parts of the world has reached the stage where the traditional architecture of states has been supplemented by what is known as state auxiliary agencies,[90] and the KPK is undoubtedly one of those.[91] In Indonesia, other state auxiliary agencies include the Election Commission, the Ombudsman and the Judicial Commission. Admittedly, complexities of contemporary state affairs need more than the executive, legislative and judicial branches, especially with regard to checks and balances that must be strengthened. State auxiliary agencies are meant to ensure that abuse of power can be avoided.

Attempts to abolish or at least undermine the KPK are challenged by anti-corruption activists, who mobilise public opinion and people's support. The forces of status quo and the corrupt seem united in weakening and ultimately dissolving the KPK with all the power and resources they have. This is what I have called the 'corruptors fight-back'.[92] However, every time the KPK is attacked, civil society, the media and the people unite to protect it and remind the government that corruption is the enemy of the people—Indonesia will not move on while widespread corruption is tolerated. It is not an exaggeration to say that in the eyes of the public, the KPK is the last bastion for eradicating corruption. As mentioned earlier, anti-corruption agencies set up under Soekarno and Soeharto did not have strong legal grounds, were not powerful enough, were attached to the executive branch, lacked comprehensive anti-corruption programs and failed to gain the trust of the public. Therefore they were not effective at all.[93] By contrast, the KPK, an independent and effective corruption eradication commission established by law, is a real threat to corruptors, and they want it destroyed, dissolved or at least weakened, which is why a coalition of corruptors in concert initiated repeated informal campaigns to destroy the KPK.

One action available under the Indonesian Constitution is to challenge the constitutionality of laws, or provisions within them, in the Constitutional Court.[94] The Constitutional Court has the power to decide whether a law or provisions of that law should be declared unconstitutional and therefore no longer enforceable. A decision of the Constitutional Court is a decision of the first and last instance—no appeal can be made. Article 24C of 1945 Constitution stipulates that: '(1) The Constitutional Court shall have the authority to make final decisions in cases of first and last instance handling the review of laws against the Constitution, to decide on authority arguments among state institutions whose competence is enshrined in the Constitution, to decide on the dissolution of political parties, and to decide on disputes regarding general election results.'

At the time of writing, the KPK Law had already been challenged on at least twenty-two occasions.[95] In fact, the KPK Law might be the most challenged law in the history of the Constitutional Court,[96] demonstrating how much hate and displeasure the KPK Law has provoked in many people, especially those directly or indirectly implicated in corruption cases (although some cases have been brought by anti-corruption activists). So far, the Constitutional Court has generally supported the KPK and the objectives of the law that established it.[97]

A key question dealt with by the Constitutional Court in many of these cases is the constitutionality or legality of the KPK itself. Its opponents have usually argued that the KPK must be declared unconstitutional because it undermines the authority of the executive, legislative and judicial branches. In some of these cases, applicants have asked how can one have an independent institution that is not subordinate to the President when it does a job that is normally conducted by the police and the Attorney General, which are subordinated to the President? Arguably, the KPK is not part of the executive, legislature or judiciary, but exists outside the normal branches of power. According to this argument, the KPK had no place in the constitutional system and the law that established it should be deemed unconstitutional.[98] Of course, as mentioned, the revised KPK Law now places the KPK as part of the executive and accountable to the President.[99] The weakening of the KPK to a certain degree has succeeded.

Another question relates to the jurisdiction of the KPK over cases that took place before the enactment of the KPK Law. This, it is argued, is a violation of the non-retroactive principle, whereby a law may not be applied to actions that took place before it was passed. The *tempus delicti* principle must be honoured. On this view, the KPK has no legal and constitutional basis by which it can investigate corruption cases that occurred before the enactment of the KPK Law. The Constitutional Court rejected this argument in one case brought before it. The court concluded that there was no violation of the retroactive principle since the KPK only took over cases that were already being investigated by the police. In other words, the KPK did not initiate new investigations.[100]

In 2006, a judicial review application questioned the 'absolute power' of the KPK to investigate corruption cases. It was claimed that this intruded upon the powers of the police and the Attorney General, and that undermined the separation of powers established in the Constitution. The Constitutional Court rejected this challenge, holding that the KPK Law did not violate the separation of powers principle.[101]

In another Constitutional Court case, also in 2006, the petitioner argued that the KPK, as a 'superbody' vested with 'excessive power', violated human rights and legal certainty, which are protected by the Constitution. Specific questions asked in this case related to the right of the KPK to wiretap and record phone conversations of persons alleged or suspected of corruption. The Constitutional Court held that the detailed procedures stipulated in the KPK Law meant that it was not possible for it to violate human rights and legal certainty, not least because fixed time limits for case handling are stipulated clearly in the KPK Law.[102]

It is important to reiterate here that the revised KPK Law has regulated the procedure for wire-tapping phone conversations so that approval from a new Board of Supervisors is needed.[103] The

KPK is thus no longer entirely free to wiretap telephone conversations of alleged corruptors as it sees fit. As explained earlier, this requirement must be considered a huge blow that weakens the effectiveness of the KPK in going after the corrupt, because it creates the possibility of delay and of offenders being warned of an imminent phone tap.

In 2007, another petition argued that the KPK Law is discriminatory in the criteria established for selection of commissioners of the KPK. However, what sort of discrimination was alleged was not clearly articulated. Legally, anyone meeting all requirements to be a commissioner of the KPK can apply, and that person could be elected as commissioner if he or she passed all the tests, including a public fit and proper test conducted by the DPR. These procedures applied to all candidates so they were not discriminatory. For this reason, the Constitutional Court rejected the judicial review application in its entirety.[104]

Those wanting to dissolve or weaken the KPK have also sought to do so by amending the KPK Law. No fewer than four amendments have been lodged in the DPR by its members, with two of the amendments being proposed jointly by the government and DPR. The reasons given for these amendments varied, but it is obvious that overall the amendments were aimed at strictly regulating the conduct of the KPK and 'domesticating' it. Amendments were proposed in 2010, 2012, 2015 and 2016.[105] As mentioned, the latest amendment eventually passed in 2019, albeit without any public participation.

The amendments have created five key changes. One concerns the KPK being able to exercise its powers without any strong, centralised supervision and control. Under the KPK Law, advisers to the KPK appointed by commissioners are meant to advise the commissioners of theKPK, but they seem to have been inadequate, in the sense that the commissioners can decide to do whatever in their opinion is the best for the KPK, regardless of contrary advice they may receive.[106] In short, the amendment was intended to establish an internal control mechanism within the KPK to ensure better accountability and compliance with due process of law—something many critics view as lacking within the powerful KPK. Therefore the amendment proposed what it called a Board of Supervisors. The authority of this board was designed as broadly as possible, requiring the commissioners of the KPK to obtain its consent before exercising some of its powers, such as intercepting or recording the telephone conversations of corruption suspects.[107] Moreover, members of the Board of Supervisors are appointed by the President, not by the KPK itself. The KPK and anti-corruption activists at large felt this was an attempt to make the KPK weaker, ineffective and unable to perform its main function, and there have been suspicions that the Board of Supervisors may serve as a gateway for political interference. It remains to be seen whether the greatest fears of the supporters of the KPK are ever realised.

The amendment of Article 12 paragraph 1 of the KPK Law regarding the authority of the KPK to intercept and record telephone conversations of suspects seems to have been the main objective of both the executive and the legislative branches. This is one of the most criticised articles of the KPK Law. As mentioned, the reality is that most corruption suspects have been discovered thanks to the interception and recording of telephone conversations. For members of the DPR, this power is seen as a violation of privacy as a fundamental human right. Essentially, this authority to intercept and record telephone conversations has frightened those involved in corruption. The amendment was not intended to revoke said authority but to regulate it closely, in the sense that any interception and recording must be approved by either the head of the district court or the Supervisory Council.[108]

As seen, the amendment of Article 12 paragraph 1 KPK Law has passed. This undermined the KPK's effectiveness. Who will guarantee that the process of obtaining consent from either the head of a district court where the suspect is domiciled or the Board of Supervisors will not result in a leak to the suspects, given widespread judicial corruption? Who will guarantee that the Board of Supervisors is acting in an independent manner given the fact that all members are appointed by the President? Who will guarantee that the consent will be given expeditiously? In October 2019, despite all these concerns, this amendment was passed by the DPR.

The amendment also granted the KPK the right to issue letters of termination of investigation (SP3) if no convincing evidence of corruption is found during an investigation. Originally, the KPK Law had no provisions on the authority to issue letters of termination of investigation (SP3); therefore a suspect, once named, must be processed all the way to the court trial.[109] The Criminal Procedural Code (KUHAP, or Kitab Undang-Undang Hukum Acara Pidana) contains a provision on the right of police investigators to issue letters of termination of investigation (SP3). The Attorney General also has similar authority.[110] In the environment of judicial corruption, the power to issue letters of termination of investigations (SP3) has often been abused, sold to the highest bidder.[111] That was why the KPK was not initially given any such right, thereby ensuring that all corruption investigations end up in court once a person is publicly named a suspect (*tersangka*). The DPR wanted this authority granted to the KPK, presumably to allow for the release or discharge of corruption suspects, especially those from the DPR and political parties. The KPK and anti-corruption activists rallied the support of the people to oppose this amendment, but they failed.

Another crucial issue is the recruitment of KPK investigators. Since its establishment, all investigators have been recruited from the police as they were already trained as investigators. The investigators then were appointed as KPK employees, but were not totally released by the police, meaning that at any time the police could recall them, thus obstructing any investigations they were handling.

A related problem arises when the KPK investigates suspects or witnesses who are police, or known to be close to the police. In this case, a dual loyalty problem is encountered in the sense that on the one hand, the investigator respects the job assigned to him, but on the other hand, he or she will also likely feel under an obligation to protect the police institution. The KPK eventually devised an interpretation of the KPK Law that allowed it to recruit its own investigators independently and not remain fully reliant on the police.[112] Needless to say, this strengthened the KPK as an institution. However, members of the DPR viewed this with suspicion and eventually amended the KPK law to ensure that all KPK investigators come from the police.[113] However, the right to recruit its own investigators independently has been previously affirmed by the Constitutional Court,[114] and affirmed by the DPR during the amendment's processes, so the KPK can still recruit its investigators from the public as well as the police.[115]

Judicial corruption is another challenge faced by the KPK in its fight against corruption, be it in the judiciary, police or the Attorney General's Office. Judges, prosecutors and police officers have been caught red-handed in clandestine operations. It is in this context that criminalisation of KPK commissioners and investigators occurred, not only as a form of retaliation but also with the ultimate objective of dissolving the KPK. Legal expert Denny Indrayana makes the following interesting observation:

> Certainly, the practice of criminalising Commissioners or employees has occurred repeatedly every time senior police officers are named suspects by KPK. When three-star police general Susno Duadji, head of national police investigation division, was investigated by KPK, two Commissioners of KPK, Chandra Hamzah and Bibid S. Riyanto, were criminalized. Then, when two-star police general Djoko Susilo was alleged to be involved in a driving license simulator corruption, an investigator of KPK, Novel Baswedan, was criminalised. Now, when three-star police general Budi Gunawan is named corruption suspect, Bambang Widjoyanto and Abaraham Samad together with Novel Baswedan are named suspects.[116]

Criminalisation of KPK commissioners and employees inevitably led to confrontation between the police and the KPK, between the supporters of the KPK and the status quo forces who feel threatened by the KPK's corruption eradication activities. Criminalisation does not mean that an offence is committed. It is more a type of retaliation by accusing commissioners of KPK of crimes, despite lacking evidence or legal grounds. The supporters of the KPK *en masse* succeeded in capturing public opinion, forcing the police to reconsider their position. Presidents Yudhoyono and Jokowi also intervened to resolve tensions and guarantee the independence of the KPK, exploiting anti-corruption politics for their political benefit. However, the criminalisation of the KPK's commissioners and staff has, to some extent, demoralised them, in the sense that there is no security for them in their day-to-day work. For this reason various people have urged the government and DPR to grant immunity to all KPK commissioners and employees in performing their duties during their terms of office. Unfortunately, this has not happened.

In a nutshell, what has been described above are various attempts to dissolve or weaken the KPK by those who felt threatened by corruption eradication activities spearheaded by the KPK. This 'corruptor fight-back phenomenon' will never stop, simply because Indonesia has never had a corruption eradication institution as strong and independent as the KPK. The KPK Law has now been revised to render the KPK much weaker, but from a corruptor's perspective, the KPK still must be destroyed. Massive and widespread support for the KPK will presumably remain, but that might not be enough. It must remain resilient and not underestimate future threats.

Decline of political support?

The KPK Law has granted all necessary powers to the KPK to function properly and independently as Indonesia's core corruption eradication agency. However, the KPK does not exist in a political vacuum, and since inception it has been repeatedly attacked by various parties such as the police, the Attorney General's Office, the DPR, political parties and the business community, as explained above. All parties seem to act both individually and jointly in attacking the KPK with the common objective of dissolving or at least weakening it. Presumably, these attacks will never stop, and therefore the survival of the KPK, to a large extent, depends on the support of the executive, the legislature and the judiciary, which, in turn, is offered only as a result of organised and concerted lobbying and agitation by civil society, especially anti-corruption activists.[117] After more than a decade of attacks on the KPK, it has become much weaker than initially intended. Its effectiveness now depends largely on the creativity of its leadership and the discretion of the President.

Certainly, political support is profoundly important, but to what extent can it last? This is something very difficult to secure, and regime changes can be expected to determine what sort of support the KPK will receive, depending on the priorities of new rulers. Therefore Jemadu is right when he states that, 'unless the executive and legislative powers share the commitment to eradicate corruption, the promotion of good governance [*corruption eradication*] in Indonesia will always be jeopardized by the institutional obstacles embedded in the nature of the operation of the Indonesian presidential system'.[118]

Nevertheless it is important to remember that neither the executive nor legislative branches live in a political vacuum. Their existence and priorities have oftentimes been dictated by political parties from where they received their support. In turn, the political parties have been run by political elites with all political and economic interests embedded in them, leading them to exploit any opportunities to strengthen their positions and leverage. In circumstances where politics require huge amounts of money, political parties may subordinate political ideals to competing business interests.[119] Indrayana argues that the KPK's legal standing must be strengthened by making it a constitutional body.[120] Having the KPK Law as a legal basis for the KPK is far from adequate because it is always vulnerable to change or repeal by the DPR, as happened with the revision of the law through a simple majority vote. However, if the KPK is stipulated in the Constitution, it will not be easy to dissolve or weaken it as that requires a two-thirds majority in the MPR.[121] In ASEAN, nine out of ten member countries have similar anti-corruption institutions—only in Indonesia is it not enshrined in the Constitution.[122]

Unfortunately, it is difficult to comprehend that a constitutional amendment could be made under the present circumstances, where hostility towards the KPK seems to be evenly felt within all political parties, taking into account the number of politicians across the political spectrum who have been imprisoned by the KPK.[123] In this respect, it is wise to assume that political support will never increase—rather it might gradually diminish. However, the KPK will still exist given the fact that openly opposing corruption eradication will continue to be deemed as being anti-Reformasi.[124] As mentioned earlier, historically the KPK is indeed a child of Reformasi and has become a fortress for its survival. It remains to be seen to what extent the KPK will manage to be as effective as the public expect. It is a complex situation. Ardian Maulana and Hokky Situngkir write:

> The complexity of social life has forbidden us to see a problem merely by using singular perspectives. Corruption eradication is a complex aspect of human life, while corruption itself is never simple. In Indonesia, the KPK has become an important institutional body for eradicating corruption. In her works combating corruption in Indonesia, KPK has faced the reality that corruption eradication is not as simple as law enforcement, but has also grown to be a political discourse.[125]

Since the KPK does not exist within a political vacuum, the dynamics of politics must be taken into account, but it is wrong to expect genuine political support from the political elite. Making the KPK an institution sanctioned by the Constitution is an important objective; however, the continuing support of the people at large is the main source of strength for corruption eradication. In the end corruption eradication must itself transform from an institutional-legal fight into a socio-legal one. The KPK must ensure that the fight against corruption is the fight of the people. This will give it the best chance of avoiding being held hostage to political contests.

Chapter 4

State capture corruption

> *Corruption is not a characteristic of the system in Mexico. It is the system.*
>
> Stephen Morris, *Political Corruption in Mexico*

After the thirty-two years of Soeharto's rule, a similar conclusion to that drawn by Morris about Mexico could also be made about Indonesia. Indonesia has been a republic since its inception in 1945, but at times, it has seemed more like islands of corruption controlled by the mafia.[1] Under Soeharto, Indonesia was run like a kingdom where the alleged king, queen, crown princes, loyalists and vassals shared the cake according to their positions and power. The general public, who lived at the bottom of the social strata, received less and less, barely meeting their basic needs. Fortunately, abundant natural resources, especially oil, gas, gold and coal, saved Indonesia from bankruptcy, although the majority of people, living outside the tiny ruling elite, suffered greatly.

The last ten years of Soeharto's reign was the period when economic inequality was sharpest, even if this was not obvious on the surface.[2] If the Partido Revolucionario Institucional (PRI) needed seventy-one years to bankrupt Mexico, Soeharto needed only thirty-two.[3] He seemed to be much cleverer and more cunning when it came to emptying the national coffers. In fact, in the global corruption landscape, Indonesia seemed to be in the same club as Nigeria, the Philippines, Congo and Haiti, to name a few. One only needs go through Transparency International's Global Corruption Perceptions Index year by year to find evidence of perceptions about the relative state of corruption in these states.[4]

How much money was allegedly stolen from the state coffers by Soeharto? As mentioned in chapter 3, in 1999 *Time* published a long report about Soeharto's empire, detailing how much money his family and cronies unlawfully piled up in their bank accounts, as well as luxurious houses, properties and the business enterprises they controlled in many sectors of the economy.[5] The ill-gotten wealth identified by *Time*'s investigative journalists was outrageously high: US$35 billion, but no one really knows how much ill-gotten money had been accumulated. Evidence from several sources received by the court during the trial in Soeharto v. *Time* indicated different amounts ranging from US$16 billion up to US$40 billion.[6] Soeharto, of course, denied it, claiming to have not even one cent in his account, but few could believe him. Soeharto was not alone, however. Other leaders such as Ferdinand Marcos of the Philippines, Mobutu Sese Seko of Zaire, Sani Abacha of Nigeria and Zine Al Abidine Ben Ali of Tunisia, among others, allegedly corrupted their nation's wealth outrageously.[7] Table 4 lists the ten allegedly most corrupt leaders in the modern world.

Generally, corruption is not an individual act. In many cases, it is the work of more than one individual, a concerted and collective illegal robbery. When a leader of a country corrupts the wealth of the nation, he or she often does so as the leader of a corrupt gang, where his or her family or clan, governmental officials, business partners and cronies work together to enrich themselves illegally.[8] Ironically, it is not uncommon to see corruption being justified by laws specifically designed to whiten the black, to whitewash the crime. In a situation such as this, what appeared on the surface was not rule of law but rule by law.[9]

Table 4: Ten most corrupt world leaders in recent history

No.	Name	Country	Amount embezzled
1	Soeharto	Indonesia	$5 to $35 billion
2	Ferdinand Marcos	Philippines	$5 to $10 billion
3	Mobutu Sese Seko	Zaire (DRC)	$4 to $5 billion
4	Sani Abacha	Nigeria	$2 to $5 billion
5	Zine Al-Abidine Ben Ali	Tunisia	$1 to $2.6 billion
6	Slobodan Milosevic	Serbia/Yugoslavia	$1 billion
7	Jean-Claude Duvalier	Haiti	$800 million
8	Alberto Fujimori	Peru	$600 million
9	Pavlo Lazarenko	Ukraine	$200 million
10	Arnoldo Aleman	Nicaragua	$100 million

Source: Jeremy Sandbrook, 'The 10 most corrupt world leaders of recent history', Integritas 360, 20 July 2016 (retrieved 7 August 2019), integritas360.org/2016/07/10-most-corrupt-world-leaders/

It is significant that all leaders listed as the most corrupt come from so-called developing countries. While this does not mean that leaders from developed countries are not corrupt, corruption does not find fertile ground in a country where checks and balances, rule of law, and democracy are functioning well. In developing countries where checks and balances, rule of law and democracy are still weak and not functioning well, corruption has more opportunities to become a system in itself—endemic, systemic and widespread.[10]

James Wolfensohn, former President of the World Bank, delivered his annual speech to the members of the bank in 1996 in very blunt language, arguing that the world was facing what he termed a 'cancer of corruption'.[11] For Wolfensohn, corruption is not only an economic matter but also a cross-sectoral problem, touching political, social, cultural, legal and moral areas.[12] He described what has happened in many countries:

> In country after country, it is the people who are demanding action on this issue. They know that corruption diverts resources from the poor to the rich, increases the cost of running business, distorts public expenditures, and deters foreign investors. They also know that it erodes the

constituency for aid programs and humanitarian relief. And we all know that it is a major barrier to sound and equitable development. Corruption is a problem that all countries have to confront. Solutions, however, can only be home grown.[13]

That is easier said than done. Corruption in most countries is often a product of the system and, in some cases, becomes part of state crime.[14] It may start with simple bribery, embezzlement and kickbacks sanctioned by traditional customary practices. However, in states where rules have not been well established, especially new ones or transitional states transforming themselves to become more democratic, corruption takes more sophisticated forms. These new practices are still basically bribery, embezzlement and kickbacks, but the actors are attached to the power structure—they are part of the government rank and file, the political elite, businessmen and cronies of the power-holders. Corruption can also transform itself into capital outflow through money-laundering, much of it being hidden in tax-haven countries.[15]

The post-Soeharto Reformasi that began in 1998 certainly delivered major political and legal change, but it also had many unintended consequences, including decentralisation of corruption and the rise of new local oligarchies, whereby certain families control regencies by placing members of their families in key positions of power. It is not uncommon to see a governor in a particular province having siblings, children and in-laws running the provincial legislature and regencies. Banten Province is a perfect example of a provincial or political dynasty that is also connected to the centre of power at the national level. At one point, it was run by a governor, Ratu Atut Chosiyah, whose husband, brother and sister controlled key positions in the provincial office, regencies and the legislatures (see figure 1).[16]

It is also not uncommon to see a regent succeeded by his or her spouse or brother, as has happened in the regencies of Kendal, Kediri, Cimahi and Indramayu.[17] In addition, in many cases, the governor or the head of regency (the *bupati*) is able to control the local ruling party by appointing a family member or a distant relative as its chair. In turn, the chair of the party runs the local parliament, which promulgates Provincial or Municipal Regulations (Peraturan Daerah) in support of the governor or regency head to pursue their predatory business interests. What is being described here is a portrait of local oligarchy, a local version of oligarchy that seems to be a trend in the regions imitating the oligarchies that dominate politics at the national level.

Figure 1: Political dynasty of Ratu Atut Chosiyah (Banten Province)

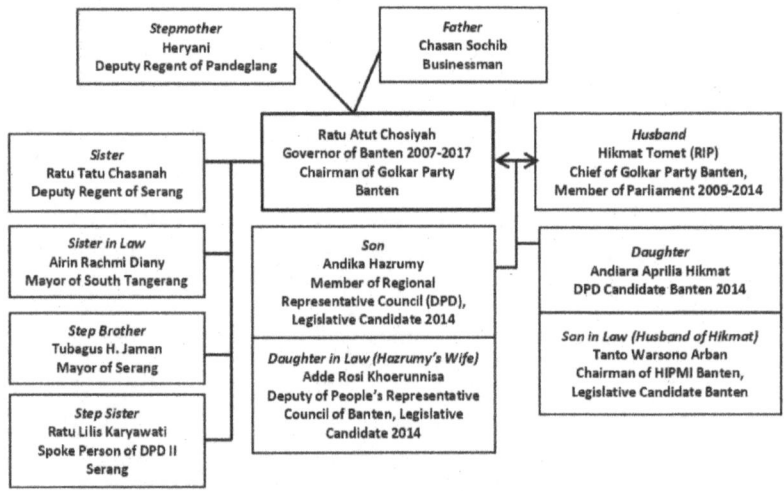

Source: Ihsanuddin, 'Dinasti Politik Ratu Atut Setelah Delapan Tahun'

Oligarchies can also be found among political parties that are run like a family enterprise, in which board members consist of family members. Of the nine political parties winning seats in parliament, four can be regarded as oligarchies because each party is effectively in the hands of a single family, which usually also established the party, often for exactly this purpose.[18] The founder, who is always regarded as the patron of the party, frequently has a continuing role as the chair, and eventually promotes his or her heir as successor when the time comes. The 'crown prince' or 'princess' will always be nominated as a candidate for the presidency, speaker of the

DPR or another top position, even if the party does have better candidates. These oligarchies are inherently corrupt, and that corruption spreads to the patron family's inner circle and cronies, depending on their proximity to the power-holders.

The corrupt state

It is useful to revisit the categories of the corrupt state described by Legvold; namely, (1) the criminal state, (2) the criminalised state and (3) public corruption. 'Criminal state' refers to a state in which the core activity is criminal, meaning that the state depends overwhelmingly on returns from illicit trade and other illegal activities to finance itself. Some former Soviet states belong to this category, and perhaps some new states or transitional countries might have engaged in criminal activities, although it would require close scrutiny to conclude whether they fall into the category of criminal state.[19] For example, many emerging countries have covertly engaged in the opium or drug business to fill their national coffers,[20] and in the early days of independence, the newly born and weak Indonesian government also engaged in the smuggling business from Singapore to earn revenues, although that had stopped by the 1950s.

A 'criminalised state' is one in which corruption is practised extensively and systematically; that is, reflecting the terminology used by Transparency International, it is endemic, systemic and widespread. In such a state, corruption is practised in many sectors and levels of government to the extent that it erodes the public's confidence in the state. It is also important to add that corruption here may be done by individuals, small groups of officials and, in many cases, in concert with the private sector. The corruption is so visible that it insults ordinary people's sense of justice, with demonstrations of illegal wealth being obvious throughout the country. Legvold refers to Russia as a criminalised state.[21] Indonesia can also be categorised as a criminalised state for the simple reason that corruption has always been rampant, widespread and well beyond what might be acceptable to the public. Under Soeharto, Indonesia suffered massive and blatant corruption driven by the ruling party and its cronies,[22] and sadly, two decades of Reformasi have failed to change Indonesia into a corruption-free state. The latest Corruption Perceptions Index of Transparency International still places Indonesia among the countries where corruption is one of the most serious problems faced.[23]

The third category of corruption is 'public corruption', whereby unscrupulous people abuse their power and connections, personal and professional, to enrich themselves illegally. Legvold does not attempt to define this term more specifically; however, it is not difficult to understand its meaning: corruption is widespread and practised by people to enrich themselves by exploiting legal loopholes and the opportunities available. This description could be applied to Indonesia, but it really belongs to the more serious category of the criminalised or kleptocratic state.[24]

As mentioned earlier, Reformasi paved the way for decentralisation, a must considering the size of the country. It has been argued that competition among the provinces and regencies will inevitably make Indonesia more advanced.[25] There is a new division of power in the sense that the regions have been given certain powers to issue licences for mining and estate farming. However, procurement of infrastructure projects, imposition of local taxes and levies, and equity participation in certain business ventures have made the provinces and regencies susceptible to bribery, 'gratification' and other forms of corruption. Decentralisation of power or authority has ironically also decentralised corruption because power and authority are priced according to the market, supply and demand. It is no longer centralised as in the past under Soeharto's government where some sort of control was in place. In decentralised corruption, virtually no rules are applied, so it is not surprising to see chaotic situations in many regions, with the anti-corruption agency catching many corrupt officials or businessmen red-handed.[26]

The level of corruption has also inevitably increased. There are various factors contributing to this, including the changes that have taken place in the regulation of the economy, the political opportunity for public and private actors to engage in corruption, and the willingness of new actors to indulge in corrupt practices.[27] After taking office, President Joko Widodo launched a massive infrastructure development program in the regions to implement his connectivity policy. This included the construction of toll roads, seaports, airports, railways, power plants and telecommunications. Significant increases in state budget were therefore directed to the regions. This was unprecedented in scope and scale. The regions suddenly found themselves running vastly bigger budgets. In the absence of effective control mechanisms, corruption crept in. Those who have little experience in running huge infrastructure projects could not resist temptation and fell into corruption's trap. That explains why so many governors, mayors and heads of regencies have been caught red-handed by the KPK in its clandestine operations.[28]

Former Vice President Jusuf Kalla has argued that Indonesia has not succeeded in combating corruption, particularly in the regions.[29] So many public officials have been detained by the KPK owing to corruption that some see Indonesia as the undisputed champion of detaining corrupt officials.[30] It is obvious that corruption is no longer a peripheral phenomenon. It is a national disease and has become Wolfensohn's 'cancer',[31] infiltrating political processes, power and social relations, and eventually hampering the Reformasi that was meant to transform Indonesia into a more democratic nation, relatively free from corruption. In these circumstances, it will be extremely difficult to eradicate corruption, even if thousands of corrupt officials are sent to prison. Corruption has become a type of mental state, fixed in people's thought process, so that even in prison, corruptors continue their criminal behaviour. Reports of corrupt inmates bribing prison guards to be able to leave the prison temporarily have been widespread. It seems that corruption no longer recognises Indonesian prison walls.[32]

State capture corruption

As explained earlier, a criminalised state is created when corrupt perpetrators exploit the weakness of the state and abuse every opportunity for personal, elite or group gain, be it political party, business association, religious organisation or others. Corruption in a criminalised state is often the result of collaboration between power-holders and either a company acting as vehicle or the corrupt perpetrator him/herself. Ruling political parties or a coalition of parties work together, taking and dividing the cake, playing by the rules but exploiting loopholes in regulations. This is the result of dysfunctional governance that fails to prevent corruption. As the World Bank has said:

> The search for effective methods of combating corruption has led to an increasingly wide recognition that corruption is fundamentally a problem of governance. Corruption thrives where states are too weak to control their own bureaucrats, to protect property and contract rights, and to provide the institutions that underpin an effective rule of law. Consequently, recent studies of corruption have tended to focus on key characteristics and policies of the state, especially the extent of state intervention in the economy and the degree of discretionary power of bureaucrats. Yet the recognition that corruption is a symptom of the underlying weakness of the state, while important, has shifted the focus of analysis away from the firms. The link between corporate governance and national governance have been largely unexplored. Moreover, empirical efforts to assess governance and corruption across countries have generally overlooked the critical information that firms can provide about the nature and extent of those problems.[33]

The relationship between the state and businesses is obviously complex and, in many cases, also suspicious. The ultimate objective of maximising profit has led the businesses to find means and ways to exploit poor governance by the state, leading to state capture. According to Hellman and colleagues:

> ... the firm-level perspective provides one of the first opportunities to analyse empirically the problem of 'state capture', that is, the efforts of firms to shape and influence the underlying rules of the game (i.e. legislation, laws, rules and decrees) through private payments to public officials. There has been analysis of how firms in the transition economies use their political influence to distort both the legal framework and the policymaking process in an effort to gain concentrated rents with detrimental consequences for the economy and society at large.[34]

What aspects of the state are typically captured by corrupt businesses? Among others, the key elements and institutions of the state such as the legislative body, the central bank, the judiciary and the election commission.[35] Political scientist Samuel Huntington believes that, particularly in Asian countries, economic development grew impressively owing to the synergy between certain forms of corrupt behaviour, including by businesses, and economic expansion enabled by cutting red tape.[36] For lack of a better word, the term 'functional corruption' is sometimes used to explain the phenomenon of treating corruption as an economic lubricant.[37] In newly independent and transitional states, the notion that some degree of corruption must be tolerated might be true; however, over the long run, the cost of corruption far outweighs the gain accumulated. That explains why those who aspire to have economic, sustainable and equitable growth denounce corruption by declaring zero tolerance of it.[38]

The rationale is self-explanatory; that is, the complexities and quantum of corruption have been significantly growing. Therefore zero tolerance is a *conditio sine qua non*. Economic regulations are often drafted in favour of economic growth, opening doors for corruption both by business firms and power-holders, either through political parties or rank and file of the bureaucracy. Political opportunities emerge as economic regulations are enacted by the legislature. It is obvious here that interaction between the actors of corrupt practice can, consciously or unconsciously, lead to an unholy alliance of the corrupt.[39] Mobutu's Zaire can be taken as a perfect example of such an alliance between high-ranking officials led by Mobutu and businesses, both national and international.[40] The E-KTP (Electronic ID) case involving Setya Novanto, then Speaker of the DPR, is another example of an alliance between political parties, legislators, high-ranking officials from the relevant Ministry (Home Affairs) and businesses to corrupt a major project.[41]

Policies play a role in facilitating corruption, and many have been translated into pieces of legislation. Therefore it is crucial to assess critically every piece of economic legislation to identify loopholes intentionally or unintentionally drafted during deliberation of the said legislation.[42] For example, one may find a provision that creates an opportunity to engage in self-enrichment or corruption. Alternatively, there is a provision that might be considered 'grey', meaning that its interpretation could go either way depending on who interprets the provision. Decentralisation as mandated by the Law on Regional Government, for instance, has conferred considerable power on heads of regencies, among others, to issue licences for mining or plantations. In a regency where governance is weak, power vested in the regency head can be abused for personal or group gain with relative ease.[43] Another example is legislation that requires an implementing regulation, but such a regulation is not issued, so corrupt actors are able simply to ignore the new law. These three problems are common in Indonesia, where ambiguity seems to be inserted into almost all legislation, making enforcement difficult.[44]

Although the main corrupt actors in Indonesia are Indonesians or Indonesian legal entities, their practice of corruption (through a series of transactions or investments) is often assisted by foreign elements through their business and professional work. International financial institutions, financial advisers, transnational criminal organisations or legal consultants all play a role in transnational transactions and investments that may originate from the proceeds of illicit enrichment or corruption.[45] These business entities and/or professionals are often complicit in this professionalisation of transactions and investments, making the transaction look as though it is in compliance with the prevailing law when it should be regarded as illegal capital flight or transnational corruption. Therefore it is appropriate to argue that in many cases, analysis of corruption and political corruption can only be done transnationally and not restricted within the boundaries of a state.[46]

Clearly foreign elements play a role in facilitating corruption through professional services, and many also collaborate as business partners.[47] However, the root of corruption is domestic and, with decentralisation, it is spreading to the regions. What is important to monitor seems to be the government's policy in promoting and expanding business involving deregulation and privatisation.[48] It is in the implementation of the policies that loopholes for corruption emerge. Synergy between businessmen and politicians often plays a role in pushing the government to introduce deregulation and privatisation, and if legislation is needed, it is often quickly enacted. State capture finds its form here as legislative corruption;[49] however, it is important to underline that it is not only the legislature that is captured. The judiciary and other state agencies are also captured eventually.

Political oligarchy and political dynasty

Oligarchs are business groups or leaders that have exceptionally large amounts of material wealth, that control many segments of the economy and that to some extent exercise political power as power-holders or part of the inner circle of power-holders. Oligarchy is not a new phenomenon in Indonesia, but its role became increasingly significant during the New Order, a process in which Soeharto played an instrumental role. It took the form of the rise of what are known in Indonesia as *konglomerat* (conglomerates, meaning 'company group' or sometimes 'tycoon'), when power became married to wealth.[50]

Under the New Order, most conglomerates were controlled by successful Chinese-Indonesian business families, and a few were exceptionally close to Soeharto. This is not by any means to say that no native Indonesian conglomerates arose, but their number was far less than the Chinese-Indonesian conglomerates. Together, however, conglomerates ran and controlled the Indonesian economy in what was called at that time 'Indonesia Incorporated'.[51] Interestingly, the Chinese-Indonesian heads of a few Indonesian conglomerates have been listed as among the richest people in the world. Michael and Robert Budi Hartono, the owners of Djarum Group, are listed as the second richest family in the world. Djarum Group controls the largest private bank in Indonesia, a cigarette company, properties, construction and many other businesses.[52] There are many other Indonesian-Chinese conglomerates that stand tall in the world of Indonesian business, such as the Salim Group, Sinar Mas, Wilmar, Lippo, Sampurna, Artha Graha, Astra and others.[53] There are also non-Chinese-Indonesian tycoons such as Aburizal Bakri, Arifin Panigoro, Hasyim Djoyohadikusumo and Sandiaga Uno, although their wealth and size is usually less than their Chinese-Indonesian counterparts.[54]

The bigger the oligarch, the riskier they are because they will always be subject to public scrutiny. There is a saying that the taller the tree, the more prone it is to the wind. Oligarchs everywhere on earth face similar risks. Therefore the oligarchs must get closer to the centre of power and be willing to share some of their fortune with power-holders. Oligarchs cannot rely solely on the certainty of law because the law will not be enough if power-holders oppose them. The art is how not to be too close or too far from the power centre, but political involvement, whether direct or indirect, is usually the price that must be paid to maintain great wealth, and wealth, in turn, is often necessary for the exercise of power: 'Wealth is the most potent and flexible of all power resources for influencing political outcomes during non-crisis periods, and those who deploy wealth power have a political impact far out of proportion to their numbers in society.'[55]

Reformasi's democratisation made political contests exorbitantly expensive by requiring election campaigns, so oligarchs become a source of funds for those taking part in elections at local and national levels.⁵⁶ The Law on Political Parties as well as the Law of General Elections have paved the way for conglomerates or oligarchs to channel their funds to political parties as donations.⁵⁷ Under the latter law, an individual may donate up to Rp 2.5 billion, while a corporation can donate up to Rp 25 billion. A conglomerate that consists of 200 corporations may therefore donate 200 times Rp 25 billion. Needless to say, the oligarchs have become cash cows of political parties and therefore have been dragged into donating more than the maximum amount for donations. Political parties, especially the ruling parties, have always found ways to ask oligarchs for more, as if donations are premiums for political insurance.⁵⁸ During political campaigns, it is not strange to read about shadow organisations campaigning that are apparently not attached to political parties but seem to have access to funding to cover their costs, which are usually significant. Where does this funding come from? Allegedly, it comes from oligarchs or their proxies, which is why the oligarchy must be investigated seriously to fully understand Indonesian politics and its relation to corruption.⁵⁹

Political donations are never free. They are always rewarded with business licences or contracts and eventually become part of business practice, a vicious circle that has no end. Heads of regencies grant mining and plantation licences to oligarchs and, at the national level, countless business contracts have been given to oligarchs by the central government.⁶⁰ From the outside, these appear to be normal business deals, but if one goes deeper and analyses the causal relationship between power and business, it would be difficult to escape the conclusion that a lot of those business licences and contracts are the result of political corruption in which the elected regents, mayors, governors and presidents reward their political donors handsomely. Business becomes unavoidably tainted with corruption.

Arguably, the oligarchs have succeeded in accumulating their wealth as a result of their support for power-holders. Their political donations are claimed as a business cost in their books through manipulation by accountants. This has been a continuing practice that is mutually beneficial both for the oligarchs and the power-holders. The resulting vicious circle has led oligarchs and politicians into a mutually symbiotic dependency over a long period. Eventually, the oligarchs have paved the way for the birth of political dynasties, especially at the regional level, and it is not uncommon to see marriages of convenience between oligarchs, making them stronger economically and politically.[61] These grant them access to almost every level of government. In these circumstances, both power-holders and oligarchs engage in predatory behaviour, exploiting whatever procurements or business licences become available.

Reformasi has also produced some non-ethnic Chinese political oligarchs who directly or indirectly engage in politics through their media enterprises,[62] which are used as conduits for political campaigns and propaganda on behalf of preferred candidates or parties. They are 'non-financial donations', given in the expectation of a political and business pay-off once their chosen candidates emerge as winners. Again, this creates a mutually symbiotic relation that breeds corruption, albeit in a more subtle and indirect way. This is not to say there are no media businesses that always play by the rules, fighting hard not to surrender to unethical and unlawful business practices. However, many media moguls have intentionally and systematically used the mass media outlets they control to go after business transactions.

Political parties are unable to avoid oligarchs completely, primarily because most parties are creatures of their founders, who are themselves oligarchs. Most Indonesian political parties began as family enterprises and are run as such. Democracy, which is intended to be the rule within Indonesian political parties, has never entirely been enforced, or is merely enforced in a pro forma manner, and therefore one should not be surprised to see parties chaired and run by the founders or their families. There is no meaningful change of leadership; there are no genuine elections of party chair. Founder domination is the law in such parties that are effectively 'owned' by oligarchs, even if the owners refuse to be called oligarchs.

PDI-Perjuangan, the party that won the greatest number of votes in the last two elections (both presidential and legislative elections in 2014 and 2019 respectively), was historically established (albeit under a different name) by the founding father of the republic, Soekarno, and has long been in the hands of his daughter, Megawati Soekarnoputri.[63] Megawati has never been replaced as chair of the party. The reason used to justify this is that there has been no alternative candidate who could replace her and unite the party. She controls the party, and even though she refuses to be called an oligarch, she is one in fact. She might not own or run any enterprise, but her access to material and immaterial wealth bestows immense power upon her.[64] Many oligarchs offer support to Megawati as political insurance in case political protection is needed.

The second largest party, Gerindra, is chaired by Prabowo Subianto, a former army general, once married to the daughter of Soeharto, Siti Hediyati Haryadi.[65] Under the presidency of Susilo Bambang Yudhoyono, and in the first term of Jokowi's presidency, Gerindra was not part of government. In the second term of Jokowi's government, however, Gerindra decided to join the government coalition. Prabowo runs the party the way one runs an army battalion: with military discipline. Prabowo and his younger brother, Hasyim Djoyohadikusumo, own a group of companies engaged in trading, mining and plantations. Prabowo and Hasyim pour money into the party to cover its activities. With their money funding the party, it is clear that Prabowo and his brother are oligarchs. Neither has ever admitted this, but no one could sensibly deny it. In the past two elections (presidential elections of 2014 and 2019), Prabowo has been supported by other oligarchs, including Aburizal Bakri and Sandiaga Uno, with the latter running as vice-president candidate alongside Prabowo in the 2019 presidential election.[66]

Partai Demokrat is run by Susilo Bambang Yudhoyono and his family. Yudhoyono served as Indonesian President from 2004 until 2014. Partai Demokrat was the largest party when Yudhoyono ran for re-election in 2009. It must be assumed that the party received many political donations from conglomerates or oligarchs, and some, such as CT Corps, Djarum and Rajawali, became close to the party.[67]

Yudhoyono is another senior political figure who refuses to be called an oligarch, but he is indeed one, in his own way.

Nasdem is a party owned and run by Surya Paloh, a charismatic oligarch, an eloquent orator and a media mogul.[68] Surya pioneered the first news television channel in Indonesia, and managed to cultivate a vast loyal audience, making his station an important political instrument. Surya gave his support to Yudhoyono and now offers it to Joko Widodo, which made him a member of the inner circle of both presidents. Directly and indirectly, his closeness to the epicentre of power has also helped him to expand his business empire.[69] Surya has always claimed to be a democrat and bound by democratic principles in running the party, but he is too dominant as the owner of the party for that to be realistic.

Other political parties, such as Golkar, PKB, PKS and PPP, do not belong to the club of oligarchs. However, it is perhaps inaccurate to categorise them as democratic parties. Golkar under the New Order was synonymous with Soeharto, and for thirty-two years Soeharto ran Golkar as if running a corporation. Since Reformasi, leadership of Golkar has changed from one congress to another congress, although it has twice been in the hands of oligarchs, Jusuf Kalla and Aburizal Bakri. PKB is another political party, but it was set up by Abdurrachman Wahid, a former president and leader of the Muslim mass organisation Nahdlatul Ulama (NU). There is no reason to associate the party with oligarchs. PKS has been regarded as a modernist Islamic party consisting of intellectuals, religious leaders, small merchants and professionals, while PPP is also an Islamic party, a home for politicians from Nahdlatul Ulama, Muhammadiah and other Islamic groups. Currently, these parties are run by traditional politicians not directly connected with the oligarchs. None has a dominant leader who dictates how their party runs.

Aside from the nine parties mentioned above, there are also parties that failed to pass the parliamentary threshold; that is, they failed to win at least 4 per cent of the seats of the DPR, although they have won seats in regional elections.[70] These parties, PSI, Perindo, PBB and Hanura, for instance, are to be closely watched because there is a possibility that they might join the nine parties that currently have seats in parliament. From the outset, none of these small parties seems to be run by oligarchs except for Perindo, which is owned by another media mogul, Harry Tanusudibyo, who controls several television, radio and social media outlets.[71]

Reformasi paved the way for regional autonomy whereby both regency and provincial governments enjoyed greater autonomy. Practically speaking, the regions run their own governments except for matters related to defence, foreign policy, religion, monetary affairs and the judiciary. As might be expected, local oligarchies are also gradually arising, and in some cases, these seem to resemble dynasties, family dynasties and political dynasties.[72]

At the regency level, small local dynasties can also be found in many places where the head of regency handed over his or her position to a spouse or children in addition to controlling key positions within the local bureaucracy.[73] In some cases, local dynasties seem to be expanded by assigning relatives and cronies to positions in national or local legislative bodies to guarantee the survival and continuity of the dynasty. Legally, there has been no violation of the law, but morally, one can argue that controlling and dominating public offices is, in itself, a conflict of interest. Moreover, domination of the bureaucracy by those close to the oligarch will weaken internal control within the bureaucracy, and eventually pave the way for manipulation, corruption and money-laundering.

In conclusion, it is not an exaggeration to argue that oligarchies and dynasties, political and commercial, have gradually emerged and expanded throughout the country. At the national level, oligarchies and political dynasties emerge through big political parties, while in the regions they appear through the heads of regencies or governorships, and there are many more lesser oligarchs and dynasties engaged in politics from the sidelines.

From culture to system

As discussed previously, corruption is no longer just a cultural problem. It has become endemic, systemic and widespread. Referring to 'petty corruption', offenders as a rule have been motivated by the low remuneration received; in order to survive, to have a decent life, petty corruption seems to be inevitable.[74] The majority of civil servants apparently engage in petty corruption in varying degrees through all manner of covert means, and sometimes openly. Initially, corruption appeared to be a cultural phenomenon. The rationale is that if everybody commits corruption, then corruption is acceptable, so what is the point of being discreet? This eventually leads to the phenomenon of *korupsi berjamaah* (collective corruption).[75] It is not uncommon to see a group of civil servants or local parliamentarians arrested by the police or prosecutors because of *korupsi berjamaah*. In North Sumatra Province, almost all provincial legislators were jailed by the KPK owing to *korupsi berjamaah* of the annual provincial budget.[76] In West Sumatra Province, *korupsi berjamaah* also took place involving forty local legislators, again related to annual provincial budgets.[77]

But more alarming is what is referred to as 'grand corruption'. This can be accomplished either individually or in concert by those who have power, and obviously, this type of corruption is not simply to ensure survival or a decent life. Grand corruption aims at self-enrichment or group enrichment, or often for a political party to strengthen its participation in political contestation. What happened in Mexico under the rule of the Partido Revolucionario Instituciona (PRI), where corruption was the central theme of the party's activities, is a perfect example of grand corruption.[78] The same thing has happened in many other countries, including Japan, Italy, Russia and Indonesia,[79] where political parties are some of the most corrupt institutions in the country.[80]

Oligarchs exploit the state much more effectively than the state exploits them. In Russia, oligarchs use violence, going after their victims by taking over competitors or new business lines in order to enlarge their business empire.[81] The collapse of the Soviet Union did not turn Russia into a 'lawless state'; however, political contestation appeared and became extremely brutal and costly, forcing power groupings to nurture their own oligarchs to accumulate funds.[82]

Michael Khodorkovsky and Boris Abraham Berezovsky, two big oligarchs in Russian business circles, were prosecuted, imprisoned and later forced into exile, with the former settling in Zurich while the latter committed suicide in London.[83] These two oligarchs made their fortunes after the collapse of the Soviet Union through privatisation undertaken by the government at that time as an attempt to transform the economy from a command economy to a market economy.[84]

In the Philippines, oligarchs have a long history dating back to when Spain and then the United States colonised the country. Johnston asserts that generally the Philippine economy has always been under the control of a few oligarchs, approximately eighty in number, mostly engaged in industry and property.[85] Initially, the oligarchs derived their wealth from outside the state, although they were assisted by the state owing to the fact that it was the oligarchs who gave birth to the political elite of the nation.[86] Since Ferdinand Marcos came to power, the oligarchs entered into more mutually dependent relationships, dividing the big economic cake among themselves. Marcos and his wife Imelda succeeded in elevating their status jointly to become a sort of joint mafia godfather to the oligarchs. Marcos in the end entrenched his name as one of the most corrupt leaders in the world.[87]

Indonesia has experienced corruption since colonial times and perfected it during the Soeharto period. Of the 1 per cent of richest people in the country today, many are oligarchs who got their start during the Soeharto era.[88] The oligarchs or cronies of Soeharto later emerged as conglomerates controlling the economy. In the 1950s, big businesses were also born out of Soekarno's Banteng policy,[89] however, their wealth did not dramatically increase. They may have been regarded as kleptocrats abusing their power for self-enrichment, with some portion trickling down to their loyal friends, but their wealth did not usually anger the public at large.[90] However, under Soeharto, the oligarchs controlled the daily lives of the public by dominating the businesses that provided their basic needs, expropriating people's land and outrageously building mountains of illicit wealth. Salim Group, for instance, controlled a number of basic industries that are linked to the needs of the people such as cement and flour.[91] The term 'oligarch' was not known then; they were simply called *konglomerat*, or *cukong*.[92] Moreover, it was under Soeharto that the marriage between power and wealth became so obvious in its penetration of state institutions, almost without any hindrance. Corruption and political corruption became the rule, not the exception.

As described earlier, the oligarchs mostly come from political parties. They employ predatory behaviour partly to finance the party and partly to enrich themselves.[93] There is also another analysis linking the oligarchs to the global capitalist system in which the oligarchs' function is to perpetuate that system.[94] The oligarchs have often transformed to become political dynasties; that is, national political dynasties and local political dynasties. Unexpectedly, twenty years of Reformasi has succeeded in creating a fertile environment in which oligarchs and political dynasties can thrive and expand more than ever before.

Although thousands of corrupt individuals have been imprisoned since the KPK was established, corruption persists. It seems that a deterrent effect has not been achieved. The description of corruption as endemic, systemic and widespread is still applicable in Indonesia's case. The *modus operandi* of corruption has become public knowledge, disseminated to those interested in repeating it. Sharing experiences of the corrupt perpetrators to some extent has perfected the techniques of corruption in terms of eliminating evidence and footprints. This is the time when state capture corruption begins, when all agencies within the government are being controlled and used to ensure that corruption duly takes place. In this type of megacorruption, all agencies are abused: the government, the legislature and the judiciary have been conditioned to facilitate corruption.[95]

State capture corruption is still evolving. The mechanisms and technologies of corruption are constantly being improved upon in anticipation of growing social discontent and social activism. Indonesia's new architecture of state, where checks and balances have been complemented by state auxiliary agencies, such as the Judicial Commission, the Ombudsman, the Election Commission and the KPK, prompt the actors of corruption, corrupt political and business oligarchs and dynasties to adapt and update. It remains to be seen whether empowering checks and balances and law enforcement is enough to combat highly advanced practices of corruption with new technologies.

Chapter 5

Political corruption cases and criminalisation

> *Rapid increase in corruption cases will bring disaster to economic as well as national life as a whole. Widespread and systematic corruption violates both the social and economic rights of the people, therefore, it should not be treated as ordinary crime but must be considered an extraordinary crime. Likewise, in its eradication, it cannot be fought normally but must be fought with extraordinary means.*
>
> Elucidation to Law No. 19 of 2019

The aggressiveness of corruption eradication efforts led by the KPK has caused widespread anger among status quo forces, especially politicians and high-ranking officials. Their anger has been transformed into outrage and a desire for revenge, leading to blatant abuses of power and law to silence, tame, injure or kill corruption eradication activists, including the KPK, its leadership and those working as investigators and prosecutors. Additionally, academia, the Judicial Commission, the National Commission of Human Rights, former Supreme Court judges, and NGO leaders have been attacked or named suspects.[1] Arguably, this has badly demoralised corruption eradication activists, especially those working at the KPK.

It is fair to conclude that political corruption is the umbrella term for various types of corruption, be it administrative, judicial, legislative, educational, environmental, or business. In many cases, these forms of corruption are interconnected, although in non-political corruption, they are often committed individually and independently by the corrupt for self-enrichment. Classification really depends on where the corruption takes place. It may be in the legislature in relation to the passing of a bill, in one of the ministries when procurement is being processed, or in the judiciary when a court order needs to be enforced. It is also possible for corruption to take place in business transactions, entirely out of the realm of the government.

One small political corruption case in East Kalimantan is a good example of inter-connectivity that occurred among local political elite, businessmen, local government and the judiciary in Jakarta.[2] In this case, the head of Gunung Mas Regency, Hambit Bintih, was running for a second term. He was aided by a campaign team that conspired with a businessman who operated palm oil plantations. The businessman happened to be a Malaysian involved in the palm oil business in Gunung Mas Regency who acquired local companies (shell companies) that already had business licences for local palm oil plantations. These companies financed the Bintih campaign with all means necessary, including—but not limited to—buying votes (money politics). Hambit Bintih decisively won the election, but his opponent filed a claim in the Constitutional Court, claiming that the election had been rigged, preceded by fraud, manipulation, intimidation and bribery.[3] The claim failed. Hambit Bintih won the court battle, but then he began to lose—he was arrested with his legal team and the Chief Justice of the Constitutional Court, Akil Mochtar, who had presided over the Constitutional Court hearings. It turned out that Bintih's court victory had been tainted by bribes paid to the Chief Justice. Hambit Bintih was a victim of his own over-confidence in believing that his power and money could save his political position. He was wrong.

According to Richard Sakwa, 'Russia is moving from mega-corruption, that is, a system which is corrupt in its very essence, to "normal" corruption; from a corrupt system to a system with corruption.'[4] The term 'mega-corruption' has rarely been used in analysis of corruption in Indonesia, but reading corruption news in the media as well as reports of the KPK, one cannot escape the fact that mega-corruption has been a reality for quite a long time already.[5] As mentioned earlier, the focus of this book is political corruption, the mother of all corruption. In this regard, the main issues are always power that must be acquired and owned. Power will grant legality, and legality will generate money, but in order to acquire power, one needs money. Money politics is not as simple as vote-buying; rather it is about controlling every branch of power in addition to co-opting elites inside and outside the power circle. Labourers, farmers, fishermen, teachers, women and youth must be co-opted in order to minimise dissent and resentment. In addition, media criticism must be silenced by buying out media owners. What happened during the thirty-two years of the New Order can be cited as a perfect example of the concentration of power in one hand controlling all branches of government, business associations, labour and farmer associations, and youth and religious communities. In short, the absolute power of the President became law that could justify whatever actions were taken. Reformasi, which began in 1998, has not really succeeded in changing the system. Democracy and corruption eradication seem to be working on the surface, but that does not reflect the actual situation. The fact is that tensions between appearance and essence, or tensions between procedure and substance, have led to substantial compromises, which contribute to the weakening of both democracy and corruption eradication.

It is important to reiterate that political parties in Indonesia are not funded through membership dues.[6] The government directly or indirectly provides some degree of funding, but it is insubstantial, so most of the funding comes from donations and income provided by party leaders and corporations that donate their money in return for business projects. Therefore illicit funding and other forms of corruption became common practice, exploiting the weakness of law enforcement and institutional defects in the democratic system.[7] The fact that in the fifteen years between 2005 and 2020 so many politicians were sentenced to imprisonment apparently has not deterred others from corruption. It is business as usual.

One further problem is the phenomenon of self-enrichment of corrupt individuals. The lifestyle of most politicians is openly luxurious, not in line with the amount of remuneration they receive as members of the legislature or as governors, for instance. It seems obvious that a significant portion of corruption goes to their personal coffers—not all the proceeds of corruption go solely to the accounts of the parties.

Below, three political corruption cases are explored in order to present a more complete picture of the relationship between corruption and the existence of oligarchies. Oligarchy in many cases must be seen in the plural because it is common to see more than one oligarch in a particular party. The first case is Ratu Atut Chosiyah, a senior politician in the Golkar Party, who at that time happened to be Governor of Banten Province. The second case is Muhammad Nazaruddin, treasurer of the Demokrat Party, who happened to be a member of parliament in Jakarta. The third case is Setya Novanto, a senior politician in the Golkar Party, who at the time was chairman of Golkar as well as Speaker of parliament. There are, of course, many other political corruption cases, but these three can be considered representative of major political corruption cases in Indonesia. Additionally, a brief explanation about Soeharto's case will demonstrate the magnitude of corruption and the power behind it.

Ratu Atut Chosiyah

Ratu Atut Chosiyah (commonly known as Ratu Atut) is known as a member of a political family whose father has been engaged in politics for quite some time. Their family controlled many governmental positions in the province of Banten: regents, mayors, speakers of local legislatures and other related positions. When Ratu Atut was elected Governor of Banten Province, she was immediately elevated to become 'matriarch' of the family. It is no secret that the family controlled various business operations and had accumulated a great fortune, so Ratu Atut became the single most powerful politician in Banten Province. Coincidentally, her first name, Ratu, translated to English means 'queen', and she was undoubtedly the 'queen' of her own province.

The province of Banten consists of four regencies and cities, each headed by a regent and mayor respectively. Ratu Atut had planned to have her own people in all those regencies and cities through elections, and for that very reason, she had done almost everything possible to assist her people to win elections by whatever means possible. She would then be able to direct both the regents and mayors to appoint her trusted cadres to strategic positions. Consequently, she would be able to engineer all procurement projects to be awarded to her designated companies. She would also be in a position to grant business licences to her cronies.

The annual expenditure of Banten Province, direct and indirect, is relatively high. In 2018, total expenditures were slightly higher than Rp 11 trillion.[8] However, this was not the only amount at stake. Business transactions in Banten are very significant as there are so many large industries located in the province. Its strategic location, next to Jakarta, has made Banten almost an extension of Jakarta, attracting many enterprises to conduct business there. Banten is also the gateway to the neighbouring island of Sumatra. For these reasons Banten Province is important for business connectivity in Indonesia.

As well as wanting to control the province, Governor Ratu Atut wanted to establish her own political dynasty and business oligarchy, to treat the province of Banten as her kingdom. Therefore winning all local elections was a *conditio sine qua non*. With considerable resources in her hands, and with the political apparatus behind her, she would have thought that she could succeed in concentrating power in her hands, or those of her family. She could not accept electoral defeat, and tried to defy the fact that, in a democracy, it is ultimately the people who decide. Democracy requires power to change hands in order to usher in new blood and prevent monopolisation of the system by a small elite. Political parties might have pledged their support to the dynasty, but political parties also must listen to their constituents. Governor Ratu Atut seemed to have forgotten this.

In 2013, Lebak Regency held an election for head and deputy head of the regency (regent and vice regent). Ratu Atut supported her candidates, Amir Hamzah and Kasmin, as regent and vice regent. The Golkar Party, of which she was the provincial chair, supported the candidates. She believed that her candidates would certainly win the election because they had more resources and better organised campaign teams. To her shock, Amir Hamzah and Kasmin lost convincingly to Iti Octavia and Ade Sumardi, candidates backed by a coalition of several parties; namely, Partai Demokrat, PDI-Perjuangan, Hanura, Gerindra, PPP, PKS and PPNU.[9]

The Election Commission held a plenary meeting on 8 September 2013, and based on its count of the votes,[10] Iti Octavia received more than 60 per cent of the votes while Amir Hamzah and Kasmin won just 36 per cent. Having been informed of the Election Commission's decision, Ratu Atut refused to accept defeat and instructed both Amir Hamzah and Kasmin to challenge the results by filing a claim with the Constitutional Court alleging intimidation, manipulation and fraud. Attorneys Rudy and Susi Tur Andayani were assigned to represent Amir Hamzah and Kasmin in the Constitutional Court. On 11 September 2013, a claim to challenge the outcome of the election results in Lebak Regency was duly lodged in the Constitutional Court.

On 22 September 2013, Ratu Atut met the Chief Justice of the Constitutional Court, Akil Mochtar, at the Marriott Hotel, Singapore. She directly asked him to annul the decision of the Election Commission in Lebak and declare Amir Hamzah and Kasmin the winners of the election for Regent and Vice Regent of Lebak Regency. She also asked her brother, Tubagus Chaeri Wardana Chasan, to be in charge, as her representative. All further communication went through Chasan to win the election in Lebak Regency at all costs.[11]

Chasan worked in tandem with Susi Tur Andayani, one of the attorneys assigned to handle the said case. Coincidentally, Susi Tur Andayani knew Mochtar, and through Andayani the Chief Justice requested Ratu Atut to pay Rp 3 billion if she really wanted to annul the decision of the Election Commission in Lebak.[12]

On 1 October 2013, the Constitutional Court convened a session to read out an interlocutory judgment in the Lebak election dispute, but before the session, Andayani sent a short message to the Chief Justice to advise him to prepare to receive advance payment in the amount of Rp 1 billion from Ratu Atut's brother, Chasan. Around noon, the reading of the interlocutory judgment took place, basically granting the request of Ratu Atut. The interlocutory judgment annulled the decision of the Election Commission of Lebak Regency, and instructed the commission to re-run the local election. That was indeed a big victory for Ratu Atut. A repeat election had to be conducted, which meant that another opportunity to win was open to her candidates. Ratu Atut must have conveyed her gratitude to the Chief Justice, although the Chief Justice did not have the opportunity to meet Andayani, who had no choice but to take the Rp 1 billion to her home for safekeeping until she had a chance to meet the Chief Justice.[13]

The next day, Andayani was arrested at the residence of Amir Hamzah, while the Rp 1 billion that was found in her house was confiscated by the KPK. Ratu Atut's brother, Chasan, was also arrested for facilitating the bribery. The main culprit, Chief Justice Mochtar, was arrested by the KPK at his official residence with multiple bribes he received from various parties. From his house, KPK confiscated Rp 7.2 billion.[14]

Ratu Atut was immediately named a suspect and arrested. She was charged with violating Article 6 para. 1 (a) of Law No. 31 of 1999 as amended by Law No. 20 of 2001.[15] In addition, she was charged with violating Article 13 of Law No. 31 of 1999 as amended by Law No. 20 of 2001.[16] The Prosecutor asked that Ratu Atut be sentenced to ten years imprisonment in addition to a Rp 250 000 000 fine. Failure to pay the fine would add five months to her sentence.

After a series of long hearings where submissions, cross-examinations and defence statements were presented, the judges of the Jakarta District Court issued a verdict affirming that Ratu Atut had convincingly been proven guilty of attempting to bribe the Chief Justice, in order to annul the election result. Ratu Atut was sentenced to four years imprisonment and fined Rp 200 000 000.[17]

Ratu Atut appealed to the High Court of Jakarta, which reaffirmed the verdict of the Central Jakarta District Court.[18] She then filed a cassation appeal to the Supreme Court, the highest appeal court in the republic. However, the Supreme Court increased her sentence to seven years imprisonment, with a Rp 200 000 000 fine or another six months imprisonment.[19] Her political rights were also revoked by the court, making her unable to take part in elections, locally or nationally. Ratu Atut still had another legal remedy available; namely, case review or judicial reconsideration (*peninjauan kembali*), by which the Supreme Court can re-examine the case if it can be shown that there is new evidence, that there was improper application of the law or that an error was made by the judges.[20] However, she decided not to file a case review.

Ratu Atut committed her offence together with her younger brother Chasan, the Chief Justice of the Constitutional Court Mochtar, attorney Andayani, and the candidates for head and deputy head of Lebak Regency, Amir Hamzah and Kasmin. The case therefore reveals a political oligarchy with connections to national-level institutions that could control a province and all its potential for wealth. Needless to say, a corrupt political oligarchy of this sort inherently denies the people it rules their legitimate right to a better life.

Those related to the case of Ratu Atut have been also sentenced by the court. Her brother Chasan received seven years imprisonment and a fine of Rp 200 000 000 from the Supreme Court.[21] The Chief Justice of the Constitutional Court, Akil Mochtar, was given a life sentence and fine amounting to Rp 10 000 000 000. This is the highest sentence in a corruption case in Indonesian history.[22] The regent candidate, Amir Hamzah, received three years and five months imprisonment and a fine of Rp 150 000 000.[23] The vice regent candidate, Kasmin, received three years imprisonment and fine of Rp 150 000 000.[24] Both accepted the sentence and decided not to appeal. The attorney Andayani, who was instrumental as a bridge to the Chief Justice, was sentenced to five years imprisonment and a fine of Rp 150 000 000.[25]

Power tends to corrupt, and that is what happened in Banten Province.[26] Allegations of corruption committed by Ratu Atut and her associates have been reported in various media, and it was only a matter of time before more political corruption cases involving her cronies were uncovered. One by one, whistleblowers, witnesses and other offenders revealed various acts of corruption involving Banten's provincial oligarchy, gradually weakening or diminishing it, perhaps even to the point of collapse.

Muhammad Nazaruddin

Muhammad Nazaruddin was a young politician, born in 1978. He was not a public figure before he joined the political party, Partai Demokrat, in Jakarta. He did not come from a political family in his hometown, Simalungun, North Sumatra. His father was known as a successful local businessman, but when he died, the business rapidly declined. The family lost the wealth it had enjoyed and was forced to move to Pekanbaru, the capital of Riau Province, just as Nazaruddin finished high school. It was in Pekanbaru that he began his business activities.[27]

Perhaps Nazaruddin inherited his father's determination and business acumen. In any case, he quickly became involved in a number of businesses, including, among others, plantations, trading of medical equipment, and construction.[28] He did not need much time to earn himself recognition as a talented businessman, and that recognition led him to join the boards of a number of companies. At such an early age, sitting on a number of boards of corporations, including his own, PT Anak Negeri, was a significant achievement, and his success in business opened the door for him to local politics, joining the local political elite.

Nazaruddin became famous for his role in Partai Demokrat, but he actually began his political involvement with Partai Persatuan Pembangunan (PPP).[29] He ran for the DPR in 2004 (for PPP) but was not elected. His failure to enter the DPR did not stop him from doing business. In fact, he was now doing business beyond Pekanbaru, ambitiously and rather recklessly, and at a number of points, he stumbled, when his name appeared in the media in some corruption cases related to the construction business. It was not clear to what extent he was involved, but the cases were too small to attract much public scrutiny at the time. Perhaps the media restrained themselves from digging up more about the cases. In any case, Nazaruddin seemed able to escape the scrutiny of the media and civil society organisations as well as the legal apparatus. His ability to outmanoeuvre the law might have convinced him that anything can be bought and anyone silenced. His confidence overwhelmingly increased.

By now, Nazaruddin clearly dreamt of becoming a national politician, as that would raise his stature and would eventually open more doors for him, doors to business and power. In 2009, he ran for a seat in DPR by joining the Partai Demokrat whose chairman, Susilo Bambang Yudhoyono, was President of Indonesia at the time. Nazaruddin was assigned to represent East Java, and was elected a member of DPR. Undoubtedly a smart person, he had made a calculated gamble and succeeded.

His rise to power was spectacular. Having been elected as a member of DPR, he became close to both Yudhoyono and Anas Urbaningrum, who chaired Partai Demokrat after Yudhoyono. In a new line-up of Partai Demokrat's leadership, Nazaruddin was appointed treasurer, obviously a highly strategic position. His tasks were to raise funds for the party because, as mentioned, all political parties depend on political donations and 'other sources' (e.g. proceeds of business secured by party members), since there are no membership dues.[30] Proceeds of business have always been linked to proceeds of corruption, directly or indirectly. Nazaruddin had no difficulty in understanding what to do to raise funds because he had frequently done so in his business dealings. If in the past, he did it with limited capability, now as treasurer of a major political party that governed the nation, he had all the power necessary, and Nazaruddin in fact quickly became a major power broker. At the same time, he became a target of envy and hatred—he was immediately in the spotlight, monitored by various competing interests within and outside his party.

The young politician worked hard to fix deals, secure projects and raise funds. It is no surprise that he succeeded in securing a great number of procurement projects from various governmental agencies and, from those projects, certain percentages were allocated to business entities directly or indirectly controlled by him. His name did not appear in any those business entities, but he had his wife and assistants running the businesses. It is not clear how many projects Nazaruddin secured, but it is clear that of every project, at least 10 per cent of the total value would go to business entities designated by him. It goes without saying that those working with him—be they members of DPR, officials from governmental agencies or party officials—had their own shares. Everybody involved in the projects received their fair share. It is hard to generalise the percentage of corruption that occurred, but it is clear that corruption was committed collectively (*korupsi berjamaah*).[31]

Nazaruddin was notoriously involved in more than one corruption case. His dossiers found their way to the KPK, and he faced trial many times, appearing in courts as both defendant and witness in a series of corruption cases. He soon became a familiar face on television and newspapers—a celebrity in the negative sense. The first case to come to public attention involved Wisma Atlet in Jakabaring, Palembang, South Sumatra.[32]

What did Nazaruddin actually do? Some time in January 2010, he met a fellow DPR member, Angelina Sondakh, a member of the Budgetary Committee, to discuss construction of the Wisma Atlet (athletes' accommodation) in Jakabaring. He wanted to engineer the grant of the project to PT Duta Graha Indah Tbk, a company that had promised to pay him a huge reward as 'compensation' for the procurement.³³ Nazaruddin introduced Sondakh to Mindo Rosalina Manulang, marketing manager of PT Anak Negeri, a company allegedly belonging to the Permai Group that was controlled by Nazaruddin and his wife, Neneng Sri Wahyuni.³⁴ Manulang's task was to win the construction of Wisma Atlet from the Ministry of Youth and Sports, which was managing the procurement process. Sondakh, who would be in charge of securing the budget in the Budgetary Committee, agreed to work jointly to win them the procurement project.

In April 2010, at a restaurant in Arcadia, Senayan, Nazaruddin, together with Mindo Rosalina Manullang, met Wafid Muharam, secretary of the Ministry of Youth and Sports. Muharam was asked to help PT Duta Graha Indah Tbk win the construction of Wisma Atlet, and he agreed to do so provided that the DPR's Budgetary Committee supported the project. Nazaruddin assured Muharam that there was no problem with the Budgetary Committee. Everybody was on board. Nazaruddin even used the term 'clear and clean' in describing the solid support of the Budgetary Committee. It was not made clear how big the project was at that time, but constructing a huge, multilevel accommodation for large numbers of athletes would certainly require a considerable investment, and Muharam was told he would get a substantial cut. The judges later sentenced Muharram to three years imprisonment and a fine of Rp 150 million. According to the court documents, Muharam received Rp 3.5 billion as a reward for his assistance in securing the procurement of Wisma Atlet's construction to PT Duta Graha Indah Tbk.³⁵

In August 2010, at the Ministry of Youth and Sport, Manullang, together with the president, director and marketing manager of PT Duta Graha Indah Tbk, Dudung Purwadi and Mohamad El Idris, met with Rizal Abdullah, representing the committee chair of the Wisma Atlet project in Palembang. Both Manullang and Idris asked for PT Duta Graha Indah Tbk to be awarded the construction contract. It is my belief that Abdullah knew who Manullang was because she was so close to Nazaruddin.³⁶ In principle, Abdullah agreed to award the project to PT Duta Graha Indah Tbk. The rest of the meeting was limited to discussion concerning details of the Memorandum of Understanding between the Ministry of Youth and Sport and the Procurement Committee of Wisma Atlet in which the agreed contract value for the purpose of tender was of Rp 199.6 billion. It was a done deal.

The next step was a faked bidding process. Idris and one of his staff, Wawan Karmawan, prepared all required documentation, design, personnel information, equipment and other necessary documents to be submitted to Abdullah and Arifin as representatives of the Procurement Committee. Interestingly, at the same time, the Procurement Committee had been provided with a list of other companies invited to take part in the tender process, but on the condition that the construction of Wisma Atlet would be awarded to PT Duta Graha Indah Tbk. The participation of other companies was a sham, aimed only at formally satisfying the requirements of an open tender process. PT Duta Graha Indah Tbk could not win the construction project without an open tender in which other companies participated without the collusion involved being obvious.

Arifin provided an estimated amount of Wisma Atlet's construction to be used in a tender process. Based on the estimated amount provided to them, the tender process commenced, and PT Duta Graha Indah Tbk was duly declared the winner with the total value of the project set at Rp 191.6 billion, as agreed.[37] PT Duta Graha Indah Tbk won the tender because their price was lower than those of other bidders. Nazaruddin then demanded a fee or compensation from PT Duta Graha Indah Tbk for his successful engineering of the entire fraudulent process.[38]

In January 2011, Nazaruddin instructed Manullang to disburse 'fees' of 13 per cent to himself, 2.5 per cent to the Governor of South Sumatra, 2.5 per cent to the Development Committee of Wisma Atlet, 2.5 per cent to the Procurement Committee, 2 per cent to Wafid Muharam as Secretary to the Minister of Youth and Sport, and 0.2 per cent to Manullang. In total, the fees—or, more properly, the bribes—deducted from the total value of the contract amounted to almost 23 per cent.

On 30 June 2011, Nazaruddin, who had already left for Singapore on 24 May 2011,[39] was named a suspect by the KPK.[40] He was put on the wanted list since he moved from one place to another before ending up in Colombia. It took the KPK several months to detect his hiding place. It was suspected that he wanted to change his citizenship, but after several attempts, the KPK, with the assistance of Interpol, finally arrested him in Cartagena, Colombia, and brought him home.[41] He was charged primarily with violating Article 12(b) of Law No. 31 of 1999 as amended by Law No. 20 of 2001.[42] He was also charged in the alternative with violating Article 5(2) in conjunction with Article 5(1)(a) of Law No. 31 of 1999 as amended by Law No. 20 of 2001.[43] In addition, he was charged with violating Article 11 of Law No. 31 of 1999 as amended by Law No. 20 of 2001.[44]

Prosecutors demanded seven years imprisonment minus time in detention, in addition to a fine of Rp 300 000 000, arguing that the judges should take into consideration the fact that Nazaruddin had been uncooperative, at one point hiding in Columbia to avoid punishment.[45] But the Jakarta District Court imposed a sentence less than that demanded by the prosecutors. Even though the panel of judges held it had been proven that Nazaruddin violated the law by corrupting the money of the state and engineering a bribe for the procurement of the Wisma Atlet contract, the judges handed down a sentence of just four years and ten months imprisonment and a fine of Rp 200 000 000.[46]

Nazaruddin appealed the decision, but the Jakarta High Court affirmed the Central Jakarta District Court decision.[47] Nazaruddin then appealed again to the Supreme Court, the highest court in the country. Appeal to the Supreme Court is known as cassation, and the panel of judges examines the application of the law, not the facts. Interestingly, although the Supreme Court also accepted the cassation, it decided that Nazaruddin should receive a heavier sentence, sentencing him to seven years imprisonment and a fine of Rp 300 000 000.[48]

As mentioned, Nazaruddin was assisted by his wife as well as Manullang, Wafid Muharam, Muhammad El Idris, Rizal Abdullah,

Machfud Suroso and a few others. Corruption here was not an opportunistic corrupt enrichment but the intentional plunder of the state's wealth for broader objectives; namely, financing political parties, enriching the senior political elite, sharing the cake with bureaucrats and retaining some portion of it. That is why Nazaruddin could not do it alone; it had to be jointly accomplished by his group of people from various backgrounds, who were accomplices or co-offenders or assisted in commission of the crime.[49] Angelina Sondakh was therefore sentenced to twelve years imprisonment and fined Rp 500 000 000, in addition to compensation amounting to Rp 12 580 000 000 and US$2 350 000.[50] Before she was sentenced to twelve years, Sondakh was sentenced to four years and six months imprisonment in addition to a fine of Rp 250 000 000 at the court of first instance,[51] while at the appeal level her sentence was reaffirmed.[52]

Muharam of the Ministry of Youth and Sport received his final sentence of five years imprisonment and a fine of Rp 200 000 000.[53] Deddy Kusdinar Mpd was sentenced to six years imprisonment and a fine of Rp 100 000 000 in addition to compensation of Rp 300 000 000.[54] Manullang received four years imprisonment in addition to a fine of Rp 200 000 000.[55] Mohammad El Idris from PT Duta Graha Indah Tbk was sentenced to two years imprisonment and a Rp 200 000 000 fine,[56] while Rizal Abdullah was sentenced to three years imprisonment and a Rp 100 000 000 fine.[57] Machfud Suroso, another defendant, received six years imprisonment and compensation amounting to Rp 36 818 625 793,[58] and Teuku Bagus Mokhamad Noor was sentenced to six years imprisonment and a fine amounting to Rp 300 000 000.[59]

Muhammad Nazaruddin's case is a perfect example of political corruption. Among those involved were two senior politicians; namely, Anas Urbaningrum and Andi Alfian Malarangeng, respectively the chair and a member of the board of the Partai Demokrat of Susilo Bambang Yudhoyono, who was then President of Indonesia. Malarangeng, in addition, was also Minister of Youth and Sport. Allegedly, some of the proceeds from the corruption went to the coffers of this party to finance its operations. As mentioned before, no one single party can exist solely on membership dues because they are so insignificant. Hence one of the key sources of financing is politicians who form the leadership of the party.[60] Every political party therefore becomes a political predator, abusing its power to collect as much money as possible. Mietzner has even argued that an inherent part of such behaviour is the strengthening and perpetuation of the wider oligarchic system because it is key to the extraction of corrupt funds.[61]

In this case, Anas Urbaningrum as chair of Partai Demokrat tacitly endorsed the aggression of Muhammad Nazaruddin in collecting money to finance the party. Whether Urbaningrum himself received a share is difficult to say, but from the court proceedings and media reporting, it was evident that some of the money was channelled to an account he controlled.[62] In the construction of the Wisma Atlet case, Urbaningrum was sentenced to fourteen years imprisonment and a fine of Rp 5 billion.[63] He is just one of four chairs of political parties who have now been imprisoned for corruption: Partai Demokrat, Partai Persatuan Pembangunan (PPP), Golkar and Partai Keadilan Sejahtera (PKS). The chairman of Partai Persatuan Pembangunan (PPP), Suryadharma Ali, was sentenced to ten years imprisonment and payment of replacement money amounting to Rp 1 821 000 000 for corruption of Haj funds.[64] The chairman of Golkar, Setya Novanto, masterminded corruption of the Electronic Identification Card (E-KTP). He was sentenced to fifteen years imprisonment, a fine of Rp 500 000 000 and payment of compensation of US$7 300 000 (less Rp 500 000 000 already paid to the state).[65] The president of Partai Keadilan Sejahtera (PKS), Lutfhi Hasan, was sentenced to eighteen years imprisonment and a fine of Rp 1 000 000 000 for corruption in importing beef. In addition, his political rights were revoked by the court.[66]

Andi Alfian Malarangeng was, at one point, Urbaningrum's rival for the position of chair of Partai Demokrat. Malarangeng lost, but he was appointed by the founder and patron of Partai Demokrat, Yudhoyono, to the Board of Supervisors (Dewan Pembina) and

Minister of Youth and Sport.[67] He was a rising star in politics, known to be bright and believed to be honest. Ironically, it was Malarangeng who was instrumental in facilitating the award of Wisma Atlet's construction to PT Duta Graha Indah Tbk.[68] Muharam, secretary of the Ministry of Youth and Sports, seemed to be acting as Malarangeng's proxy in arranging for the construction contract to be assigned to PT Duta Graha Indah Tbk.[69] Malarangeng was eventually tried and sentenced to four years imprisonment and a Rp 200 000 000 fine.[70] The cassation judgment rendered by the Supreme Court in his case upheld the earlier Central Jakarta District Court[71] and Jakarta High Court decisions.[72]

This was not the only corruption case involving the elite of the Partai Demokrat. Nazaruddin, Malarangeng, Urbaniningrum and other notable names from the DPR, cabinet and business were also involved in grand corruption related to the construction of a sports centre in Hambalang, West Java.[73] The amount stolen here was allegedly much greater than in the Wisma Atlet case, and more people served time in prison. Partai Demokrat's image became tarnished in the eyes of the public, and its decline was inevitable.

Setya Novanto

Setya Novanto is a famous name in Indonesia—a senior politician and businessman. For years, his name saturated Indonesia's media, even if not all reporting about him was positive.[74] He eventually became notorious for violating the public's sense of justice, even though some cases seemed unclear.[75] Novanto is a tough and, to some extent, cunning person. When he was young, he worked as a small rice merchant, driver, house servant and model. He worked extremely hard to save money to finance his university studies. He succeeded and managed to finish his studies, obtaining an undergraduate degree.[76] Novanto then entered political life by joining the Golkar Party, the ruling party under Soeharto. He worked hard, competing with other politicians to gain opportunity and position. At the same time, he found ways to become close to Soeharto's inner circle and managed to win business deals from the children of

Soeharto. His hard work and persistence led to success and opened more political doors within Golkar.

In 1998, Setya Novanto was appointed vice treasurer of Golkar and subsequently elected as a member of the DPR representing East Nusa Tenggara province (NTT).[77] That was the beginning of Novanto's spectacular rise. He did not look like a political star and his political views did not impress many people, but his ability to lobby and network was his strength. A likeable person and known to be generous, he was elected four times to the DPR.[78] His career slowly but surely took him towards the top leadership of DPR, from junior member in several commissions, to chair of Golkar's faction, and finally the prize, Speaker of the DPR. Golkar itself, a party that dominated Indonesia's politics during New Order, gradually lost its dominant position after Reformasi began. But while not emerging as the winner of general elections during the Reformasi era (1999, 2004, 2009, 2013 and 2019), Golkar remained strong, within the top three parties in the DPR, so its vote has frequently been a decisive factor in passing and endorsing key policies and legislation. For better or worse, every single president from Soeharto has needed Golkar's support, including the government of Jokowi.

The cost of being a politician is substantial, especially if one aspires to become a top politician. Predatory power and corruption seem essential to exist, let alone progress. That explains why so many politicians have been engaged in corruption, although most of them managed to escape investigation. Novanto's name has been mentioned by the media many times, but he always managed to avoid legal accountability. So corruption was not new to him. Several big corruption cases had Setya Novanto's footprint; namely, Bank Bali, the illegal import of rice from Vietnam, cases described earlier involving Ratu Atut Chosiyah and Akil Mochtar, PON Riau, the importation of toxic waste, the purchase of seaplanes and the single identity system (E-KTP) case. For a long time, however, he managed to escape investigation.[79] In the eyes of many, this meant Novanto had become a legend in the field of corruption, escaping accountability while climbing to one of highest political positions in the country. But clever and cunning though he was, few criminals can run free forever. The E-KTP case proved to be Novanto's downfall. In 2018, he was tried in the Central Jakarta District Court and sentenced to fifteen years imprisonment and fined Rp 500 000 000. He was required to pay compensation of US$7 300 000, less Rp 5 000 000 000 already paid to the state. He also suffered revocation of political rights while serving his sentence.[80]

The background to the E-KTP case is as follows. In late November 2009, Minister of the Interior Gamawan Fauzi sent a letter to the Minister of Finance and the head of the National State Development Planning Agency (Bappenas) regarding a proposal for a single identity system for citizens, together with an application of a public electronic identification card (E-KTP) funded by foreign loans. This was viewed as an important project for a country in the process of development; therefore the Minister of Finance and head of National State Development Planning Agency approved the project in its entirety, agreeing to fund it fully through the state budget. However, the project had to go to the DPR to be endorsed.[81]

Irman, the Director General of Population and Civil Registry of the Ministry of the Interior, together with Andi Agustinus (Andi Narogong), a businessman who was struggling to win the project, lobbied the DPR to approve the project. They promised to reward a group of parliamentarians for their support for the project, and when the project was approved, a disbursement of kickbacks would follow—bribery, in other words. In the eyes of Narogong and Irman, for a megaproject in the amount of Rp 5 952 083 009 000, a substantial amount for bribery seemed appropriate. Everyone at the Ministry of the Interior and DPR who endorsed and approved this project was rewarded handsomely.[82]

Collective corruption, in the sense of sharing the proceeds of corruption, seemed to have become the new norm within business and bureaucracy. In the DPR, the recipients of bribery crossed party lines. Several big names from the Ministry of the Interior and DPR were soon being mentioned in the media, such as Diah Angraini, Secretary General of the Ministry of the Interior, Gamawan Fauzi,

Minister of the Interior, Chairuman Harahap, chair of Commission II of parliament,[83] and of course Setya Novanto, who at that time was a chair of the Golkar faction in the DPR. Gamawan Fauzi and Chairuman Harahap belonged to Partai Demokrat and Golkar respectively.

The tender for the project was processed accordingly with three participants: Konsorsium PNRI, Konsorsium Astragraphia and Konsorsium Murakabi.[84] Konsorsium PNRI consisted of companies ultimately designated the winners of the tender, while Konsorsium Astragraphia and Konsorsium Murakabi seem to have participated in the tender simply in order to comply with regulations and good governance principles. Konsorsium PNRI was managed and controlled by Narogong and eventually by Novanto, while Konsorsium Murakabi was controlled by Irvanto Hendra Pambudi Cahyo, who happened to be a nephew of Novanto.[85] As planned, Konsorsium PNRI was selected as the contractor to procure the E-KTP project.

Throughout the years, even though the budget had been allocated in the annual state budget, disbursement of the budget was often delayed for various reasons. A megaproject such as this would require compliance with significant administrative procedures. A disbursement application must be submitted with detailed appropriation based on a reasonable market price and a timeline. In this regard, it is common to see a time-consuming process owing to several approvals that need to be secured. In the meantime, there had also been intentional delays on the part of certain officials who implicitly demanded payment for the project to get moving again, what Huntington calls a 'lubricant'.[86] Delays of this type kept occurring throughout the project, thus disrupting its realisation. In this situation, normally Novanto came forward, intervening in order to expedite the disbursement of funds. He was thus a saviour of the project. Without him, there would have been no E-KTP project.

Promises made by Narogong, and seemingly endorsed by Novanto, were made to various parties, ranging from officials of the Ministry of the Interior, members of parliament, businessmen and others. The bribes paid to them were allegedly the most in any corruption case handled by Indonesian law enforcement agencies. According to an audit by the state audit agency (BPK), at a minimum, the state lost approximately 50 per cent of the total budget of the project: Rp 5 841 896 144 993.[87] Evidently, so much was stolen that the allocated budget was not enough to complete the project. Allocating additional budget to finish a project has been a common practice in this type of situation, but the resulting public scepticism appeared to contribute to the ambivalence of the government and the DPR about allocating more budget, despite the fact that the E-KTP was undoubtedly a vital project for the country. This is the first electronic identity card in Indonesia, which is used in the national census, general elections and other national programs.

Interestingly, when Novanto was convicted, he did not appeal the decision, and therefore it became final and binding. Perhaps he was afraid that, if he appealed, the appellate court decision would be much more severe, as in many other cases.[88] At the time of his trial, Supreme Court Justice Artidjo Alkostar was still in charge of corruption cases, especially high-profile corruption cases. He was well known for the long prison sentences he routinely imposed on corruption offenders, and he would undoubtedly have treated Novanto's case as one of most serious cases of corruption in Indonesian history.

Novanto was the main offender but, as explained above, he certainly did not act alone in the E-KTP scandal.[89] Other recipients of bribes were tried, but most of them remain free, and it is unclear whether they will ever be tried. Among those who have been prosecuted were Made Oka Mas Agung, Irvanto Hendra Pambudi, Sugiharto, Irman, Markus Nari and Andi Narogong. Their sentences varied depending on their involvement in the scandal. At the court of first instance, a close friend of Novanto, Agung, was sentenced to ten years imprisonment and a Rp 500 000 000 fine.[90] Novanto's nephew, Pambudi, also received ten years imprisonment and a Rp 500 000 000 fine.[91] Sugiharto, director of Management of Population and Administrative Information, Ministry of the Interior, received five years imprisonment in addition to a fine of Rp 400 000 000. Sugiharto had to pay compensation amounting to US$50 000, less US$30 000 and Rp 150 000 000 paid already to the KPK.[92] Another high-ranking official from the Ministry of the Interior, Irman, was sentenced to fifteen years imprisonment, a Rp 500 000 000 fine and compensation amounting to US$500 000 and Rp 1 000 000 000.[93] Nari, who was a member of DPR, received imprisonment of six years in addition to a fine of Rp 300 000 000,[94] while Andi Narogong was sentenced to eight years imprisonment and Rp 400 000 000 fine.[95] All accepted their sentences except Sugiharto and Narogong, who challenged their decisions in the Supreme Court. Sugiharto at the Supreme Court level was sentenced to fifteen years imprisonment, a fine of Rp 500 000 000, and compensation of US$450 000 and Rp 460 000 000 less US$430 000 already paid to the KPK.[96] Narogong received thirteen years imprisonment, a fine of Rp 1 000 000 000, compensation of US$2 150 000 and Rp 1 186 000 000.[97]

It is important to add that there are many politicians and high-level officials who allegedly received bribes in the course of the E-KTP project, and most have been questioned by investigators from the KPK. They remain mere witnesses. Despite the fact that their names were mentioned by defendants in many court proceedings, they have, as mentioned, never been taken to court. The limited number of investigators and prosecutors within the KPK forces the commission to prioritise other cases that urgently need attention. The investigators and prosecutors were therefore not able to proceed with prosecution of these individuals, and that has created uncertainty and delayed justice.

Soeharto Inc.

Soeharto Inc. is not a legal term.[98] It refers to a cluster of Soeharto's businesses involving his immediate family, relatives and cronies. This group amassed an exorbitant fortune spread out across many places in many forms, including property, equity, deposits and others. The judgment of the Jakarta District Court in *Time* v. Soeharto in 2000 listed companies belonging to the family, although many companies were undetected owing to transfers of ownership.[99] The court judgment also did not mention the many *yayasan* controlled by Soeharto to run business projects, fund his supporters and pocket revenue for the family. In his long period in power, Soeharto amassed a considerable fortune, but nobody can determine the exact sum with certainty. Amounts ranging from US$5 billion to US$35 billion have been suggested,[100] but Soeharto denied these claims outright.

As a lawyer for *Time* at the trial, I submitted evidence based on investigations by *Time* reporters about what was called a 'staggering sum of money'.[101] The cover story of *Time* had captured wide attention and was seen as reflecting public anger about abuse of power, corruption, collusion and nepotism (KKN), but *Time*'s editor called all the evidence 'journalistic evidence' that needed to be verified. However, investigating and publishing reports about abuse of power have always been considered public interest issues. As long as investigation and publication reflected journalistic rules and ethics, there should not be any reason to be afraid, *Time* believed. If for one reason or another *Time* was sued, its leaders believed that it was the price it must pay for publishing on public interest issues.

In 1998, one year after Reformasi, the People's Consultative Assembly (MPR) issued Decision No. XI/MPR/1998 reinforcing public sentiment against abuse of power, corruption, collusion and nepotism (KKN). Article 4 stipulates, 'Attempts to combat corruption, collusion and nepotism must be undertaken firmly against anyone be it a public official, a former public official, family and cronies including but not limited to the private sector/conglomerates and former President Soeharto …'.

This MPR Decision tasked President Habibie with initiating legal action against Soeharto. Habibie, who had replaced Soeharto, was caught in a dilemma, given that he himself was indebted to Soeharto. If not for Soeharto, Habibie would have remained in Germany working as an engineer in an aircraft company. Soeharto brought him back to Indonesia and appointed him a member of his cabinet, and he subsequently rose to the position of vice president. As discussed earlier, when the economic crisis badly hit Indonesia in

1998, forcing Soeharto to step down, Habibie, in accordance with the Constitution, stepped into the presidency and launched a series of major reforms in many fields. It must be emphasised that Habibie had almost no choice but to 'reform'; he was under huge public and political pressure to do so. In the eyes of the public, combating corruption, collusion and nepotism was high on the agenda, and that required Habibie to clean up the government, introduce new laws on corruption eradication and set up an agency to fight corruption.

Initially, Habibie was hesitant to touch Soeharto and his family. Facing intense public pressure, however, he was forced to instruct the Attorney General, Andi Ghalib, to investigate Soeharto.[102] The Attorney General identified seven *yayasan* run by Soeharto owning assets amounting to Rp 4.1 trillion and numerous bank accounts under Soeharto's name, totalling US$3 million. The Attorney General also investigated a national car project run by Soeharto's youngest son, Hutomo Mandala Putra, as well as the family's assets in Indonesia and other countries.[103] While leading the investigation, Andi Ghalib was forced to resign since he himself had committed corruption, as was widely reported in the media. He was replaced by the acting Attorney General Ismudjoko, who later issued an SP3, a letter of termination of the investigation.[104] The reason for the termination was never made clear, but many suspect that Soeharto was still very powerful within the government. No one should be surprised that he and his family were extremely influential after thirty-two years in power.

After the general election in 1999, Habibie was, as mentioned, replaced by Abdurrachman Wahid (Gus Dur), who faced strong demand from the public to bring Soeharto to trial. Wahid was required to use his office to implement MPR Decision XI/MPR/1998 and bring Soeharto to court for his abuse of power and corruption. It was clear that no president could ignore the widespread protests against corruption, collusion and nepotism. Soeharto was duly named a suspect and later, defendant, facing charges of abuse of power in his management of the *yayasan* under his control. He had been placed under house arrest, and the Attorney General

Marzuki Darusman seized all *yayasan* assets and bank accounts before the trial.[105] When the trial commenced, Soeharto failed to appear at the initial hearing because he was ill. The same thing happened at the second, third and fourth hearings. In fact, no hearing ever took place. Submissions by Soeharto's lawyers to the court seemed merely to inform the judges that Soeharto was not fit to stand trial owing to his illness; therefore no trial could be held. To support the submission, a certificate of illness from Soeharto's medical team was handed over to the panel of judges.

Regardless of whether Soeharto was really ill or only pretending, the South Jakarta District Court's panel of judges issued a decision that the case could not proceed for the reason that Soeharto, because of his illness, was not fit to stand trial.[106] The prosecutor appealed the decision, and the Jakarta High Court accepted the appeal and ordered the South Jakarta District Court to resume the trial and reinstate Soeharto's house arrest. However, Soeharto continued to claim illness, and there was no way the court could hear the case if the defendant did not appear. One may argue that a trial in absentia could be conducted, but the said opinion has no legal basis because the defendant in this case did not disappear. A trial in absentia could only be held if the defendant disappeared.[107] And when the case went to the Supreme Court, the panel of judges held that the absence of the defendant meant the panel of judges in the District Court could not determine the abuse of power and corruption of Soeharto alleged by the prosecutor.[108] To conclude, Soeharto was never convicted of corruption by the court, demonstrating the extent of influence and loyalty the former President enjoyed to the end of his life.

Earlier it was stated that Soeharto Inc. covered Soeharto, his immediate family, relatives and cronies. To make up for Soeharto's apparent impunity, the Attorney General, Marzuki Darusman, went for the 'low-hanging fruit'; namely, the youngest son of Soeharto, Hutomo Mandala Putra (Tommy), and a close friend of Soeharto, businessman Muhammad Bob Hasan. Both were tried for corruption, charged with causing losses to the state of Rp 96.6 billion and Rp 75 billion respectively.[109] Tommy's case related to a fraudulent land swap while Bob Hasan's case was about corruption of a reforestation fund. Tommy was sentenced to eighteen months imprisonment and a fine of Rp 30 600 000 000, while Bob Hasan received six years imprisonment and fine of Rp 24 000 000 000.[110] Tommy refused to accept the court judgment and subsequently orchestrated the killing of the presiding judge, Syafiuddin Kartasasmita, ten months after the verdict was rendered. He was sentenced to fifteen years imprisonment having been proven guilty of masterminding the murder.[111]

Soeharto died in 2008, and the case was closed. Nothing more can be done; now only history can judge him. There have been initiatives to name Soeharto a 'national hero', but these have always been opposed by many people and organisations, mainly for his abuse of power and corruption.[112] The collective memory of the people, especially those fighting for eradication of corruption, remains, as an indictment against Indonesia's longest serving ruler.

Criminalisation and revenge

For all its shortcomings, Indonesia's war on corruption has shaken political elites both inside and outside power. Politicians, businessmen and high-ranking public officials have come to the conclusion that the anti-corruption movement, especially the KPK, must be stopped. In their opinion, the KPK has excessively broadened its mandate beyond what is stipulated in the KPK Law; ultimately it must be dissolved, and corruption eradication needs to be completely recaptured by the police and prosecution services. In addition, the civil society groups that support the KPK must be curtailed and silenced. To achieve these aims, the political elite started its own war—against the KPK.

Numerous actions to weaken the KPK and the civil society were taken time and again in many formats. The KPK Law, for instance, has been challenged in the Constitutional Court for various reasons, among others the allegedly excessive power it grants the KPK, the KPK's place outside and above other legal institutions, and the KPK's lack of accountability. They also claim that the KPK is an *ad hoc* institution but is treated as though it is a permanent institution. In the DPR, attempts to revise the KPK Law have been undertaken many times. Intimidation and threats against the KPK took the form of threats of budget cuts and the withdrawing of investigators. Many of these attacks failed, but some have been successful, weakening the KPK.

What triggered these attacks? In 2015, President Jokowi, in the process of forming his cabinet, nominated three-star Police General Budi Gunawan to become National Chief of Police. The KPK was also in a process of investigating several police generals who had been accused of having *rekening gendut* or 'fat accounts', allegedly the result of corruption.[113] Abraham Samad and Bambang Widjoyanto named Budi Gunawan as a suspect of corruption not long after President Jokowi nominated him National Chief of Police. Immediately, the news blew up, polemics against Gunawan went viral, and that forced Jokowi to drop the nomination. At this stage, Budi Gunawan felt publicly shamed by the KPK and orchestrated his revenge by naming Abraham Samad and Bambang Widjoyanto as suspects, along with others such as Novel Baswedan, Kombes Endang, Eko Marjono and Ari Widiatmoko.[114]

Widjoyanto was named a suspect on 22 January 2015 for allegedly giving false testimony to the Constitutional Court in 2010 in a local election case in Kotawaringin Barat. The panel of Constitutional Court judges admitted the testimony of Widjoyanto in its entirety. There has never been any statement from the panel of judges that the testimony was inadmissible because of misrepresentation, inaccurate or slanderous—not to mention a false—testimony. Interestingly, after Budi Gunawan was named a suspect, accusation that Widjoyanto made a false testimony came up. Therefore it is hard to digest what was meant by false testimony in this case. The only explanation that can be offered here is that the naming of Budi Gunawan as suspect has to be retaliation. After Widjoyanto was named a suspect, he was detained the next day by the police.[115] I was with him at police headquarters during his interrogation and was informed that the investigation was 'stuck' owing to lack of evidence, and his file was eventually transferred to the Attorney General's Office.[116] If the file were deemed complete, the case should be sent to the court for trial; otherwise the prosecutor can either return the file to the police or conduct additional interrogation or investigation to complete the file. None of these things happened.

Interestingly, objections to this type of criminalisation became widespread, which forced President Jokowi to mediate the tensions between the police and KPK. If the file were sent to court and trial began, the KPK would lose its chairman and a deputy chairman, and that would certainly weaken the eradication of corruption. There was a public interest issue here. Hence, in the name of public interest and in order to save the KPK, the investigation had to be stopped. This could be done by the issue of a letter of termination of the investigation (SP3). As public discontent grew, to the extent of worrying the political elite, President Jokowi was forced to consider this option.[117] However, the Attorney General's Office refused to issue the letter. Instead, it issued what is called a *pengesampingan hukum* or a waiver of the case in the name of public interest.[118] It meant that the case was closed, although the effectiveness of the KPK undoubtedly had been diminished.

Next, the chair of the KPK, Abraham Samad, was named a suspect on 9 February 2015 for document falsification. Allegedly Samad falsified a document in 2007, a family card, stating that he resided in the subdistrict of Masale in Panalkukang, South Sulawesi, although he has never lived there. It has been argued that Samad had an affair with Feriyana Liem, but Samad denied it. The accusation that Samad intended to assist Feriyana Liem to obtain a passport by using Samad's address in Panalkukang had no ground whatsoever. The fact of the matter is that Samad did not live there and had never met Feriyana Liem. Imran Samad, head of the subdistrict Masale, who happened to be a sibling of Samad, claimed that the case was groundless, and indeed there was no evidence that supported the allegation and no witness confirmed it. Therefore the case was closed because it could not be transferred to court. How could a case be tried if there is no legal basis and evidence? Despite this, the case re-emerged once Samad and Widjoyanto named Gunawan a suspect.[119]

Samad was never detained, but he faced no fewer than five criminal complaints. One worth mentioning was filed by the Secretary General of the political party PDI-P, accusing Samad of corruptly attempting to become a vice presidential candidate with Jokowi by facilitating a trade-off in the form of the release of Emir Moeis from prison.[120] This was absurd because there was in fact no way the chair of the KPK could release a corrupt convict from prison—the KPK has no authority to do so. This complaint was clearly contrived simply to shame and humiliate Samad in order to have him removed from his position as chair of the KPK. Of course, Samad denied it outright, saying the allegations were defamatory.[121]

Samad not only faced legal complaints filed by his opponents but also was the subject of public humiliation, with his personal life and 'love affair' exposed in a vulgar manner. Faked photos of him in bed with a lover were circulated, which damaged his reputation despite the facts and his denials. But the weight of these attacks was significant, and sufficient to see him temporarily suspended from his chairmanship of the KPK.[122] Widjoyanto faced similar suspension temporarily.[123]

Like Widjoyanto, Samad's case did not go to court. The Attorney General issued another *pengesampingan hukum* or waiver of the case in the name of public interest.[124] But the KPK as an institution was tarnished and demoralised; the damage went deep. The war against corruption needed recharging, and the support of both the government and the public at large had to be mobilised. In the meantime, actions to weaken or dissolve the KPK continued, directed at the KPK and those supporting it, be it intellectuals or civil society organisations.

Criminalisation is a form of malicious investigation and malicious persecution, but it will be used more often in the future to silence anyone attempting to undermine the police or the Attorney General's Office. The police and the Attorney General's Office are well equipped to launch these attacks, and politicians nervous about aggressive corruption eradication will back them up in such a way as to diminish the effectiveness of the KPK. At the same time, the attempt to weaken the KPK Law will continue in the DPR and the Constitutional Court.

The infamous cases of Ratu Atut Chosiyah, Muhammad Nazaruddin and Setya Novanto are only the tip of the iceberg. So many among the political elite, political parties, religious leaders, military or former military officers, judges, prosecutors, lawyers, businessmen, celebrities and civil society are involved in corruption, be it in Jakarta or in the regions. It is difficult to obtain exact numbers, but the names of many must be listed with the police, prosecutor, judicial commission, state audit agency and the KPK. In addition, there are of course large numbers who manage to escape investigation for one reason or another. No one questions the fact that the number of people involved in corruption is extraordinarily high.

In almost every mega-corruption case, big names remain untouchable. Statements from legal officials often emphasise that there has not been enough evidence to prosecute them. According to the prevailing criminal procedural law, two pieces of evidence are necessary to name someone a suspect and then to prosecute and convict, and this requirement must be satisfied by investigators, prosecutors and judges in accordance with Article 183 and Article 184 of the Criminal Procedure Code (KUHAP).[125] It has been argued that it is difficult to collect evidence of corruption, even though in many cases, the evidence already exists and has been used in the trials of other related defendants. But the authority to determine whether the requirement that two pieces of evidence has been met is legally in the hands of the police, prosecutors and judges, and practically nothing can be done if they take the view that the evidence is inadequate. Transparency and accountability are obviously absent. Many important cases have evaporated for these reasons, such as the BLBI and Bank Century cases, discussed earlier.

The possibility of political interference also cannot be excluded. The fact that a famous politician, top official, military general or super-wealthy businessman remains untouched demonstrates that law enforcement agencies are not really free and independent.[126] These famous and untouchable people are often referred to as 'big fish', and in the mega-corruption cases involving Ratu Atut Chosiyah, Muhammad Nazaruddin and Setya Novanto, 'big fish' have been mentioned or even questioned by the investigators. Interestingly, they have sometimes also appeared as witnesses in court and their names even mentioned in the court judgments, but they are not pursued by the legal apparatus, either because legally the two pieces of evidence have not been collected or because law enforcers were ambivalent owing to possible defamation actions that might be brought against them.[127]

In short, political corruption saturates the history of Indonesia, and the war against corruption launched by the government at different times has not stopped it. Political corruption is not only a grand corruption or mega-corruption; it is also the mother of all corruption.

Chapter 6

Conclusion

Corruption has always been part of Indonesian society, even if justified and rationalised by cultural notions of gift-giving:[1] the belief that gratitude for assistance rendered must be manifested in the form of gifts or monetary gratuity, or both. *Upeti* (tribute) presented to the king or power-holder was also a form of submission to the king or power-holder, and therefore a contribution to strengthening him or her.[2] This might sound like an in-kind tax payment, but it is not really a tax. Moreover, *upeti* was not paid by every member of the population but only by village heads, informal leaders or merchants and others whose existence was dependent, in many instances, on the king or power-holder.[3]

In the literature on corruption, *upeti* is always understood as a form of corruption, but in many traditional communities (*masyarakat adat*), *upeti* has been accepted as normal practice and, over time, treated as the norm in line with so-called Asian values.[4] After Indonesia's political independence was won, the practice of *upeti* continued as payment by subordinates to their head of department or agency. This was cultural, but more than that. People who ran the bureaucracy then were in dire need of additional income because remuneration was insufficient. Salaries were far from adequate and never enough for a decent life, forcing civil servants into different forms of corruption. As a result, corruption to meet basic needs became accepted as a matter of necessity, even if it were a violation of the prevailing law. When almost every civil servant commits corruption, a stage is reached where corruption is being committed collectively, despite the fact that the amounts stolen are relatively small, such as pilfering paper, ink, gasoline, rice and other goods.[5] In modern Indonesia, this type of petty corruption persists, and has spread into a wide range of forms of bribery paid by people to mid-level civil servants who procure or issue identification cards, marriage certificates, death certificates, birth certificates and others. As this suggests, the number of people involved in petty corruption in Indonesia has always been extremely high.

The Corruption Perceptions Index should not be interpreted as actual corruption since it is only a perception. However, it allows us to imagine the level of corruption in a given state. On a scale of 0 to 100 where a score of 0 refers to the most corrupt and a score of 100 is no corruption, Indonesia has been languishing near the bottom for a long time. It has never been able to cross the middle line, 50, which would indicate that corruption is decreasing.[6] The highest score for Indonesia on the Corruption Perceptions Index was 40, achieved in 2019, but in 2020 the score dropped to 37.[7]

Most corruption in Indonesia probably remains the same: petty corruption or corruption motivated by need, not greed.[8] However, rapid economic development under Soeharto opened more opportunities for people such as politicians, civil servants and businessmen to enrich themselves by abusing their power and leverage.[9] These rent-seekers grasped every opportunity for self-enrichment, as the volume of business grew rapidly, with corruption following economic development.[10] Needless to say, the amount of money stolen or corrupted has increased enormously, indicating that much of what occurs is no longer petty corruption but now includes major corruption driven by greed. The case of Setia Novanto is a good example of grand and political corruption in which the amount corrupted was 50 per cent out of the total E-KTP project, more than Rp 2 900 000 000 (see chapter 5). This type of corruption undoubtedly has insulted our common sense of justice, so exorbitant is it. This happened as a new middle class, the new rich, was emerging in Indonesia. It is not wrong therefore to argue that grand and political corruption such as this will badly poison the mind of the middle class.

This created the new phenomenon of overt corruption, whereby the proceeds of corruption are evidenced by a luxurious lifestyle, even though the salary of the corrupt person was known to be limited, making these super-rich lifestyles unaffordable to an honest person. In fact, the twenty years since Reformasi (1998–2018) saw an evolutionary increase in corruption in Indonesia. In the past, there was never corruption where the proceeds exceeded a few billion rupiahs, but it is no longer out of the ordinary to see corruption involving more than a trillion rupiahs.[11] Of course, inflation and exchange rates must be taken into consideration, but that does not change the fact that the amount of corruption committed has dramatically increased beyond common sense.

One should not be surprised to see how much corrupt money has been parked overseas, including in tax havens or offshore financial centres.[12] This is tied to the fact that the common close link between corruption and the political elite or parties began to emerge only in the 1990s, although they have become much more obvious in more recent high-profile cases such as the Hambalang Project, the E-KTP case and the imported meat case.[13] In addition, it is appropriate to mention two mega-corruption cases: namely, Century Bank and Jiwasraya, allegedly linked to powerful politicians and power brokers. Now corruptors come from the legislature, government, judiciary and business communities, and they are not simply thieves but rent-seekers, benefiting from rapid economic development and weak law enforcement,[14] and collusion among them seems common in most of the cases that are exposed.

This is not to say that petty corruption not related to politics has been eradicated. Those who commit petty corruption should not be perceived as 'bad apples' because they mostly are not. Of course, petty corruption is bad; however, this type of corruption has always been dictated by one single objective: to have a decent life, given the fact that many salaries—government and private sector—still fail to meet basic needs. By contrast, political corruption usually has to do with excessive greed or power and the idea of staying in power permanently, or both. Therefore it is a type of grand corruption, although one might also have grand corruption that is not associated with political power.[15]

The noted political scholar Samuel Huntington argues that 'corruption may be more prevalent in some cultures than in others, but in most cultures, it seems to be most prevalent during the most intense phases of modernization'.[16] Modernisation is undoubtedly a key objective of every nation, whether colonised or not. Modernisation is often called 'economic development', by which a nation tries to advance the economic well-being of its people. In this process, investments are poured into such projects as infrastructure, housing, transportation and telecommunications. The source of investment can be the state budget or the private sector in the form of both domestic and foreign investment. In addition, foreign governments and international financial institutions such as the World Bank, IMF and ADB may also offer forms of loans or economic assistance. The objective is to transform the country from a less developed country into a more developed one, so that money continuously flows into the market and the government. However, running a country and modernising its economy have never been easy. Not many countries succeed in managing the economy and keeping a close track on investments. Investment and development money can evaporate anywhere.

As a result, modernisation or economic development often breeds corruption.[17] Arguably, it involves a change in the basic values of the society by which they become more materialistic, more exposed to new things owing to frequent interaction with foreign visitors, connectedness and increased cross-border mobility. Modernisation also contributes to corruption by opening the doors to wealth and power,[18] and corruption transforms from petty to grand, from self-enrichment to accumulation of wealth, from individual, family or clan corruption to political corruption, including corruption aimed at staying in power for as long as possible. The cost of staying in power permanently is enormous because the opposition must be bribed or criticism must be silenced, and every intellectual must be tamed. This is corruption in its very essence: political corruption, the mother of all corruption, which cannot be confined by simple legal definition.[19]

Political corruption normally occurs more often under authoritarian governments that allow it in order to maintain and reward loyal subordinates and cronies. When checks and balances do not function properly, there is also room for political corruption. For the same reason, political corruption finds fertile ground in countries where democracy is still weak and flawed.[20] Political corruption still occurs in advanced democratic countries, but since checks and balances function well and the judiciary enjoys independence, it does not flourish. Political corruption has been restrained owing to the fact that the parties have logistical and financial independence in the sense that they have more than sufficient funds from membership dues. Nevertheless, if political parties have no logistical and financial independence, they inevitably must look for opportunities to accumulate funds to finance their operations. Almost everywhere, contemporary politics evidently has become outrageously expensive. Political contestation becomes more and more costly, and only those parties having liquidity can cover all political expenses; otherwise they end up as cheerleaders, not players, on the periphery, not the centre.

Grand corruption is not just stealing money from the state. It involves planning, strategising, lobbying, executing, investing and laundering the money. It therefore requires a team among which to divide labour, and in such corrupt circumstances, partners in crime can be found in almost every government institution, including, of course, legislatures and judiciaries. It is important to emphasise here that often everything appears to be in compliance with the law—to an external viewer at least. The E-KTP project, for instance, was proposed by the Minister of the Interior, approved by the Minister of Finance and endorsed by DPR, but the total budget was exorbitantly marked up to enable the corruption perpetrators to take shares of the spoils as planned.²¹ So, from the outset, everything appears legal and no law seems to be violated because in these more sophisticated modes of corruption, the state has been captured.²² Actually, what has been captured is not really the state in its entirety but only certain state functions, depending on where and what corruption project is being created.²³

In a country such as Indonesia, the phenomenon of political corruption and, especially, state capture corruption is related to emerging political oligarchies and political dynasties because Indonesian politics in the post-Soekarno era (1965–2015) has been dominated by families and groups with vast resources and power bases. So, for example, many grand corruption perpetrators reported in the media have obvious links to a political oligarch or dynasty. In most cases, those involved in corruption cases were immediately discharged from their affiliation to political party or group, but they will always be part of the inner circle of the political oligarchy or dynasty.²⁴ Legacies of the past, when patrimonialism functioned strongly, contribute to the presence of 'strong men', who, in line with modernisation and democratisation, have transformed themselves into political parties. This helps explain why political oligarchies and dynasties have succeeded in perpetuating themselves.²⁵

In the provinces, state capture corruption follows what happens in the capital, Jakarta. Those running regional governments come from national-level political parties, and most serve on the board of parties in their region. Although the amount of corruption may be relatively lower, the pattern of corruption—the *modus operandi*—is the same: local political oligarchies and political dynasties have emerged and state officials have been captured, co-opted and bought. The KPK, since its establishment, has imprisoned at least 121 governors, mayors and heads of regency, something unprecedented in the history of corruption eradication.²⁶ What happened in Banten Province under Governor Ratu Atut Chosiyah is a model of what is happening more widely (see chapter 5).

Reformasi in 1998 led the way to devolution of power by central government, changing centralised government to decentralised government under the umbrella of the unitary state.[27] A series of constitutional amendments changed the Indonesian state from a centralised state to a decentralised one, even though it failed to become a federal state.[28] However, decentralisation conferred unprecedented vast power on the regions, with governors, mayors and heads of regency as elected officials governing their respective regions under a new constitutional mandate. They have guaranteed autonomy and independence to the extent that the central government cannot discharge them. It can be said that this is one of the unintended results of Reformasi: decentralised corruption.

Does Indonesia belong to a criminal state, to use the term used by Legvold?[29] The answer to the question is that Indonesia is definitely not a criminal state. The 1945 Constitution, laws and regulations, regional regulations and presidential or ministerial decrees have been very firm in their rhetorical commitment to uphold the rule of law, fight corruption and realise social justice for all the people. There are many state organs that directly or indirectly deal with eradication of corruption, such as the state audit agency, judicial commission and anti-money-laundering agency. The KPK also still fights corruption, although its power and authority have been significantly weakened.[30] A commitment to eradicate corruption has always been part and parcel of the existence of the Indonesian state, even if it has rarely been implemented.

Another category mentioned by Legvold is the criminalised state. Corruption in a criminalised state is certainly extensive, endemic, systemic and widespread, and entwined with the state where bribery (corruption) works within some agencies and public officials, and turns up more than sporadically. Expectation that most core institutions remain uncontaminated can no longer be sustained. Corruption seems to penetrate almost every state and local institution, despite the fact that within those institutions there are many decent and uncorrupted people who are powerless and trapped. The rise of political oligarchies and dynasties, especially in the regions, shows that most governmental agencies are controlled and domesticated in order to accumulate funds to perpetuate power. In the capital, the controlling and domesticating of governmental agencies also happens on a larger scale, but there is only so much that can be controlled and domesticated. Media, civil society and honest people within the government have always managed to a certain extent to withstand the deterioration.

What to do to succeed in combating corruption? This is a question that has haunted Indonesia. Corruption seems to be a vicious circle, impossible to eradicate. Any answer provided will be incomplete and imperfect, but one should not lose hope. No country can ever eradicate corruption completely. The most it can do is to minimise corruption by strengthening governance and supremacy of law. Narrowing the income gap between the 'haves' and 'have-nots' will be important, and if the welfare of the people can be guaranteed, room for corruption will be significantly reduced.[31] Thus the answer should be detailed and comprehensive.

First, empowering the KPK is *conditio sine qua non*. The KPK has been effective and successful in its work since its inception, unlike all other agencies that preceded it.[32] Corruption eradication stopped being mere lip service as part of a political public relations effort to satisfy anti-corruption critics. However, in 2019, Law No. 30 of 2002 regarding the KPK was amended by Law No. 19 of 2019. This has significantly weakened the KPK to the extent that it no longer has teeth. The KPK, once regarded as a superbody, has been transformed into an ordinary law enforcement agency, governed by general criminal procedural law that practically ties its hands. The KPK's past successes catching 'big fish' corruption perpetrators will likely not be repeated, although this remains to be seen. Small fish—petty corruptors—may be caught, but political corruption will be largely untouchable. Indonesia seems to be back where it started. Therefore the KPK must be re-empowered if corruption eradication is to be continued.

Additionally, the law dealing with corruption eradication must be strengthened. Legal reforms are needed to enable the KPK and other law enforcement agencies to succeed in reclaiming the illegal wealth of the corrupt perpetrators. Abdurachman Wahid, when he was President, proposed *pembuktian terbalik* (reverse burden of proof) in the sense that the corrupt perpetrator must prove that the assets or wealth he/she possessed did not originate from corruption.[33] Failure to do so would reinforce the presumption that the assets and wealth in question are indeed the result of corruption. However, this proposal died quickly because for many people, especially conservative legal academia and practitioners, the reverse burden of proof violates the principle of presumption of innocence adhered to in criminal law systems in almost every state.[34] In limited form, however, a reverse burden of proof actually has been stipulated in Article 37 para.1 of Law No. 31 of 1999 on Corruption Eradication (as amended).[35]

There has also been a proposal for non-conviction asset forfeiture; namely, that the assets can be forfeited despite the fact that there has not been any verdict from the court. The assets are taken by the state on the basis of the assumption that the investigators and prosecutors have already gathered all evidence concerning the corruption, and in case the judges examined all the evidence, the decision to confiscate the assets will absolutely be taken. Submission of all evidence by the prosecutors will force the judges to conclude that beyond any reasonable doubt, the corruption occurred and the assets must be confiscated.[36] Another reason to forfeit the asset is in order to prevent the defendant or their proxy from transferring the asset; therefore it is justified to seize the assets on the basis of the principle of non-conviction based asset forfeiture. Arguably, this proposal sounds controversial and too far-reaching. It is for this reason that many people, including conservative legal academics and practitioners, have criticised this as a violation of the legal principle that an asset can only be forfeited by a court decision.[37]

Another action that can be taken is asset tracing in cooperation with other countries or international agencies.[38] Transparency International has long campaigned for this, knowing that many assets are transferred overseas, and used to purchase real estate, ranches, hotels, corporations and other valuable assets. Multilateral cooperation must be institutionalised if this form of corruption eradication is to be effective. Sadly, asset-tracing by law enforcement agencies, including the KPK, has been limited to assets in Indonesia, while assets in other countries unfortunately still remain untouched.[39]

There has also been discussion concerning an impoverishment penalty, meaning that those who corrupt the state money should be made poor by means of their wealth being confiscated by the state.[40] This idea, however, was rejected by many people, including those from the legal fraternity.[41] The rationale for rejection, as with rejection of the reverse burden of proof and non-conviction based assets forfeiture proposals, is based on the legal principle that the impoverishment penalty is not stipulated in Indonesian legislation. Moreover, whose assets are to be seized? The corrupt in most cases share the illegal wealth or money with their family and friends, so it is likely to be mixed with wealth and money that have nothing to do with corruption. It would not be fair to confiscate wealth and money not coming from corruption, but how are they to be distinguished?

Despite these difficulties, legal reform is essential if law enforcement agencies and the KPK are to be effective in their fight against corruption. Aggressive legal actions must be allowed. Corruption eradication must dare to think outside the box, with the results tested and adopted into law if necessary, provided the rule of law is always firmly upheld. What has been absent in the history of corruption eradication in Indonesia is the supremacy of the law, the rule of law. No matter how strong the KPK is as a superbody, without the rule of law, it will never be as effective as it should be. Without the rule of law, political oligarchies and political dynasties will be able to free themselves from the risk of civil and criminal liability. As a country constitutionally based on law—a *Rechtsstaat*—the supremacy of law should never be compromised.

Lastly, it must be reiterated again and again that, on its own, the legal fight against corruption will never be able to achieve the objective of corruption eradication in its entirety. Imprisoning corruption perpetrators will not deter all those tempted by corruption, and economic inequality will always function as a justification for corruption. In addition, a dysfunctional democracy will contribute to weaknesses in control mechanisms, and cultural permissiveness will play a role in perpetuating corruption. For all these reasons, corruption, especially political corruption, can only be fought by bringing more people to the anti-corruption movement.

Notes

1 Political corruption in Indonesia

1. Pramoedya Ananta Toer published four novels, namely: *Bumi Manusia* [This earth of mankind], 1980; *Anak Semua Bangsa* [Child of all nations], 1980; *Jejak Langkah* [Foodsteps], 1985; and *Rumah Kaca* [House of glass], 1988. These novels have been translated into more than twenty languages and won him a nomination for the Nobel Peace Prize.
2. It should be noted that Transparency International has changed its methods of indexing, and a score of 37 in 2020 is equivalent to a 3.7 under the previous methods of indexing (before 2012). Transparency International, 'Corruption Index 2020'.
3. See Transparency International, 'Corruption Perceptions Index [2021]'.
4. Regencies (*kabupaten*) are an administrative division immediately below the level of province (*provinsi*). Regencies are governed by *bupati* or regents. In an interview with the Commissioner of the KPK, Bambang Widjojanto, on 10 May 2013, he said that KPK received more than 50 000 complaints/reports of alleged corruption charges committed by many individuals, including regents, mayors and governors. In each province, a regent, mayor or governor has been reported on corruption allegations. Tim Penyusun Laporan Tahunan KPK, *Annual Report 2018*, pp. 14–64.
5. In its 2012 Annual Report, 'Towards corruption-free Indonesia' was changed to 'To become the leading corruption eradication institution that works with integrity, effectively and efficiently'. It seems the KPK realised that it is almost impossible to be completely free from corruption, but it is possible to be an effective and efficient institution for combating corruption. Tim Penyusun Laporan Tahunan KPK, *Annual Report 2012*, p. ii.
6. Transparency International Indonesia as a chapter of Transparency International campaigned for 'zero tolerance against corruption'. As a founder and chairman of Transparency International Indonesia (2006–11), I waged a campaign to maintain 'zero tolerance against corruption'. Other anti-corruption NGOs, such as the Indonesian Corruption Watch and Masyarakat Transparansi Indonesia (Indonesia Transparency Society), joined our campaign.
7. Tim Penyusun Laporan Tahunan KPK, *Annual Report 2018*, p. 72.
8. Johnston, *Syndromes of Corruption*, pp. 177–85.
9. In addition to using corporations and joint venture corporations where foreign investors are involved, it was common practice for Soeharto and his cronies to use

yayasan (foundations) as vehicles to extract money. The *yayasan* itself is a legal entity that can only be used for charitable and social activities, not for business activities. However, it played an important role in Soeharto's dubious business practices.

10 Robertson-Snape, 'Corruption, collusion and nepotism in Indonesia', pp. 589–602.
11 Van der Eng, *Business in Indonesia*, pp. 1–20.
12 Law No. 40 of 1999 regarding the Press. Article 4 of the Press Law guarantees freedom of the press, including, but not limited to, the right to publish, no censorship, no banning and no closure. Indonesia, *Undang-Undang Pers*, UU No. 40 of 1999, LN. No. 166 of 1999, TLN. No. 3887, Articles 5–16.
13 Hosen, 'The Habibie government and anti-corruption reform in Indonesia', pp. 53–68.
14 One bold presidential decision made by Habibie was allowing an independence referendum to take place in East Timor, resulting in the breakaway of East Timor from Indonesia. This was diametrically contrary to the policies of Soeharto. See Simpson, 'Some reflections on the case concerning East Timor', pp. 381–99.
15 Nasution, *The Aspiration for Constitutional Government in Indonesia*. See also Lubis, *In Search of Human Rights*. These two books describe in great detail the long period of authoritarian government from Soekarno to Soeharto.
16 Indrayana, *Indonesian Constitutional Reform*, pp. 143–320.
17 See Komisi Pemberantasan Korupsi, www.kpk.go.id/id/.
18 Manion, *Corruption by Design*, pp. 27–83.
19 Established on 16 August 1999.
20 Established on 21 November 2001.
21 See UN Convention against Corruption, 'Signature and ratification status', www.unodc.org/unodc/en/treaties/CAC/signatories.html, which Indonesia signed and ratified on 18 December 2003 and 19 September 2006 respectively.
22 Pusat Pelaporan dan Analisis Transaksi Keuangan (PPATK), *Regulasi Terbaru Di Bidang Pencegahan dan Pemberantasan Tindak Pidana Pencucian Uang dan Pendanaan Terorisme* [Current regulations in the field of prevention and eradication of acts of money-laundering and the funding of terrorism]. PPATK is an agency in charge of the eradication of money-laundering. This book is a comprehensive collection of regulations concerning money-laundering in Indonesia.
23 Indonesia, *Instruksi Presiden tentang Rencana Aksi Pencegahan dan Pemberantasan Korupsi Tahun 2013*, Inpres No. 1 of 2013. Before Inpres No. 1, of 2013, there was Inpres No. 17, of 2011, containing all preventive and eradication actions to fight corruption. An evaluation of the effectiveness of Inpres No. 17, of 2011, has been conducted and submitted to the President. Indonesia, *Instruksi Presiden tentang Aksi Pencegahan dan Pemberantasan Korupsi Tahun 2012*, Inpres No. 17, of 2011.
24 See Law No. 30 of 2002, Articles 5–16. Indonesia, *Undang-Undang Komisi Pemberantasan Korupsi*, UU No. 30 of 2002, LN. No 137 of 2002, TLN. No. 4250, Articles 5–16.
25 See ibid., Article 11.
26 As of 2019, the KPK employed 1629 people, and approximately 306 of them are in charge of preinvestigation, investigation and prosecution operation for the whole of Indonesia. Tim Penyusun Laporan Tahunan KPK, *Annual Report 2019*, pp. 11–12. Similar agencies in Hong Kong, Thailand and Malaysia, all much smaller countries than Indonesia, employ 1300, 1300 and 2600 people respectively.
27 Law No. 8 of 2010 regarding Prevention and Eradication of Money Laundering Act in conjunction Law No. 3 of 2011 regarding Funds Transfer. Indonesia, *Undang-Undang Pencegahan dan Pemberantasan Tindak Pidana Pencucian Uang*, UU No. 8 of 2010, LN. No. 122 of 2010 TLN. No. 5164. Indonesia, *Undang-Undang Transfer Dana*,

LN. No. 39 of 201, TLN. No 5204.
28 Law No. 22 of 2004 regarding Judicial Commission. Indonesia, *Undang-Undang Komisi Yudisial*, UU No. 22 of 2004, LN. No. 89 of 2004, TLN. No. 4415.
29 Law No. 13 of 2006 regarding Witness and Victim Protection Agency. Indonesia, *Undang-Undang Perlindungan Saksi dan Korban*, UU No. 13 of 2006, LN. No. 64 of 2006, TLN. No. 4635.
30 Law No. 15 of 2006 regarding Financial Audit Body. Indonesia, *Undang-Undang Badan Pemeriksa Keuangan*, UU. No. 15 of 2006, LN. No. 85 of 2006, TLN. No. 4654.
31 Indonesia, *Keputusan Presiden Badan Pengawasan Keuangan dan Pembangunan*, Kepres No. 31 of 1983. Presidential Decree No. 31 of 1983 regarding Financial and Development Audit Body.
32 There are many civil society organisations supporting the anti-corruption fight. Among them are the Indonesian Corruption Watch and Transparency International Indonesia. See www.antikorupsi.org.
33 Alkostar, *Korupsi Politik Di Negara Modern* [Political corruption in modern states], pp. 51–85. Alkostar describes Indonesia's long history of failed attempts to eradicate corruption.
34 According to KPK *Annual Report 2019*, seventy new cases were handled in 2019; thus the total cases handled by KPK reached 957. However, detailed statistics of the cases could not be retrieved as the ACCH KPK official website could not be accessed. Therefore the number of cases used in this book is 887.
35 Wedeman, *Double Paradox*, pp. 10–11.
36 Antara News, 'Aulia Pohan Tersangka Kasus Dana BI'. See also *Detik News*, 'Sudah Jelas Bersalah, Aulia Pohan Jelas Koruptor'.
37 *Tempo*, 'Burhanuddin Abdullah: Kasus BLBI Kewengangan Penegak Hukum'.
38 Kumoro, 'Mantan Ketua MK Akil Mochtar Divonis Seumur Hidup'. See also BBC News Indonesia, 'Setya Novanto dihukum 15 tahun, denda Rp 500 juta, dicabut hak politik 5 tahun', and see also *Tempo*, 'Terbukti Terima Suap, Irman Gusman Dihukum 4,5 Tahun'.
39 MacIntyre, 'Investment, property rights, and corruption in Indonesia', p. 37.
40 Rose-Ackerman, *Corruption*, pp. 1–14.
41 De Leon, *Thinking About Political Corruption*, p. 22. See also Ahmed, *The Dilemma of Corruption in Southeast Asia*, pp. 1–37.
42 Rose-Ackerman, 'Political corruption and reform in democracies', pp. 45–6.
43 Ibid. See also Bull and Newell, 'New avenues in the study of political corruption', pp. 169–73. Bull and Newell argue that aside from seeing corruption from a legal or moral rule, agent and principal, they also see it as a characterisation of behaviour that may be deemed corrupt. See also Hansen and Stanusch, 'Varieties of corruption control', p. 116. See also Chipkin, 'Whither the State?', p. 211. Chipkin argues that in the late eighteenth century, Montesquieu and Edmund Burke attempted to define corruption as failing to act according to the core principles of, or to subvert the integrity of, a public office. Since then, the definition has evolved into what we now generally view as a misuse of public office for private gain.
44 Bhargava and Bolongaita, *Challenging Corruption in Asia*, pp. 209–34.
45 Klitgaard, *Controlling Corruption*, p. 75.
46 International Council on Human Rights Policy, 'Corruption and human rights', p. 5. See also Nichols et al., *Corruption and Misuse of Public Office*, who note (pp. 1–13) that the *Oxford English Dictionary* defines 'corruption' as the perversion or destruction of integrity in the discharge of public duties by bribery or favours.
47 Kim, 'Do Asian values exist?', pp. 315–44. See also Lindsey, 'History always repeats?', pp. 1–23, as well as Uhlin, *Asian Values Democracy*, pp. 1–26, and Ahmed, *The Dilemma*

of *Corruption in Southeast Asia*, pp. 26–37. Ahmed acknowledges that Islam does not recognise the word 'corruption'. A thorough study of Islam is obligatory to understand what corruption is, which in Arabic is called *fasad*, meaning 'every act dispraised by the Shariah (Islamic Law) or by those minded people'. The term connotes mischief, corruption, exploitation, wrong, all forms of injustice, anarchy and chaos.

48 Bhargava and Bolongaita, *Challenging Corruption in Asia*, pp. 209–15. See also International Council on Human Rights Policy, 'Corruption and human rights', p. 15.
49 Kang, *Crony Capitalism*, p. 16.
50 Huntington, 'Modernization and corruption', pp. 253–63.
51 Heidenheimer, 'Perspectives on the perception of corruption', p. 161.
52 Legvold, 'Corruption, the criminalized state, and post-Soviet transition', pp. 196–7.
53 United Nations Development Programme [UNDP], *Tackling Corruption, Transforming Lives*, pp. 21–2.
54 The full text of Article 2 of Law No. 31 of 1999 states, 'Anyone who illegally commits an act to enrich oneself or another person or a corporation, thereby creating losses to the state finance or state economy, is sentenced to life imprisonment or minimum imprisonment of 4 (four) years and to a maximum of 20 (twenty) years, and fined to a minimum of Rp 200 000 000 (two hundred million rupiah) and to a maximum of Rp 1 000 000 000 (one billion rupiah).' Indonesia, *Undang-Undang Pemberantasan Tindak Pidana Korupsi*, UU No. 31 of 1999, LN. No. 140 Year 1999, TLN. No. 3874.
55 The full text of Article 3 of Law No. 31 of 1999 states, 'Anyone [who] with the aim of enriching oneself or another person or a corporation, abuses the authority, opportunity or facilities given to him related to his post or position, which creates losses to the state finance or state economy, is sentenced to life imprisonment, or minimum sentence of 1 (one) year and maximum sentence of 20 (twenty) years or the minimum fine of Rp 50 000 000 (fifty million rupiah) and maximum fine of Rp 1 000 000 000 (one billion rupiah).' Ibid.
56 See Indonesia, *Undang-Undang Pencegahan dan Pemberantasan Tindak Pidana Pencucian Uang*, Articles 3–10.
57 UN Convention against Corruption, 'Signature and ratification of UN Convention against corruption'.
58 See Law No. 22 of 2004, regarding Judicial Commission, Law No. 13 of 2006, regarding Witness and Victim Protection Agency, Indonesia, *Undang-Undang Perlindungan Saksi dan Korban*, UU No. 13 of 2016, LN. No. 64 of 2006, TLN. No. 4635. See also Law No. 15 of 2006, regarding Financial Audit Body, Indonesia, *Undang-Undang Badan Pemeriksa Keuangan*, and Presidential Decree No. 31 of 1983, regarding Financial and Development. Indonesia, President, *Keputusan Presiden Badan Pengawasan Keuangan dan Pembangunan*, Audit Body.
59 *Undang-Undang Pemberantasan Tindak Pidana Korupsi*, UU No. 31 of 1999, as amended by UU No. 20 of 2001, LN. No. 134 of 2001, TLN. No. 4150.
60 See UN Convention against Corruption, 2003, Articles 15, 16, 17, 18, 19, 20, 21, 22, 23, 24 and 25. Articles 21 and 22 stipulate bribery and embezzlement of property in the private sector. These two belong in the category of bribery and embezzlement.
61 At least 154 states have already fully ratified the Convention. See also www.unodc.org/unodc/en/treaties/CAC/signatories.html.
62 UNDP, *Tackling Corruption, Transforming Lives*, p. 19.
63 Chipkin, 'Whither the State?', pp. 211–31.
64 Additionally, there is also a price for nomination of a candidate. Any person aspiring

to be a member of Parliament, regent, mayor, governor or president must be nominated by a party or a coalition of parties. The cost for nomination differs from place to place and from position to position. For those coming from outside a party, the price is much higher. It also depends on the party. Small parties will charge small nomination prices, but bigger parties or ruling parties might charge higher prices. Whatever the amount, this is another form of electorate corruption.

65 Badoh and Diani, *Korupsi Pemilu* [Electoral corruption], p. 12. See also Badoh and Dahlan, *Korupsi Pemilu di Indonesia* [Electoral corruption in Indonesia], p. 13. See also Johnston, *Syndromes of Corruption*, p. 10.
66 A number of politicians in Jakarta and within the regions have been jailed for their involvement in generating funds for their own parties and for themselves. Cases involving the Governor of Riau Province, Rusli Zainal, and the brother of Banten Provincial Governor, Tubagus Chaeri Wardana, are examples of raising funds on behalf of themselves and their parties by accepting commissions, bribery and other forms of payment.
67 In 2005, the government regulated (issued) Government Regulation (Peraturan Pemerintah) on Financial Assistance for Political Parties, whereby only political parties that have a seat in parliament will receive yearly financial support (25 million rupiah per seat).
68 Mietzner, 'Party financing in post-Soeharto Indonesia', p. 246.
69 Ibid., p. 246.
70 Yadav, *Political Parties, Business Groups, and Corruption in Developing Countries*, p. 42.
71 Della Porta and Vannucci, 'Typology of corrupt networks', p. 30.
72 Mietzner, 'Party financing in post-Soeharto Indonesia', p. 248.
73 Media reporting on the trials of Nazaruddin, Treasurer of Partai Demokrat, and Luthfi Hasan Ishaaq, President of Partai Keadilan Sejahtera, provided all the links of corruption to parties' fund-raising. See Afrilianti, 'Nazaruddin Juga Sebut Menpora Terlibat dalam Kasus Wisma Atlet'. See also Fahmi, 'Luthfi Tampik Ijonkan Proyek Kementan untuk Danai PKS'.
74 Legvold, 'Corruption, the criminalized state, and post-Soviet transition', pp. 195–8.
75 Ibid., p. 196.
76 Ibid. p. 196.
77 See chapter 4, 'State capture corruption'. Transparency International also uses the term 'state capture' in describing the practice of using and misusing the state for corruption. See also www.ti.or.id/en/index.php/press-release/2010/11/11/money-politics-and-state-capture.
78 Legvold, 'Corruption, the criminalized state, and post-Soviet transition', pp. 196–7.
79 Ibid., pp. 197–8.
80 Friedrichs and Friedrichs, 'The World Bank and crimes of globalization', pp. 1–12, 13–36.
81 In human rights literature, such international financial institutions as the World Bank, IMF, IFI and others have been included as part of actors in crimes of globalisation. See Rothe, 'Facilitating corruption and human rights violations', pp. 457–76.
82 Greenhill, 'Kleptocratic interdependence', pp. 196–223.
83 Ibid., p. 101.
84 Ibid., p. 97.
85 Shore and Haller, 'Introduction—Sharp practice', pp. 1–28.
86 Interview with Susi Pudjiastuti, former Minister of Maritime Affairs and Fisheries, 6 June 2018.
87 Cox, 'A primer in political pathologies', p. 3. See also Chipkin, 'Whither the State?', pp. 213–14.

88 Harris, *Political Corruption*, p. 30.
89 Funderburk, 'Political corruption', p. 1.
90 Huntington, 'Modernization and corruption', p. 261. See also Mauro, 'World Bank researchers and the study of corruption', pp. 67–71.
91 Huntington, 'Modernization and corruption', p. 255.
92 Werner, 'The development of political corruption in Israel', p. 199.
93 Jimenez and Cainzos, 'Political corruption in Spain', p. 21.
94 Tim Penyusun Laporan Tahunan KPK, *Annual Report 2012*, pp. 14–15.
95 *Jawa Pos*, 'Selain Gayus Tambunan, Ini Sederet Kasus Suap Melibatkan Pegawai Pajak'. See also Maharani, 'Luthfi Hasan Ishaaq Divonis 16 Tahun Penjara', 5 May 2021, and Maharani, 'Rudi Rubiandini Divonis 7 Tahun Penjara'.
96 Interviews with Abraham Samad, 17 May 2013; Bambang Widjoyanto, 10 April 2013; and Busro Muqoddas, 15 May 2013. Samad, Widyoyanto and Muqoddas have been chairman and deputy chairman of the KPK.
97 De Leon, *Thinking About Political Corruption*, pp. 40–3.
98 Bhargava and Bolongaita, *Challenging Corruption in Asia*, pp. 3–5.
99 Goodpaster, 'Reflections on corruption in Indonesia', p. 104.
100 Hansen and Stanusch, 'Varieties of corruption control', pp. 115–16.
101 Mietzner, 'Party financing in post-Soeharto Indonesia', p. 240.
102 Bull and Newell, 'New avenues in the study of political corruption', pp. 169–73. See also Legvold, 'Corruption, the criminalized state, and post-Soviet transition', pp. 208–9.
103 Wedeman, *Double Paradox*, pp. 6–7.
104 Chipkin, 'Whither the State?', p. 225.
105 Legvold, 'Corruption, the criminalized state, and post-Soviet transition', pp. 194–238. The history of many nations, including Indonesia, has shown that corruption has been a significant reason for state collapse. Poverty is the product of corruption in its various forms. When poverty grows unchecked, it is only a matter of time before the state collapses.
106 KPK Law No. 30 of 2002 has been amended by KPK Law No. 19 of 2019. In this book, KPK Law refers to both the law and its amendment unless it is mentioned separately.
107 The Attorney General's Office and the police, for instance, have always complained that they could not do much to fight corruption because the prevailing laws give them less power and authority than the KPK.
108 Goodpaster, 'Reflections on corruption in Indonesia', pp. 87–108. See also Bhargava and Bolongaita, *Challenging Corruption in Asia*, p. 217. It was a senior economist, Sumitro Djoyohadikusumo, who first suggested that up to 30 per cent of the national budget 'evaporated' annually.
109 See Komisi Pemberantasan Korupsi [Anti-Corruption Clearing House], 'Tindak Pidana Korupsi Berdasarkan Jenis Perkara'.
110 Goodpaster, 'Reflections on corruption in Indonesia', pp. 64–78.
111 Their cases mostly relate to the procurements of goods, budget abuse and bribery. Tim Penyusun Laporan Tahunan KPK, *Annual Report 2011*, and Tim Penyusun Laporan Tahunan KPK, *Annual Report 2012*.
112 Among others they were involved in corruption of Hambalang sport facilities (Andi Malarangeng), PON Sport Facility (Rusli Zainal), oil trading (Rudi Rubiandini) and local election disputes (Akil Mochtar). Politicians Luthfi Hasan Ishaq and Police General Djoko Susilo were imprisoned in cases related to illegal beef importation and procurement of driving licence simulation equipment respectively.
113 Mietzner, 'Party financing in post-Soeharto Indonesia', p. 248.

114 See Tim Penyusun Laporan Tahunan KPK, *Annual Report 2012*, pp. 64–71. The report does not use the term 'political corruption' and does not describe the corporations used by defendant Nazaruddin to raise funds for the party. But the media have published the *modus operandi* clearly. In my interview with KPK Commissioner Bambang Widjoyanto on 10 April 2013, he confirmed that corporations were used as vehicles to raise funds for parties. This was not only in the case of the ruling party, Partai Demokrat, but other parties as well.
115 Greenhill, 'Kleptocratic interdependence', pp. 96–115. See also Shore and Haller, 'Introduction—Sharp practice', pp. 1–46.
116 Greenhill, 'Kleptocratic interdependence', p. 106. Greenhill mentioned Sierra Leone, Guinea-Bissau and the Democratic Republic of Congo as states in the bandit states category.
117 See Law No. 32 of 2009, regarding Protection and Management of Environment. Indonesia, *Undang-Undang Perlindungan dan Pengelolaan Lingkungan Hidup*, UU No. 32 of 2009, LN. No. 140 of 2009, TLN. No. 5059.
118 The author, as a partner in the law firm Lubis, Santosa & Maramis (LSM), represented Chevron at trial. We disagreed with the Attorney General's Office view that corporate corruption occurred, but the District Court and High Court sentenced executives of Chevron to imprisonment for violating the anti-corruption laws. However, in the Supreme Court, the convicted executives were acquitted. It is our opinion that if the alleged corruption were considered corporate corruption, then the President Director of Chevron was the one who must be tried and held accountable for the alleged violation of anti-corruption laws. The executives were merely acting as persons in charge, not the ones legally responsible and accountable under the Company Law.
119 See UN Convention against Corruption, Article 12.
120 Ibid.
121 Greenhill, 'Kleptocratic interdependence', pp. 98–9.
122 Friedrichs and Friedrichs, 'The World Bank and crimes of globalization', pp. 1–12.
123 Nelken and Levi, 'The corruption of politics and the politics of corruption', p. 6.
124 See among others Presidential Regulation No. 55 of 2012. Indonesia, *Peraturan Presiden Strategi Nasional Pencegahan dan Pemberantasan Korupsi Jangka Panjang Tahun 2012–2025 dan Jangka Menengah Tahun 2012–2014*, Perpres No. 55 of 2012, LN. No. 122 of 2012; and Presidential Instruction No. 1 of 2013, Indonesia, *Instruksi Presiden tentang Rencana Aksi Pencegahan dan Pemberantasan Korupsi Tahun 2013*. See also Presidential Decree No. 54 of 2018, Indonesia, *Peraturan Presiden Strategi Nasional Pencegahan Korupsi*, Perpres No. 54 of 2018, LN. No. 108 of 2018.
125 See Instruksi Presiden No. 1 of 2013, point 3.
126 See Attachment to Instruksi Presiden No. 1, of 2013. See also Attachment to Presidential Decree No. 54 of 2018.
127 Ibid.
128 See Tim Penyusun Laporan Tahunan KPK, *Annual Report 2012*, pp. 16–19. See also Tim Penyusun Laporan Tahunan KPK, *Annual Report 2018*, pp. 18–20.
129 In interviews with deputy chairman of KPK, Laode Syarif, on 8 May 2019, he underlined this policy of going after oligarchs in Jakarta and the regions.
130 See BBC United Kingdom, 'Indonesian taxman Gayus Tambunan jailed for corruption'.
131 Safitri, 'Pemerintah masih teruskan penyuap Gayus'.
132 *Republika*, 'Kasus Gayus Tambunan Pengaruhi Kepercayaan Wajib Pajak'.
133 See Merdeka, 'Kasus Luthfi Hasan Ishaaq, KPK Periksa Sekretaris Mentan'.
134 See Amindoni, 'Mengapa Harga Daging Sapi di Indonesia Mahal?' See also Finance

Detik, 'Harga Daging Sapi di 3 Negara ini Jauh Lebih Murah dari RI'.
135 See *Tempo*, 'Surya Eka Perkasa corporate secretary'.
136 Umah, 'Jokowi Curiga'.
137 CEIC Data, 'Indonesia oil consumption', www.ceicdata.com/en/indicator/indonesia/oil-consumption.
138 See JG News Channel, 'Former lawmaker Angelina Sondakh denies intimidation in Hambalang case'.
139 See BBC News Indonesia, 'Akil Mochtar Divonis Hukuman Seumur Hidup'. See also CNN Indonesia, 'Orang Dekat Akil Mochtar Divonis 4,5 Tahun Penjara'.
140 See Hidayat and Fadhil, 'Terbukti Korupsi e-KTP, Setya Novanto Divonis 15 Tahun Penjara'.
141 Legvold, 'Corruption, the criminalized state, and post-Soviet transition', pp. 194–8.
142 Interviews with Abraham Samad, Chairman of KPK, 17 May 2013; Bambang Widjojanto, Deputy Chairman of KPK, 10 April 2013; and Laode Syarif, Deputy Chairman of KPK, 8 May 2019.

2 Historical perspective

1 Wahyu, 'Cegah Korupsi Jadi Budaya'.
2 Movanita, 'Komisioner KPK'.
3 Jackson, 'The political implications of structure and culture in Indonesia', pp. 40–2.
4 Liddle, *Leadership and Culture in Indonesian Politics*, p. 80.
5 When Indonesia's founders drafted the first Constitution, one article stipulated that 'the economy is managed based on family principle', meaning 'togetherness, for the people as a whole'. In practice, however, that article was intentionally misinterpreted and abused by politicians and the business community to justify collusion and nepotism. See Article 33 of the 1945 Constitution: Indonesia, *Undang-Undang Dasar 1945*, Article 33.
6 Jackson, 'The political implications of structure and culture in Indonesia', pp. 40–2.
7 Klitgaard, *Controlling Corruption*, pp. 13–51.
8 Alatas, *The Problem of Corruption*, p. 43.
9 Ahmed, *The Dilemma of Corruption in Southeast Asia*, p. 10. Lindsey, 'History always repeats?', p. 19.
10 Dhakidae, 'Korupsi dalam Relasi Modal Negara', pp. 4–27.
11 Volksraad was established in order to be a sounding board for the people, especially the 'natives'; however, the majority of its members were non-native.
12 Dhakidae, 'Korupsi dalam Relasi Modal Negara', pp. 8–10.
13 Alkostar, *Korupsi Politik Di Negara Modern*, pp. 75–6.
14 Indonesia, *Kitab Undang-Undang Pidana* [Wetboek van Straftrecht], Article 362.
15 Ibid., Article 424.
16 Alisyahbana, 'The grievances of the region', p. 321.
17 The Indonesian Communist Party (PKI) was dissolved and banned by the government of Indonesia for Aidit's alleged involvement in the coup in 1965. See Tap MPRS No. XXV/1966. Indonesia, Ketetapan Majelis Permusyawaratan Rakyat Sementara, Tap MPRS No. XXV/1966 of 1966.
18 Aidit, 'Mismanagement, corruption, and bureaucratic capitalist', p. 400.
19 Feith, *The Decline of Constitutional Democracy in Indonesia*, p. 422.
20 Juwono, *Melawan Korupsi*, p. 81.
21 Ibid.
22 Feith, *The Decline of Constitutional Democracy in Indonesia*, p. 423.
23 Thee Kian Wie, 'The Indonesian government's economic policies towards the ethnic

Chinese', pp. 80–4.
24 Feith, *The Decline of Constitutional Democracy in Indonesia*, p. 423.
25 Ibid., p. 423.
26 Ibid., p. 509.
27 Ibid., p. 509.
28 Juwono, *Melawan Korupsi*, p. 99.
29 Ibid., p. 99.
30 Alisyahbana, 'The grievances of the region', pp. 323–5.
31 Legvold, 'Corruption, the criminalized state, and post-Soviet transition', pp. 195–6.
32 The Emergency Anti-Corruption Law was similar in form to the Government Regulation in Lieu of Law (*Perpu*, or *Peraturan Pemerintah Pengganti Undang-Undang*). The Perpu was not known at the time, but essentially it is the same concept: that the President could issue an emergency anti-corruption law without going through the legislature, although the legislature must now review such laws after a period of time.
33 Juwono, *Melawan Korupsi*, p. 83.
34 Ibid. See also Alkostar, *Korupsi Politik Di Negara Modern*, pp. 53–6.
35 Pompe, *A Study of Institutional Collapse*, p. 35.
36 Ibid., p. 52.
37 Schwarz, *A Nation in Waiting*, pp. 65–6.
38 Pompe, *A Study of Institutional Collapse*, p. 36.
39 Ibnu Sutowo under Soeharto's New Order ran the state-owned oil company Pertamina, which became a cash cow for the New Order government, before coming close to collapse owing to losses caused by corruption. Juwono, *Melawan Korupsi*, p. 101.
40 Ibid., p. 101.
41 Ibid., pp. 103–4.
42 The greatest tensions seemed to be between the army and the PKI, the Indonesian Communist Party, which had now emerged as one of the strongest parties and was backed by President Soekarno. Ideologically, the military, especially General Nasution, opposed communism.
43 Juwono, *Melawan Korupsi*, p. 107.
44 Ibid., pp. 107–11.
45 Provisions on corruption can be found in Section 1 of Criminal Code, Articles 209, 210, 415, 416, 417, 418, 419, 420, 423, 425 and 435. Indonesia, *Kitab Undang-Undang Pidana* [Wetboek van Straftrecht].
46 Owing to local rebellions in West and North Sumatra as well as North Sulawesi, the government had declared an emergency, and in this situation authority was in the hands of the military commander, allowing him to promulgate Peperpu to deal with corruption eradication. Alkostar, *Korupsi Politik Di Negara Modern*, pp. 79–80. The position of Central War Commander was held by the Army Commander while that of Supreme War Commander was held by President Soekarno. The Peperpu was issued and signed by the Army Commander.
47 Ibid., pp. 79–80.
48 This is only a small part of elucidation of the Law No. 13 of 1965. Indonesia, *Undang-Undang Pengadilan dalam Lingkungan Peradilan Umum dan Mahkamah Agung*, UU No. 13 of 1965, LN. No. 31 of 1960, TLN. No. 2767. This law, together with its elucidation, is discussed at length in Pompe, *A Study of Institutional Collapse*, pp. 52–66. Article 23 of the Law No. 13 of 1965 stipulates that the President could interfere in the judicial process.
49 Lindsey, 'From rule of law to law of the rulers', p. 13.

50 Ibid., p. 13.
51 Pompe, *A Study of Institutional Collapse*, p. 58. The word *pengayoman* refers to 'protection'. The judge's principal duty under Guided Democracy was to protect state and society, not to provide justice.
52 Production of fertiliser per kilogram was approximately Rp 69, but when it was sold, the farmers had to pay Rp 400. Similar practices took place with respect to copra. See Aidit, 'Mismanagement, corruption, and bureaucratic capitalist', pp. 400–4.
53 Legvold, 'Corruption, the criminalized state, and post-Soviet transition', pp. 194–8.
54 G30S stands for Gerakan 30 September (Movement of 30 September). From the Soeharto government's point of view, G30S was a movement of the Indonesian Communist Party, together with some elements of the military, to overthrow the government. This version has been refuted by many groups and academics, who argued that the G30S had been engineered by the military through the Dewan Jenderal (Military General Council). See Notosusanto and Saleh, 'The coup attempt of the "September 30 Movement" in Indonesia'. See also Anderson and McVey, *A Preliminary Analysis of the October 1, 1965 Coup in Indonesia*, pp. 15–217.
55 Pompe, *A Study of Institutional Collapse*, pp. 77–80. Read also Lindsey, 'From rule of law to law of the rulers', pp. 17–18. See also Lubis, *In Search of Human Rights*, pp. 91–6.
56 Juwono, *Melawan Korupsi*, pp. 121–2.
57 Ibid., pp. 128–30.
58 Ibid., pp. 128–30.
59 Ibid., p. 129.
60 Ibid., pp. 130–1.
61 Ibid., p. 131.
62 Ibid., p. 131.
63 Bhargava and Bolongaita, *Challenging Corruption in Asia*, pp. 209–15. See also International Council on Human Rights Policy, 'Corruption and human rights', p. 5.
64 Juwono, *Melawan Korupsi*, pp. 131–5. I was a second-year law student at the University of Indonesia and attended a few meetings of the Komite Anti Korupsi, where I witnessed the frustration and anger of the students. They began to keep their (political) distance from Soeharto thereafter.
65 Ibid., p. 122.
66 Together with other student activists at that time, we named our movement Gerakan Penghematan (Austerity Movement), calling for cancellation of mega-projects not directly related to the needs of the people.
67 Febrian, 'The bittersweet love story of Pak Harto and Ibu Tien'.
68 Many Presidential Decrees were issued to facilitate the business projects of Soeharto's children such as the case of clove monopoly and the National Car Project, both controlled by Hutomo Mandala Putra, known as Tommy Soeharto. Alkostar, *Korupsi Politik Di Negara Modern*, pp. 83–5.
69 Among those brought to court were Hariman Siregar, Syahrir and Aini Chalid, who were all students leading the big demonstrations in various cities.
70 Juwono, *Melawan Korupsi* [Fighting Corruption], p. 160.
71 President Soeharto allegedly issued seventy-two Presidential Decrees in favour of his family's businesses. Indonesia, *Keputusan Presiden Pembuatan Mobil Nasional*, Kepres No. 42 of 1996. Juwono, *Melawan Korupsi*, p. 160. See also Alkostar, *Korupsi Politik Di Negara Modern*, pp. 83–5.
72 Juwono, *Melawan Korupsi*, pp. 140–2.
73 Alkostar, *Korupsi Politik Di Negara Modern*, p. 79. See also Juwono, *Melawan Korupsi*, p. 122.

74 Juwono, *Melawan Korupsi*, pp. 135–75. See also *Time* (special edition), 24 May 1999. *Time* was published with a cover of Soeharto titled 'Special Report Soeharto Inc.'.
75 Schwarz, *A Nation in Waiting*, pp. 135–44.
76 Lubis, *In Search of Human Rights*, pp. 86–126.
77 Legvold, 'Corruption, the criminalized state, and post-Soviet transition', pp. 195–8.
78 *Time*, 24 May 1999. *Time* exposed the alleged corruption of the families in a comprehensive cover story.
79 Tempo, 'Soeharto Koruptor Terkaya di Dunia'. See also Institute for Criminal Justice Reform, 'Time vs H.M. Soeharto (PK)'.
80 *Time*, 24 May 1999.
81 Lubis, 'Soeharto vs *Time*', pp. 349–444.
82 The judges took the view that *Time* covered both sides of the issue and had no malicious intent. Its coverage of the alleged corruption has always been in line with general public interest. Ibid., pp. 301–444. See Decision of Central Jakarta District Court No. 338/PDT.G/1999/PN.JKT.PST, 6 June 2000.
83 See Decision of Jakarta High Court No. 551/PDT/2000/PT.DKI, 16 March 2001.
84 See Supreme Court Decision No. 3215K/PDT/2001. The public apology was to be published in five national news outlets, five national magazines and *Time* itself three days consecutively. See Liputan6, '12 Tahun Lalu, Soeharto Menang Lawan Majalah Time'.
85 See Batubara, 'Edaran MA, Sinar Terang bagi Pers'. See also Mahkamah Konstitusi—Dewan, *Nota Kesepahaman antara Mahkamah Konstitusi Republik Indonesia dan Dewan Pers tentang Peningkatan Pemahaman Hak Konstitusional Warga Negara*, No 56/PK/2019—No 07/DP/MoU/IV/2019.
86 See Supreme Court Decision No. 273 PK/PDT/2008, 16 April 2008.
87 Juwono, *Melawan Korupsi*, pp. 179–94.
88 Ibid., pp. 194–7.
89 Decree No. XI of 1998 regarding State Official who are Clean and Free from Corruption, Collusion and Nepotism, Article 4 para. 1. Indonesia, *Ketetapan Majelis Permusyawaratan Rakyat Penyelenggara Negara yang Bersih dan Bebas Korupsi, Kolusi dan Nepotisme*, Tap MPR XI/MPR/1998 of 1998, Article 4 para. 1.
90 Juwono, *Melawan Korupsi*, p. 197.
91 Members of Habibie's campaign team who were involved in the Bank Bali Case included, among others, Setya Novanto and Akbar Tanjung. Ibid., p. 198. Both Tanjung and Novanto were senior politicians of Golkar Party, which was then still the largest party. Tanjung served as Habibie's Minister of State Secretariat, a key role.
92 Indonesia, *Undang-Undang Pemberantasan Tindak Pidana Korupsi*. Text in Bahasa Indonesia can be downloaded from www.kpk.go.id/images/pdf/Undang-undang/uu311999.pdf.
93 The election of the president in 1999, before amendment of the 1945 Constitution, was conducted by the People's Consultative Assembly (MPR). The first direct election of President took place in 2004 based on the amended 1945 Constitution. Under the rules in place for 1999, a candidate did not need to win the general election to win the presidency; he or she simply had to have the support of the MPR. Wahid managed to gather this support from a number of parties in the MPR.
94 Juwono, *Melawan Korupsi*, pp. 203–24.
95 Ibid., p. 204.
96 Ibid., pp. 207–8.
97 Ibid., pp. 210–13.
98 Tempo, '20 Tahun Pembunuhan Hakim Agung Syafiuddin yang Melibatkan Tommy Soeharto'.

99 Juwono, *Melawan Korupsi*, p. 208.
100 Tri/Apr, 'Yahya Harahap Dapat Dituntut'.
101 Juwono, *Melawan Korupsi*, pp. 216–17.
102 *Tempo*, 'Kasus Bruneigate dan Buloggate Bisa Dibuka Lagi'.
103 Butt and Lindsey, *The Constitution of Indonesia*, pp. 1–25. Detailed anatomy of the Constitution can be seen in pp. 260–7.
104 Juwono, *Melawan Korupsi*, pp. 235–9. See also Komisi Pemberantasan Korupsi, 'Lahirnya Komisi Pemberantasan Korupsi KPK'.
105 Juwono, *Melawan Korupsi*, pp. 224–7.
106 Ibid., pp. 228–9. See also *Tempo*, 'Akbar Tandjung Divonis 3 Tahun di Pengadilan Tinggi'.
107 Aji, 'Kasus BLBI, Mantan Kepala BPPN Dituntut 15 Tahun Penjara'.
108 Zhafira, 'KPK terus Lanjutkan Usut Kasus Korupsi BLBI'.
109 Juwono, *Melawan Korupsi*, p. 238.
110 Hukum Online, 'Senin, Presiden Lantik Pimpinan KPK'.
111 Juwono, *Melawan Korupsi*, p. 269. See also *Detik News*, 'SBY Minta Timtas Tipikor Sedikit Bicara Banyak Bekerja'.
112 Juwono, *Melawan Korupsi*, p. 269. See also Detik, 'Said Agil Jadi Tersangka Korupsi, Tetangga Juga Terkaget-Kaget'.
113 Hukum Online, 'Divonis Delapan Tahun Penjara, Mantan Dirut Jamsostek Ngamuk'.
114 Juwono, *Melawan Korupsi*, pp. 270–1. See also Priyambodo, 'Terbukti Korupsi, Komjen Suyitno Landung Divonis 18 Bulan Penjara'.
115 Juwono, *Melawan Korupsi*, pp. 271–3. (See also Hukum Online, 'KPK Tetapkan Abdullah Puteh sebagai Tersangka Korupsi'.)
116 Juwono, *Melawan Korupsi*, p. 273. See also *Detik News*, 'Kronologi Kasus Mulyana Versi BPK'.
117 Juwono, *Melawan Korupsi*, p. 273. See also Indonesia Corruption Watch, 'Korupsi KPU; MA Kurangi Hukuman Nazaruddin Sjamsuddin'.
118 Juwono, *Melawan Korupsi*, pp. 275–6. See also *Detik News*, 'Rokhmin Divonis 7 Tahun Penjara', and *Tempo*, 'Theo Toemion Divonis 6 Tahun'.
119 Juwono, *Melawan Korupsi*, pp. 274–5. See also Hukum Online, 'Pilih Antasari sebagai Ketua KPK, DPR Dihujani Kritik'.
120 Novianti, 'Kontroversi Seputar Terpilihnya Antasari Azhar Sebagai Ketua KPK'.
121 Juwono, *Melawan Korupsi*, p. 275. See also Firdaus, 'Ini Penyebab Rusdiharjo Divonis Rendah'.
122 Juwono, *Melawan Korupsi*, p. 275. See also *Kompas*, 'Burhanuddin Abdullah Divonis Lima Tahun'.
123 Ibid., pp. 275–6. See also *Detik News*, 'Sudah Divonis Bersalah Aulia Pohan Jelas Koruptor'.
124 Ibid., p. 276. See *Warta Kota*, 'Ingat Rani Juliani Caddy Golf yang Terlibat Kasus Antasari? Kabarnya Terkini Mengejutkan'. See also Gatra, 'Antasari Azhar Bebas Bersyarat, Ini Perjalanan Kasusnya'.
125 *Detik News*, 'Polisi Perpanjang Penahanan Antasari Azhar Hingga 31 Agustus'.
126 Juwono, *Melawan Korupsi*, pp. 277–8.
127 The members of Tim Delapan were: Adnan Buyung Nasution, Todung Mulya Lubis, Denny Indrayana, Amir Syamsuddin, Anies Baswedan, Hikmahanto Juwana, Kusparmono Irsan and Komaruddin Hidayat.
128 BBC News Indonesia, 'Rekomendasi Tim Pencari Fakta'.
129 Ibid., pp. 300–4. See BBC News Indonesia, 'Nazaruddin Diperiksa Penyidik KPK.' See also *Kompas*, 'Angelina Sondakh Divonis 4,5 Tahun Penjara'; *Kompas*, 'Andi Mallarangeng Didakwa Korupsi Rp 4 Miliar dan 550 000 Dollar AS'; BBC News

Indonesia, 'Anas Urbaningrum Divonis 8 Tahun Penjara'.
130 *Tempo*, 'Daftar Kader Partai Demokrat yang Terlibat Korupsi'.
131 Juwono, *Melawan Korupsi*, pp. 300–3. See also Wardah, 'KPK tetapkan Miranda Goeltom sebagai Tersangka'.
132 Juwono, *Melawan Korupsi*, pp. 304–5. See also Maharani, 'Luthfi Hasan Ishaaq Divonis 16 Tahun Penjara'.
133 Ibrahim, 'Nur Mahmudi Tersangka Korupsi, Fahri Hamzah Berkicau Soal Sosoknya'.
134 Juwono, *Melawan Korupsi*, pp. 300–1. See *Republika*, 'Rugikan Negara Rp 33,7 Miliar Bachtiar Chamsyah Hanya Divonis 1,8 Tahun'; and Revianur, 'Hukuman Mantan Mendagri Hari Sabarno Jadi 5 Tahun'.
135 Dhakidae, 'Korupsi dalam Relasi Modal Negara', pp. 3–18. See also Affan, 'Korupsi Massal di DPRD'.
136 Juwono, *Melawan Korupsi*, pp. 307–8. See also Oke News, 'Akil Mochtar Tidak Menyesal Dihukum'. The Chief Justice refused to admit that he corrupted money belonging to the state. In other words, he said he did not corrupt.
137 Butt, *The Constitutional Court and Democracy in Indonesia*, pp. 1–8.
138 *Kompas*, 'Patrialis Akbar Divonis 8 Tahun Penjara'.
139 *Tribun News*, 'Sebut Korupsi Ibarat Kanker Bagi Negara, Artidjo Alkostar'. See also Fatmawati, 'KPK Soal Artidjo Pension'.
140 Lubis, *Recrowning Negara Hukum*, pp. 5–17.
141 Paat, 'ICW'.
142 Amrullah, 'Kasus Suryadharma Ali'. See also BBC News Indonesia, 'Menteri ESDM Jero Wacik Resmi Tersangka'; Hukum Online, 'KPK Geledah Rumah di Depok Terkait Kasus Sutan Bhatoegana'; *Kompas*, 'Ini Detail Kasus Dugaan Korupsi Pajak yang Diduga Menjerat Hadi Poernomo'.
143 Paat, 'ICW'.
144 Firdaus, 'KPK Tetapkan Gubernur Sumut Gatot dan istri Mudanya sebagai Tersangka'. See also Sitompul, 'Kasus Ratu Atut, KPK Periksa Pihak Swasta'; Rodzi, 'Tiga Kali Gubernur Riau Korupsi, Ada Apa Dengan Riau?'
145 *Kompas*, 'Syamsul Arifin-Gatot Pujo Nugroho Resmi Menang'. See also Rodzi, 'Tiga Kali Gubernur Riau Korupsi, Ada Apa Dengan Riau?'
146 *Tribun Medan*, 'Daftar Nama-Nama 38 Anggota DPRD Sumut yang Tersangka KPK masa Penahanan Diperpanjang'. See also *Investor Daily Indonesia*, 'KPK Tahan Tujuh Anggota DPRD Riau'; Ali, '5 Politikus Terjerat Korupsi Sepanjang 2015'.
147 Lestari, 'ICW, Vonis Bebas Terdakwa Kasus Korupsi Meningkat'.
148 Reily, 'Ada 19 Kasus Korupsi Selama 2017, KPK Cetak Rekor OTT Terbanyak'.
149 *Kompas*, 'Kaleidoskop 2016'.
150 Ibid.
151 BBC News Indonesia, 'Ketua DPD Irman Gusman Ditetapkan Sebagai Tersangka Setelah Operasi Tangkap Tangan KPK'.
152 Reily, 'Ada 19 Kasus Korupsi Selama 2017'.
153 *Kompas*, 'Patrialis Akbar Divonis 8 Tahun Penjara'.
154 Fatmawati, 'Kronologi OTT Kasus Suap Gubernur Bengkulu'.
155 *Tribun News*, 'Ini 8 Kepala Daerah yang Dijerat KPK Sepanjang 2017'.
156 Risalah, 'Ini Daftar Lengkap 19 OTT KPK Sepanjang 2017'.
157 Ibid.
158 Fadhil, 'KPK Tangani 178 Kasus Korupsi di 2018, Terbanyak Libatkan Legislatif'.
159 *Kompas*, 'Infografik: 29 Kepala Daerah Terjerat kasus Korupsi Sepanjang 2018'.
160 Damhuri, 'Mengapa Idrus Marham Jadi Tersangka?'
161 *Kumparan*, 'Kaleidoskop 2019: 5 Kasus Korupsi dengan Nilai Terbesar'.
162 Interview with Laode Syarif, Deputy Chair of KPK, 6 March 2020. See also Tim

Penyusun Laporan Tahunan KPK, 2018, www.kpk.go.id/id/publikasi/laporan-tahunan (some English translation is available).
163 Legvold, 'Corruption, the criminalized state, and post-Soviet transition', pp. 195–8.
164 Lindsey, 'From rule of law to law of the rulers', pp. 1–19. See also Goodpaster, 'Reflections on corruption in Indonesia', pp. 87–107.
165 ICAC, 'Brief history'.

3 KPK: a superbody?

1 Butt, *Corruption and Law in Indonesia*, p. 12.
2 Nguyen, *The Indonesian Dream*, pp. xxix–xxxiii. See also Lubis, *Recrowning Negara Hukum*, pp. 5–17.
3 Law No. 31 of 1999 on Eradication of the Criminal Act of Corruption replaced Law No. 3 Year 1971 on Eradication of the Criminal Act of Corruption. Indonesia, *Undang-Undang Pemberantasan Tindak Pidana Korupsi*, UU No. 31 Year 1999. Indonesia, *Undang-Undang Pemberantasan Tindak Pidana Korupsi*, UU No. 3 Year 1971, LN. No. 19 Year 1971, TLN. No. 19.
4 Lindsey and Santosa, 'The trajectory of law reform in Indonesia', pp. 12–15.
5 Ibid. See also Juwono, *Melawan Korupsi*, pp. 194–9.
6 Juwono, *Melawan Korupsi*, pp. 194–202. It is important to note that the Law on Government Officials Free and Clean of Corruption, Collusion and Nepotism, Law No. 28 of 1999, had paved the way for the establishment of KPK.
7 Ibid.
8 Lindsey and Santosa, 'The trajectory of law reform in Indonesia', pp. 12–15.
9 See Government Regulation No. 71 of 2000, Articles 7–11. Indonesia, *Peraturan Pemerintah Tata Cara Pelaksanaan Peran Serta Masyarakat dan Pemberian Penghargaan dalam Pencegahan dan Pemberantasan Tindak Pidana Korupsi*, PP No. 71 Year 2000, TLN. No. 3995, Articles 7–11.
10 The Constitution does not grant the President the right to dissolve Parliament. *Tempo*, 'DPR dan TNI Akan Bereaksi Kalau Dekrit Keluar'.
11 What actually happened was an impeachment; however, the Constitution did not have a provision on impeachment at that time. Wahid was therefore discharged from the presidency on the basis of the People's Consultative Assembly (MPR) Decision No II/MPR/2001. Lindsey and Santosa, 'The trajectory of law reform in Indonesia', pp. 15–17. See also Marzuki, 'Pemakzulan Presiden/Wakil Presiden Menurut Undang-Undang Dasar 1945', pp. 15–28. See also Viva, 'Kisah Kejatuhan Gus Dur dari Kursi Presiden'.
12 Juwono, *Melawan Korupsi*, pp. 235–9.
13 Hainsworth, 'Rule of law, anti-corruption, anti-terrorism and militant Islam', pp. 129–31.
14 Juwono, *Melawan Korupsi*, pp. 269–70.
15 Indonesia, *Undang-Undang Komisi Pemberantasan Korupsi*, Article 44 para. 2.
16 Ibid., Articles 45–50.
17 Indonesia, *Undang-Undang Perubahan Kedua Atas Undang-Undang Nomor 30 Tahun 2002 tentang Komisi Pemberantasan Tinak Pidana Korupsi*, UU No. 19 of 2019, Article 40.
18 Indonesia, *Undang-Undang Komisi Pemberantasan Korupsi*, Articles 6–15.
19 Yudhoyono issued Presidential Regulation No. 55 Year 2012 on National Strategy of Prevention and Eradication of Corruption. Indonesia, *Peraturan Presiden Strategi Nasional Pencegahan dan Pemberantasan Korupsi Jangka Panjang Tahun 2012–2025 dan Jangka Menengah Tahun 2012–2014*, and P Indonesia, *Instruksi Presiden tentang*

Rencana Aksi Pencegahan dan Pemberantasan Korupsi Tahun 2013.

20 This story came up during a cross-examination of a police officer by Tim Delapan (Team of Eight), when I asked the police officer to explain what he said were the offences committed by Hamzah and Rianto. See also *Detik News*, 'Kronologi Chandra and Bibit Menuju Tahanan Rutan Bareskrim'.

21 Guanto, 'Tumpak, Mas Achmad Santosa, dan Waluyo Pimpinan KPK Sementara'.

22 I remember General Susno Duaji, answering my question in the Tim Delapan cross-examination, saying: 'Kok Cicak mau melawan Buaya?' ('Why does a lizard want to fight a crocodile?')

23 For me, it was clear that President Susilo Bambang Yudhoyono at that time supported the KPK to fight corruption, provided action was taken in order to make the KPK more credible and respected.

24 Tim Delapan examined all files related to the Bank Century case as investigated by the police. At the same time, Tim Delapan gathered all reports from the KPK regarding KPK's investigation of cases that related to Bank Century's case. Some KPK investigators were also interviewed to gather more information. On the basis of this preliminary investigation, Tim Delapan decided to cross-examine Susno Duaji, Chandra Hamzah and Bibit Samad Rianto.

25 My personal conversation with Jokowi took place when I served on Jokowi's legal team during his campaign for the presidency in 2013.

26 See Profile Corruption Eradication Commission Republic Indonesia, KPK, Section on Public Engagement, Komisi Pemberantasan Korupsi, 'Beranda KPK'.

27 The Elucidation to Article 3 stipulates: 'In this article, powers and influence shall be construed as any power that could affect the tasks and authority of the KPK or members of the Commissioners of the KPK individually, from the executive, judiciary, legislative, and any other entities connected to a corruption case, or any other circumstances and situation, for any reason.' Indonesia, *Undang-Undang Komisi Pemberantasan Korupsi*, elucidation of Article 3.

28 See Law No. 19 of 2019, Articles 3 and 25.

29 Brata, *Why Did Anticorruption Policy Fail?*, pp. 18–20.

30 Tim Penyusun Laporan Tahunan KPK, 'KPK, Demi dan Untuk Indonesia', *Annual Report 2017*, p. viii.

31 Indonesia, *Undang-Undang Komisi Pemberantasan Korupsi*, Articles 21, 29–34.

32 Indonesia, *Undang-Undang tentang Perubahan Kedua atas Undang-Undang Nomor 30. Tahun 2002 tentang Komisi Pemberantasan Tindak Pidana Korupsi*, UU No. 19 of 2019, LN. No. 197 Year 2019, TLN No. 6409, Articles 3 and 25.

33 Guritno, 'Kejanggalan Tes Wawasan Kebangsaan Pegawai KPK yang Jadi Sorotan'.

34 Agus, 'Agus Rahardjo'. See also No Man's Land, 'KPK: Lembaga Permanen atau Lembaga Ad Hoc?'

35 Lubis, *Recrowning Negara Hukum*, pp. 5–12.

36 Ibid. See also Noviyanto, 'PDIP Sepakat KPK Dibubarkan', and *Tempo*, 'Fahri Hamzah Sarankan KPK Dibubarkan, Pukat UGM'.

37 West, 'KPK Harusnya Dipermanenkan, Bukan Dihilangkan'. See also Sindo News, 'Pengamat Setuju KPK Harus Dipermanenkan'.

38 See Indonesia, *Undang-Undang Komisi Pemberantasan Korupsi*, Article 21.

39 Indonesia, *Undang-Undang Komisi Pemberantasan Korupsi*, Article 34.

40 See Kompas, 'Petahana yang Kembali Terpilih Jadi Pimpinan KPK'.

41 Corruption cases handled by KPK in 2018 consist of ninety-one cases involving parliamentarians, fifty cases involving business people, twenty-eight cases involving a governor and head of regency, and twenty cases involving other high-ranking officials. See Komisi Pemberantasan Korupsi, 'Press release: Capaikan dan Kinerja di

Tahun 2018'. See also Komisi Pemberantasan Korupsi, 'Laporan Akuntabilitas (LAKIP) KPK 2018'.
42 Tim Penyusun Laporan Tahunan KPK, *Annual Report 2017*.
43 Indonesia, *Undang-Undang Komisi Pemberantasan Korupsi*, Article 32. See also BBC News Indonesia, 'Antasari Diberhentikan Sementara'.
44 Indonesia, *Undang-Undang tentang Perubahan Kedua atas Undang-Undang Nomor 30 Tahun 2002*, Articles 12, 12B, 12C, 12D.
45 No one knows how many corruption cases exist in a country such as Indonesia where corruption is systemic, endemic and widespread. Statistics do not convey the corruption reality—perception does. As Brata says: 'After the collapse of the New Order regime, most Indonesians and non-governmental organizations such as Indonesian Corruption Watch (ICW) and Transparency International (TI Reports 2002 and 2003), perceived that the level of corruption under democratic governments of the Reform Order regime was higher than the level under the authoritarian government of the New Order regime.' Brata, *Why Did Anticorruption Policy Fail?*, pp. 1–2.
46 Indonesia, *Undang-Undang Komisi Pemberantasan Korupsi*, Article 11.
47 See Davidson, 'Politics-as-usual on trial', pp. 75–99. Davidson says, rightly: 'Rarely a day passes in the country's media without an article uncovering, describing, decrying or ruminating upon a bewildering array of corruption …'
48 Indonesia, *Undang-Undang Komisi Pemberantasan Korupsi*, Article 12.
49 See Indonesia, *Undang-Undang tentang Perubahan Kedua atas Undang-Undang Nomor 30 Tahun 2002*, Articles 12, 12B, 12C and 12D.
50 Indonesia, *Undang-Undang Komisi Pemberantasan Korupsi*, Article 15. See also Law No. 13 Year 2006, Indonesia, *Undang-Undang Badan Pemeriksa Keuangan*. Perlindungan Whistleblowers are covered by this particular legislation.
51 *Kompas*, 'Kaleidoskop 2016'.
52 Klitgaard, *Controlling Corruption*, pp. 81–97.
53 Indonesia, *Undang-Undang Komisi Pemberantasan Korupsi*, Article 13. See Komisi Pemberantasan Korupsi, 'Beranda KPK'.
54 See Indonesia, *Undang-Undang tentang Perubahan Kedua atas Undang-Undang Nomor 30 Tahun 2002*, Article 6. Prevention in this article is listed as the principal task of KPK. Presiden Jokowi stressed the importance of 'prevention' when I met him at the start of his first term and we discussed the corruption eradication program in Indonesia.
55 Indonesia, *Undang-Undang Komisi Pemberantasan Korupsi*, Articles 6 and 14. See also Indonesia, *Undang-Undang tentang Perubahan Kedua atas Undang-Undang Nomor 30 Tahun 2002*, Articles 6 and 9.
56 Most World Bank publications have emphasised good governance, good corporate governance and, more recently, good civil society governance. Those who have good governance will be able to reduce corruption significantly. See Vogl, *Waging War on Corruption*, pp. 1–33.
57 Publica News, 'Kesimpulan Pansus Hak Angket Sebut KPK Superbody'. See also Hukum Online, 'KPK Memang Dirancang Superbody Sedari Awal'.
58 Jemadu, *Challenges in Eradicating Corruption*, pp. 1–12.
59 See Klitgaard, *Controlling Corruption*, p. 88. Laws and rules in some circumstances may be used as tools for corruption, and in other circumstances they may be used also as tools to reduce corruption.
60 Jemadu, *Challenges in Eradicating Corruption*, p. 2.
61 *Tribun News*, 'Jaksa Agung Bentuk Satgas Khusus Tangani Kasus Korupsi Besar'. Why did the Attorney General form a 'special task force to deal with grand corruption

cases'? The answer is simple: the Attorney General did not genuinely accept that the KPK was now, by law, the agency that was to handle most grand corruption cases.
62 Indonesia, *Undang-Undang Komisi Pemberantasan Korupsi*, Articles 53–62. See also Butt, *Corruption and Law in Indonesia*, pp. 23–5. See also Lindsey, 'An overview of Indonesian law', pp. 18–19.
63 Butt, *Corruption and Law in Indonesia*, p. 22.
64 Santoso, 'Polri Tangani 1.472 Kasus Korupsi Selama 2017, 1.028 Selesai'. See also Taher, 'Catatan Kinerja KPK di 2017'.
65 *Kompas*, '2017, Kejagung Selamatkan Uang Negara RP 734 M dari Kasus Pidana Khusus'.
66 Indonesia, *Undang-Undang Tentang Kepolisian Negara Republik Indonesia*, UU No. 2 of 2002, LN. No. 2 Year 2002, TLN. No. 4168, Article 2.
67 Indonesia, *Undang-Undang Hukum Acara Pidana*, UU No. 8 Year 1981, LN. No. 76 Year 1981, TLN. No. 3258, Articles 1–9.
68 Sofwan, 'Ulang Tahun ke-69 Polri dan Penanganan Korupsi Kakap'.
69 Indonesia, *Undang-Undang Kejaksaan Republik Indonesia*, UU No. 16 Year 2004, LN. No. 67 Year 2004, TLN. No. 4401, Article 30.
70 Ibid.
71 Ibid. Article 30, para. 1, point 4, which stipulates that prosecutors are entitled to investigate certain criminal offences on the basis of prevailing laws.
72 *Tribun News*, 'ICW Minta Jaksa Agung Berani Tangkap Koruptor Kakap'. In criminal law, there are two categories of crime or offence, namely, general crimes and special crimes. Corruption and drug trafficking, among others, are classified as special crimes.
73 Indonesia, *Undang-Undang Kejaksaan Republik Indonesia*, Article 30.
74 KPK, 'Siaran Pers Capaian Kinerja KPK di Tahun 2018'. See also Kulsum, 'Tahun 2018, KPK Serap Anggaran Rp 744 Miliar'.
75 KPK Press Conference, 'Capaian dan Kinerja KPK di Tahun 2018'. Hakim, 'KPK Ajukan Rp 985 Miliar untuk Anggaran 2019'.
76 Aziza, 'Kemhan dan Polri Dapat Anggaran Paling Besar pada APBN 2018'.
77 Rizqo, 'Anggaran Kejaksaan 2018 Capai Rp 6,4 T, Jaksa Agung: Alhamdulillah'.
78 Indonesia, *Undang-Undang Komisi Pemberantasan Korupsi*, Article 40.
79 Hukum Online, 'Mau Tahu Biaya Penanganan Perkara Korupsi?' Actually, KPK has not specifically come up with an exact budget for each corruption case. The budget allocated is Rp 11 billion for ninety pre-investigations, Rp 12 billion for eighty-five investigations while the allocation for execution of court verdict is Rp 14 329 billion for eighty-five cases. In addition, there is also Rp 45 billion for imprisonment-related expenses. It may be that the cost per case is different from one case to another. But overall it is fair to say that KPK's budget for any single corruption case is considerably higher than for the police and prosecution service.
80 Komisi III DPR, 'Anggaran Kejagung 2020 Sebesar Rp. 6725 Triliun'. See also Chaterine, 'Kejagung Dapat Tambahan Anggaran Rp 350 M untuk Bangun Gedung Utama'.
81 Rose-Ackerman, *Corruption and Government*, pp. 198–229.
82 See Indonesia, *Undang-Undang tentang Perubahan Kedua atas Undang-Undang Nomor 30 Tahun 2002*, Article 40.
83 Anto, 'Abraham Samad, Segeralah Deklarasi Cawapres atau Bahkan Capres!'
84 Movanita, 'Kasus Simulator SIM, KPK periksa Empat Polisi'.
85 Juwono, *Melawan Korupsi*, pp. 302–6.
86 Sari, '8 Upaya Pelemahan KPK oleh DPR Menurut Catatan ICW'.
87 Jemadu, *Challenges in Eradicating Corruption*, pp. 1–12.

88 Butt, *Corruption and Law in Indonesia*, pp. 35–48.
89 Sindo News, 'Konsep KPK Dibentuk Ad Hoc, Tak Perlu Dipermanenkan'.
90 Indrayana, *Indonesian Constitutional Reform*, pp. 143–320.
91 Indonesia, *Undang-Undang Komisi Pemberantasan Korupsi*, KPK, was enacted on 27 December 2002.
92 Gabrillin, 'Ruki, Sejak 2005, Saya Sinyalir ada "Corruptor Fight Back".' The term 'corruptors fight-back' is a term I coined in 2006 at a year-end press conference of Transparency International Indonesia, which I then chaired. Attempts to weaken the KPK had been launched by a few parliamentarians, suspects and individuals who were directly or indirectly linked to corruption cases.
93 Rochman and Achwan, 'Corruption in Indonesia's emerging democracy', p. 164.
94 Indonesia, *Undang-Undang Dasar 1945*, Article 24C.
95 Indrayana, *Jangan Bunuh KPK*, pp. 99–174. My interviews of 16 March 2020 with Zainal Arifin Mochtar, anti-corruption activist from the University of Gajah Mada, and Feri Amsari, a constitutional law expert from the University of Andalas, are the sources of these data. In fact, twenty-six petitions for judicial review have been submitted to the Constitutional Court but only twenty-two registered because in some petitions there were more than one petitioner raising the same legal question.
96 Ibid., p. 99.
97 Interview with Zainal Arifin Mochtar, Constitutional Law Lecturer of Universitas Gadjah Mada, 16 March 2020.
98 Case No. 006/PUU-I/2003, Indonesia, *Mahkamah Konstitusi Putusan Perkara Nomor 006/PUU-1/2003*.
99 Indonesia, *Undang-Undang tentang Perubahan Kedua atas Undang-Undang Nomor 30 Tahun 2002*, Articles 1 and 7.
100 Case No 069/PUU-II/2004, Indonesia, Mahkamah Konstitusi Putusan Perkara Nomor 069/PUU-II/2004. See also Case No 019/PUU-IV/2006, Indonesia, Mahkamah Konstitusi Putusan Perkara Nomor 019/PUU-IV/2006.
101 Case No 010/PUU-IV/2006. Indonesia, Mahkamah Konstitusi Putusan Perkara Nomor 010/PUU-IV/2006.
102 Case No 012/PUU-II/2006, Indonesia, Mahkamah Konstitusi Putusan Perkara Nomor 012/PUU-II/2006. See also Case No 16/PUU-II/2006, Indonesia, Mahkamah Konstitusi Putusan Perkara Nomor 16/PUU-II/2006.
103 Indonesia, *Undang-Undang tentang Perubahan Kedua atas Undang-Undang Nomor 30 Tahun 2002*, Articles 12, 12B, 12C and 12D.
104 Case No. 19/PUU-V/2007, Indonesia, *Mahkamah Konstitusi Putusan Perkara Nomor19/PUU-V/2007*.
105 *Kompas*, 'Jalan Panjang Revisi UU KPK, Ditolak Berkali-kali hingga Disahkan'.
106 Indonesia, *Undang-Undang Komisi Pemberantasan Korupsi*, Articles 22–24. See also Stefanie, 'Pro Kontra DPR di Pasar Dewan Pengawas KPK'.
107 Interview with Zainal Arifin Mochtar, 16 March 2020. See also Putra, 'Ini Poin-Poin dalam RUU yang Dinilai Akan Memperlemah KPK'.
108 Interview with Zainal Arifin Mochtar, 16 March 2020. See also Firmanto, 'Revisi UU KPK, Sejumlah Indikasi Pelemahan KPK'.
109 Indonesia, *Undang-Undang Komisi Pemberantasan Korupsi*, Article 40.
110 Indonesia, *Undang-Undang Hukum Acara Pidana*, Article 109, para. 2. See Abduh, 'Penghentian Penyidikan Tindak Pidana dan Penyelesaian Diluar Pengadilan Dugaan Pemerasan dan Penyalahgunaan Wewenang'.
111 Gabrillin, 'Kewenangan SP3 bagi KPK Dikhawatirkan Diperjualbelikan'.
112 Indrayana, *Jangan Bunuh KPK*, pp. 198–200.
113 Interview with Zainal Arifin Mochtar, 16 March 2020. See Hamzah, 'Urgensi

Penyidik Independen KPK'. See also Hukum Online, 'Hakim'.
114 Case No. 109/PUU-XIII/2007, Indonesia, *Mahkamah Konstitusi Putusan Perkara Nomor 109/PUU-V/2007.*
115 Indonesia, *Undang-Undang tentang Perubahan Kedua atas Undang-Undang Nomor 30 Tahun 2002*, Article 43.
116 Indrayana, *Jangan Bunuh KPK*, p. 195. See also Mubarok, 'Inilah Alasan polisi Jadikan Bibit dan Chandra Tersangka'; *Tempo*, 'Ini Kejanggalan Penetapan Novel Baswedan sebagai Tersangka'; and *Detik News*, 'Jokowi Berhentikan Sementara Abraham Samad dan BW karena Jadi Tersangka'.
117 Jemadu, *Challenges in Eradicating Corruption*, pp. 2–12. See also Indrayana, *Jangan Bunuh KPK*, pp. 73–83.
118 Jemadu, *Challenges in Eradicating Corruption*, p. 2. My italics.
119 Rochman and Achwan, 'Corruption in Indonesia's emerging democracy', p. 167.
120 Indrayana, *Jangan Bunuh KPK*, pp. 74–83.
121 See Indonesia, *Undang-Undang Dasar 1945*, Art. 37.
122 Indrayana, *Jangan Bunuh KPK*, p. 161.
123 Della Porta and Vannucci, 'Typology of corrupt networks', pp. 23–44. Della Porta and Vannucci describe in detail the practice of 'party corruption' in several countries, and the practice is also found in Indonesia.
124 Stewart, 'Measuring up?', pp. 406–29.
125 Maulana and Situngkir, 'Dynamics of corruption eradication in Indonesia', p. 7. This paper is part of research cooperation between the Bandung Fe Institute, represented by Surya Research and Education (SURE) Indonesia and the Konsorsium Reformasi Hukum Nasional (KRHN).

4 State capture corruption

1 At one point, I wrote an op-ed in *Kompas* newspaper titled 'Republik Mafia' [Mafia republic] referring to the endemic, systemic and widespread corruption during the thirty-two years of Soeharto's government.
2 A study undertaken by Ash Center, Harvard Kennedy School, offered a general overview on the inequality and concentration of wealth in Indonesia prior to and right after Reformasi. See Harvard Kennedy School Indonesia Program, *The Sum is Greater Than the Parts*, pp. xxii–xlviii.
3 Morris, *Political Corruption in Mexico*, pp. 1–5.
4 See Global Corruption Perceptions Indexes published by Transparency International.
5 See *Time*, 24 May 1999.
6 See Evidence Item T-62. I represented *Time* at that trial, and Evidence T-62 was one of the documents I registered. Lubis, 'Soeharto v. *Time*', pp. 255–6.
7 See Sandbrook, 'The 10 most corrupt world leaders of recent history'.
8 Halaya, *Emergency*, p. 4. Referring to corruption in Soviet Union and quoting Steven Staats, Halaya notes that corruption in the Soviet Union is an integral part of the system: 'It appears that corruption may be as integral to Soviet life as vodka and kasha.'
9 Wedeman, *Double Paradox*, pp. 4–13. See also Nelken and Levi, 'The corruption of politics and the politics of corruption', pp. 1–17.
10 Scott, *Comparative Political Corruption*, pp. 1–19.
11 Wolfensohn, speech at annual meeting of World Bank, 1 October 1996. See also Harrison, *Between Morality and the Law*, pp. 135–50.
12 Wolfensohn, speech.
13 Ibid.

14 Nelken and Levi, 'The corruption of politics and the politics of corruption', pp. 1–17.
15 Scott, *Comparative Political Corruption*, p. 3. See also World Bank, 'G-20 high-level principles on beneficial ownership transparency'.
16 See also Nugroho, 'Dinasti Politik Ratu Atut Setelah Delapan Tahun Berkuasa'.
17 Aziz, 'Mereka Mewariskan Jabatan Politik Kepada Istrinya Sendiri'.
18 Purwanti, '3 Contoh Politik Oligarki di Indonesia'. See also Puspita, 'LIPI: Oligarki Parpol Perburuk Kualitas Demokrasi di Indonesia'.
19 Legvold, 'Corruption, the criminalized state, and post-Soviet transition', pp. 208-16.
20 Afghanistan has been mentioned as a country that engaged in heroin traffic to Baltic states and from the Baltic to the rest of Europe. Ibid., pp. 211–12.
21 Ibid., pp. 195–7.
22 Rochman and Achwan, 'Corruption in Indonesia's emerging democracy', pp. 159–77. See also Butt, *Corruption and Law in Indonesia*, pp. 12–48, and Lindsey, 'Black letter, black market and bad faith', pp. 278–92.
23 See Transparency International, 'Corruption Perceptions Index 2019'. See also Indonesia Investments, 'Korupsi di Indonesia'.
24 Lindsey, 'Black letter, black market and bad faith', pp. 282–5.
25 Hadiz, *Localizing Power in Post-Authoritarian Indonesia*, pp. 75–87.
26 Juwono, *Melawan Korupsi*, pp. 241–349.
27 Bull and Newell, 'New avenues in the study of political corruption', p. 171.
28 See Amrullah, 'Kasus Suryadharma Ali'. See also Habibie, 'Data 2004–2018'.
29 Fadhil, 'JK Sebut Pemberantasan Korupsi Belum Berhasil, KPK Bicara Komitmen'.
30 See *Harian Jogja*, 'JK Sebut Jumlah Kasus Korupsi Belum Berhasil Ditekan, Begini Tanggapan KPK'. See also Evani, 'Jusuf Kalla'.
31 Bull and Newell, 'New avenues in the study of political corruption', pp. 172–6, 180. See also Wolfensohn, speech.
32 See Suriyanto, 'Kontroversi Gayus Tambunan'. See also BBC News Indonesia, 'Kasus Setya Novanto "Pelesiran"'.
33 Hellmann et al., 'Measuring governance corruption and state capture', p. 4.
34 Ibid.
35 Ibid., p. 21.
36 Huntington, 'Modernization and corruption', pp. 253–63.
37 Caiden, 'Shortchanging the public', p. 295. Caiden says sarcastically, 'If a corrupt practice is truly functional, presumably it would be better to legalise it by incorporating market mechanism into public transactions but often to do so would undermine the whole rationale for government actions in the first place, particularly distributional objectives.'
38 See Bari and Naz, 'Government's "zero-tolerance policy" against corruption'. See also Office of Assistance to Deputy Cabinet Secretary for State Documents and Translation in Setkab, 'Zero tolerance for corruptors hiding their money abroad, President Jokowi says'.
39 Bull and Newell, 'New avenues in the study of political corruption', pp. 169–72.
40 See *Irish Times*, 'Mobutu leaves legacy of chaos and corruption'. See also Transparency International, 'Seize Mobutu's wealth or lose your own money, Western governments told'.
41 See Decision of Central Jakarta District Court No. 130/PID.SUS/TPK/2017/PN.JKT.PST, 17 April 2018. See also Nurita, 'Begini Kronologi Kasus Setya Novanto'.
42 Rothe, 'Facilitating corruption and human rights violations', pp. 457–9.
43 Law No. 23 Year 2014 concerning Regional Government, Articles 10–12. This law

stipulates that the central government has absolute authority on the matters of foreign affairs, defence, security, judicial, monetary and fiscal as well as religious affairs. Other matters are in the hands of the regional governments (i.e. regencies).
44 Lubis, *Catatan Hukum*, pp. 58–70.
45 RFE/RL, 'Global banks reported $2 trillion in suspicious transactions over two decades, new report shows'. See also Cockcroft, *Global Corruption*, pp. 127–38.
46 Harris, *Political Corruption*, pp. 1–31.
47 Cockcroft, *Global Corruption*, p. 11–26.
48 Rothe, 'Facilitating corruption and human rights violations', p. 460.
49 Legvold, 'Corruption, the criminalized state, and post-Soviet transition', p. 219.
50 Winters, 'Oligarchy and democracy in Indonesia', pp. 1–23.
51 See *Time*, Asia Edition, 24 May 1999.
52 See Bloomberg, 10 August 2019. The family allegedly owned US$32.5 billion.
53 Forbes Press Release, 'Wealth of tycoons on Forbes Indonesia Rich List reaches a record $129 billion'.
54 Kurnia, 'Daftar Terbaru 150 di Indonesia 27 Juli 2018'.
55 Winters, 'Oligarchy and democracy in Indonesia', p. 2.
56 Ibid.
57 See Law No. 2 of 2011. Indonesia, *Undang-Undang Perubahan Atas Undang-Undang Nomor 2 Tahun 2008 Tentang Partai Politik*, UU No. 2 of 2011, LN. No. 8 of 2011, TLN. No. 5189. See also Law No. 7 Year 2017. Indonesia, *Undang-Undang Pemilihan Umum*, UU No. 7 of 2017, LN. No. 182 of 2017. TLN. No. 6109.
58 Farisa, 'Tak Ada Batas Pengeluaran Dana Kampanye Pemilu'. See also *Tempo*, 'UU Pemilu, Jangan Ada Lagi Dana Siluman Partai'.
59 Johnston, *Syndromes of Corruption*, pp. 177–85.
60 See Tim Penyusun Laporan Tahunan KPK, *Annual Report 2018*, pp. 62–79.
61 In fact, all big oligarchs at the national level have a vast network of companies across the nation and some also regionally. Salim Group and Wilmar, for instance, have even invested beyond South-East Asia. Salim Group is a perfect example of marriage between power-holder and conglomerate, between Soeharto and Liem Sioe Liong. Borsuk and Ching, *Liem Sioe Liong's Salim Group*, pp. 130–318. Moran, *Crime and Corruption in New Democracies*.
62 See Winters, 'Oligarchy and democracy in Indonesia', pp. 15–19. Surya Paloh and Aburizal Bakri, who run Metro TV and TV One respectively, are good examples of oligarchs. Their television and other media platforms have been used to campaign for candidates they support.
63 Soekarno set up and chaired the predecessor of PDI-P, PNI. It was almost dissolved after 1965, when Soekarno was accused of being too close to the Indonesian Communist Party (PKI), which had been accused of initiating a coup on 30 September that year. The coup failed, PKI was banned and its members and sympathisers killed or detained, some for decades. PNI has always been perceived as closely associated with PKI. It was not banned, but soon collapsed. PDI-Perjuangan was set up by Megawati to replace PNI in order to erase the stigma of the PKI, and to revive the ideology created by Soekarno based around the notion of the little people (Marhaenism). See also Wicaksono, 'PKI Dibubarkan Tahun 1966, PDI Lahir 1973 Hasil Fusi Lima Partai, Versi PDIP Lahir Tahun 1970'.
64 Megawati is the longest serving chair of a political party in Indonesia. See Erdianto, 'Bakal Terpilih Lagi, Megawati Perpanjang Rekor Ketum Parpol Terlama'.
65 Nurrizki, 'Prabowo Subianto Pimpin Partai Gerindra'. See also Agence France-Presse, 'Who is Prabowo Subianto?', and Liljas, 'Here's why some Indonesians are spooked by this presidential contender'.

66 See Budilaksono, 'Gerindra'.
67 *Kompas*, 'Tiga Jabatan SBY di Partai Demokrat'. See also Perkasa, 'Harta 40 Orang Terkaya Makin "Gendut" di Rezim SBY dan Jokowi'.
68 Celebes, 'Konglomerasi Media Massa, Siapa Menguasai Apa?' See also Lifepal, 'Dari Jualan Ikan Asin Hingga Jadi Bos TV, Ini Kisah Inspiratif Surya Paloh'.
69 Ihsanuddin, 'Minta Dukungan, SBY Janjikan Surya Paloh Jabatan Menteri'. See also Armenia, 'Jokowi Resmikan Gedung Rp Triliun Milik Surya Paloh'.
70 *Warta Kota*, 'Update Survei: 7 Parpol Tak Lolos Ambang Batas Parlemen Pemilu 2019, Ini Daftar Partai Gagal'. See also Law No. 7 of 2017, Indonesia, *Undang-Undang Pemilihan Umum*, UU No. 7 of 2017, Article 414.
71 Erwanti, 'Hary Tanoe'.
72 Wedhaswary, 'Dinasti Politik Lokal Semakin Meluas'.
73 Masykuri, 'Potret Oligarki Politik di Madura'. See also Utomo, 'Politik Dinasti dalam Pemerintah Daerah'.
74 Bhargava and Bolongaita, *Challenging Corruption in Asia*, pp. 209–15.
75 Rafie, 'Begini Cerita Lengkap Soal Korupsi Berjamaan 41 Anggota DPRD Malang'. See also Thoha, 'Korupsi Berjamaah Berjamaan, Sebuah Istilah yang Tidak Pantas'.
76 *Banjarmasin Post*, 'Korupsi Berjamaan, Ini Nama 38 Anggota DPRD Sumut Ramai-Ramai Jadi Tersangka oleh KPK'.
77 Ibid.
78 Lapalombara, 'Structural and institutional aspects of corruption', p. 339.
79 Ibid. See also Lubis, *Political Corruption in Indonesia*, pp. 9–25.
80 Transparency International Indonesia, 'Global Corruption Barometer 2017'. See also Transparency International, 'Global Corruption Barometer 2009'.
81 Johnston, *Syndromes of Corruption*, pp. 120–36.
82 Ibid.
83 Michael Khodorkovsky owned a giant oil company, Yuko, while Berezovsky controlled television business. See Walker, 'Mikhail Khodorkovsky on life after prison and Russia after Putin'. See also Lopez, 'How dead oligarch Boris Berezovsky impoverished himself'.
84 Johnston, *Syndromes of Corruption*, pp. 120–36.
85 Ibid., pp. 136–44.
86 Ibid.
87 Infoplease, 'World's ten most corrupt leaders'. See also Denny, 'Soeharto, Marcos and Mobutu head corruption table with $50bn scams'.
88 Databoks, '1% Orang Terkaya Indonesia Menguasai 46% Kekayaan Penduduk'.
89 See the 'Bad Apples' section of chapter 2.
90 Feith, *The Decline of Constitutional Democracy in Indonesia*, pp. 218–24.
91 Borsuk and Ching, *Liem Sioe Liong's Salim Group*, pp. 164–209.
92 Arifianto, 'Corruption in Indonesia', pp. 6–7. The paper is unpublished, still a work in progress.
93 Mietzner, 'Party financing in post-Soeharto Indonesia', p. 239.
94 Ibid., pp. 238–40.
95 Arifianto, 'Corruption in Indonesia', pp. 1–15. The phenomenon of state capture corruption occurs when a country is a strong authoritarian state where no effective checks and balances function. The New Order under Soeharto is a good example of state capture corruption. In Hungary, alleged state capture corruption also takes place under strongman Viktor Orban, where executive, legislative and judicial powers are aligned in what Orban called the 'system of national cooperation'. *Economist*, 'Democracy's enemy within'.

5 Political corruption cases and criminalisation

1. Tim Advokasi Anti Kriminalisasi, *Buku Putih*, 2015, p. 1 (unpublished; copy in the author's possession).
2. See the Gecko Project, 'Ghost in the Machine'.
3. Ibid.
4. Sakwa, 'Russia', p. 123.
5. See Tim Penyusun Laporan Tahunan KPK, *Annual Report 2018*.
6. Mietzner, 'Party financing in post-Soeharto Indonesia', p. 240.
7. Ibid., p. 239.
8. See Badan Pusat Statistik Provinsi Banten, *Statistik Daerah Provinsi Banten 2018*, p. 3.
9. See *Tempo*, 'Hasil Hitung Cepat, Anak Bupati Lebak Unggul'.
10. See Decision of Central Jakarta District Court No. 44/PID.SUS/TPK/2014/PN.JKT.Pst, 1 September 2014. See also Decision of Jakarta High Court No. 72/PID/TPK/2014/PT.DKI, 18 November 2014 and Decision of Supreme Court No. 285K/PID.SUS/2015, 23 February 2015.
11. See Hutomo, 'Kasus Suap Gugatan Pilkada Lebab, Atut Didakwa Menyap Akil'.
12. See *Detik News*, 'Susi "Kurir Suap Akil Mochtar Dihukum 7 Tahun Penjara"'.
13. See Decision of Jakarta District Court No. 16/PID.SUS/TPK/2014/PN.JKT.PST, 23 June 2014. See also Decisions of Jakarta High Court No. 48/PID/TPK/2014/PT.DKI, 30 September 2014, and Decision of Supreme Court No 2429 K/PID.SUS/2014, 11 March 2015.
14. See *Detik News*, 'Total Uang Akil Mochtar yang Disita KPK Senilai Rp 7,2 M'.
15. Law No. 31 of 1999 as amended to Law No. 20 of 2001. Indonesia, *Undang-Undang Pemberantasan Tindak Pidana Korupsi*, UU No. 31 of 1999, as amended by Indonesia, *Undang-Undang Perubahan atas Undang-Undang Nomor 31 Tahun 1999 tentang Pemberantasan Tindak Pidana Korupsi*, UU No. 20 of 2001, Article 6 para. 1a of which stipulates: 'Anybody that promises something to a judge with the aim of influencing the decision of the case handed to him/her for trial shall be sentenced to a minimum of 3 (three) years imprisonment and a maximum of 15 (fifteen) years imprisonment and be fined a minimum of Rp 150 000 000 (one hundred and fifty million rupiah) and a maximum of Rp 750 000 000 (seven hundred and fifty million rupiah).' In practice, if the primary charge is proven, judges will not consider the secondary charges. Only when the primary charge is not proven will the secondary charge be considered. The prosecutors always use primary and secondary charges.
16. Law No. 31 of 1999 as amended to Law No 20. of 2001, Indonesia, *Undang-Undang Pemberantasan Tindak Pidana Korupsi*, UU No. 31 of 1999, as amended by Indonesia, *Undang-Undang Perubahan atas Undang-Undang Nomor 31 Tahun 1999 tentang Pemberantasan Tindak Pidana Korupsi*, UU No. 20 of 2001. Article 13 stipulates: 'Anybody giving presents or promises to a civil servant with a view to the power or authority vested in the post or position, or by the provision of present is considered vested in the post or position is maximally sentenced 3 (three) years and or maximally fined Rp 150.000.000 (one hundred fifty million rupiah).'
17. See Decision of Central Jakarta Pusat District Court No. 44/PID.SUS/TPK/2014/PN.JKT.PST, 28 August 2014.
18. See Decision of Jakarta High Court No. 72/PID/TPK/2014/PT.DKI, 18 November 2014.
19. See Decision of Supreme Court No. 285K/PID.SUS/2015, 23 February 2015.
20. See Pangaribuan, 'Tentang PK (Peninjauan Kembali'.
21. See Decision of the Supreme Court No. 2429 K/PID.SUS/2014, 11 March 2015.
22. See Decision of the Supreme Court No. 336 K/PID.SUS/2015, 23 February 2015.

23 See Decision of the Central Jakarta District Court No. 111/PID.SUS/TPK/2015/PB.JKT.PST, 16 September 2015.
24 See ibid.
25 See Decision of the Jakarta High Court No. 47/PID.SUS/TPK/2014/PT.DKI, 18 September 2014.
26 See Putsanra, 'Ratu Atut Divonis 5,5 Tahun Bui dalam kasus Korupsi Alkes'. Ratu Atut Chosiyah was imprisoned for her corruption in procurement of medical equipment in Banten Province.
27 See *Tirto*, 'Profile Muhammad Nazaruddin'.
28 Ibid.
29 See Wicaksono, 'Muhammad Nazaruddin'.
30 Mietzner, 'Party financing in post-Soeharto Indonesia'.
31 *Korupsi berjemaah* literally means collective corruption. But this is not a correct translation. *Berjemaah* comes from an Arabic word that often refers to collective prayer, mostly in mosques. Fionna, Negara and Foong, 'Indonesia in 2013', pp. 119–38.
32 *Tempo*, 'Kasus Wisma Atlet, Saksi'.
33 See Law No. 31 of 1999 as amended to Law No. 20 of 2001, Indonesia, *Undang-Undang Pemberantasan Tindak Pidana Korupsi*, UU No. 31 of 1999, as amended by Indonesia, *Undang-Undang Perubahan atas Undang-Undang Nomor 31 Tahun 1999 tentang Pemberantasan Tindak Pidana Korupsi*, UU No. 20 of 2001, Article 2 para. 1: 'Any person who illegally commits an act to make oneself rich or another person rich or a corporation that can create loss to the state finance or state economy, is sentenced to life imprisonment or minimum imprisonment of 4 (four) years and maximally 20 (twenty) years, and a fine of at least Rp 200 000 000 (two hundred million rupiah) and not more than Rp 1 000 000 000 (one billion rupiah).'
34 See Berita Satu, 'Perusahaan Nazaruddin untuk Bermain di Tender Pemerintah'.
35 See Rastika, 'Wafid Muharam tetap Divonis 3 Tahun Penjara'.
36 See Setyawan, 'Nazaruddin "Bekingi" PT DGI Garap Wisma Atlet Palembang'.
37 See *Tempo*, 'Proyek Wisma Atlet Dinilai Sudah Direkayasa Sejak Awal'.
38 Babrillin, 'Petinggi PT Wika Mengaku Diarahkan PT DGI dalam Lelang Proyek Wisma Atlet'.
39 See Berita Satu, 'Kabur ke Luar Negeri, Beratkan Nazaruddin'.
40 See BBC News Indonesia, 'Nazaruddin Resmi Tersangka Kasus Suap'.
41 See *Tempo*, 'Nazaruddin Ditangkap di Kolombia'.
42 Article 12 (b) Law No. 31 of 1999 as amended by Law No. 20 of 2001, Indonesia, *Undang-Undang Pemberantasan Tindak Pidana Korupsi No. 31 Tahun 1999*, as amended by Indonesia, UU No. 20 Tahun 2001. Article 12b stipulates, '[A]ny gratification for a civil servant or state apparatus shall be considered as a bribe when it has something to do with his/her position and is against his/her obligation or task.' The amount of gratification should be above Rp 10 000 000 (ten million rupiah). Then para. 2 of Article 12 (b) stipulates, '[A] civil servant or state apparatus who is found guilty of the criminal offence as referred in paragraph 1 shall be sentenced to life imprisonment or a minimum of 4 (four) years' imprisonment and a maximum of 20 (twenty) years' imprisonment and be fined a minimum of Rp 200 000 000 (two hundred million rupiah) and maximum of Rp 1 000 000 000 (one billion rupiah).'
43 Article 5 para. 2 in conjunction with Article 5 para. 1 (a) Law No. 31 of 1999 as amended by Law No. 20 of 2001 stipulates, 'The civil servant or state apparatus who receives a payment or promise as referred to in paragraph (1) letter a or b shall be sentenced to the same jail term as that referred to in paragraph (1).' Article 5 para. 1 (a) stipulates, 'Any person(s) who gives or promises something to a civil servant or state apparatus with the aim of persuading him/her to perform an action or not to

perform an action because of his/her position in violation of his/her obligation shall be sentenced to a minimum of 1 (one) year imprisonment and a maximum of 5 (five) years' imprisonment and/or be fined a minimum of Rp 50 000 000.00 (fifty million rupiah) and a maximum of Rp 250 000 000.00 (two hundred million rupiahs).'

44 Law No. 31 of 1999 as amended by law No. 20 of 200, Indonesia, *Undang-Undang Pemberantasan Tindak Pidana Korupsi*, UU No. 31 Tahun 1999, as amended by Indonesia, *Undang-Undang Perubahan atas Undang-Undang Nomor 31 Tahun 1999 tentang Pemberantasan Tindak Pidana Korupsi*, UU No. 20 Tahun 2001, Article 11 of which stipulates, 'A civil servant or state apparatus who receives a payment or a promise believed to have been given because of the power or authority to his/her position or prize or promise which according to the contributor still has something to do with his/her position, shall be sentenced to a minimum 1 (one) year imprisonment and a maximum of 5 (five) years' imprisonment and be fined a minimum of Rp 50 000 000.00 (fifty million rupiahs) and a maximum of Rp 250 000 000 (two hundred million rupiahs).'

45 See *Tribun News*, 'Kisah Pelarian Nazaruddin Sebelum Tertangkap di Kolombia'.
46 See Decision of the Central Jakarta District Court No. 69/PID.B/TPK/2011/PN.JKT.PST, 20 April 2012.
47 See Decision of the Central Jakarta District Court No. 31/PID/TPK/2012/PT.DKI, 8 August 2012.
48 See Decision of Supreme Court No. 2233 K/PID.SUS/2012, 22 January 2013.
49 See Litigasi, 'Turut Serta Melakukan Kejahatan Dapat Dihukum'. In legal terminology, those assisting the offender in an offence are called *mede-dader* (*pelaku pembantu*; co-perpetrator and/or accomplice).
50 See Decision of Supreme Court No. 1616 K/PID.SUS, 20 November 2013. It is important to note that some defendants had to pay compensation, which has to do with the real state losses that must be replaced. This is an additional sentence imposed by the judges on the basis of a specific consideration. See also Rohrohmana, 'Pidana Pembayaran Uang Pengganti Sebagai Pidana Tambahan Dalam Tindak Pidana Korupsi', p. 1.
51 See Decision of the Central Jakarta District Court No. 54/Pid.B/TPK/2012/PN.JKT.PST, 7 January 2013.
52 See Decision of the Jakarta High Court No. 11/PID/TPK/2013/PT.DKI, 22 May 2013.
53 See Decision of the Supreme Court No. 1393 K/PID.SUS/2012, 29 August 2012.
54 See Decision of the Central Jakarta District Court No. 62/PID.SUS/TPK/2013/PN.JKT.PST, 11 March 2014. Deddy Kusnidar did not appeal the decision, so the decision became final and binding.
55 See Decision of the Central Jakarta District Court No. 33/PID.B/TPK/2011/PN.JKT.PST, 21 September 2011. In this case, Mindo Rosalina Manullang decided not to appeal. Hence the decision became final and binding.
56 See Decision of the Central Jakarta District Court No. 31/PID.B/TPK/2011/PN.JKT.PST, 21 September 2011. Muhammad El Idris accepted the court decision. He did not appeal.
57 See Decision of the Central Jakarta District Court No. 75/PID.SUS/TPK/2015/PN.JKT.PST, 27 November 2015. The decision was appealed to the Jakarta High Court. See Decision of the Jakarta High Court No. 03/PID/TPK/2016/PT.DKI, 26 January 2016. There was no appeal to the Supreme Court, making the Jakarta High Court Decision final and binding.
58 See Decision of the Central Jakarta District Court No. 117/PID.SUS/TPK/2014/

PN.JKT.PST, 1 April 2014. The decision was not appealed and therefore became final and binding. The judges did not impose a fine in this case.
59 See Decision of the Central Jakarta District Court No. 30/PID.SUS/TPK/2014/PT.DKI, 8 July 2014. Teuku Bagus Mokhamad Noor appealed the decision to the Jakarta High Court. See Decision of the Jakarta High Court No. 58/PID/TPK/2014/PT.DKI, 28 October 2014. No cassation was filed; therefore the Jakarta High Court Decision became final and binding.
60 Mietzner, 'Party financing in post-Soeharto Indonesia', p. 240. In almost every organisation—social, business and professional—membership dues have never been that effective in Indonesia. As a president of the Indonesian Bar Association (Ikatan Advokat Indonesia—Ikadin), I experienced this problem: very few members paid their dues. Together with other board members, I ended up covering the costs and expenses of the organisation.
61 Ibid., p. 239.
62 See Detik, 'Nazaruddin Sebut Lagi Anas Otak Kasus Korupsi Wisma Atlet'. See also R Antares P, 'Elit Demokrat yang Terjerat kasus Korupsi Besar'.
63 See Decision of Supreme Court No. 1261 K/PID.SUS/2015, 8 June 2015. See also Decision of Central Jakarta District Court No. 55/PID.SUS/TPK/2014/PN.JKT. PST, 24 September 2014, in conjunction with Decision of Jakarta High Court No. 74/PID/TPK/2014/PT.DKI, 4 February 2015.
64 See Saputra, 'PK Suryadharma Ali Ditolak, Tetap Dibui 10 Tahun karena Korupsi Haji'.
65 See Decision of Central Jakarta District Court No. 130/PID.SUS/TPK/2017/PN.JKT.PST, 17 April 2018.
66 See Ridwan, 'Diganjar 18 Tahun Penjara, Mantan Presiden PKS Akhirnya Ajukan PK'.
67 See Liputan6, 'Profil Andi Malarangeng'.
68 See *Tempo*, 'Peran Andi dan Anas di Wisma Atlet Mulai Diusut'.
69 See Decision of the Central Jakarta District Court No. 48/Pid.B/TPK/2011/PN.JKT.PST, 19 December 2011.
70 See Decision of the Supreme Court No. 2427 K/PID.SUS/2014, 8 April 2015.
71 See Decision of the Central Jakarta District Court No. 23/PID.SUS/TPK/2014/PN.JKT.PST, 18 July 2014.
72 See Decision of the Jakarta High Court No. 57/PID/TPK/2014/PT.DKI, 15 October 2014.
73 See *Tempo*, 'Daftar Kader Partai Demokrat yang Terlibat Korupsi'.
74 See Permana, 'Kisah Hidup Setya Novanto, dari Tukang Beras, Model Hingga Jadi Miliuner'.
75 See Nugroho, 'Berbagai Skandal yang Membelit Setya Novanto'. See also Winarto, 'Skandal Bank Bali'.
76 See Permana, 'Kisah Hidup Setya Novanto, dari Tukang Beras, Model Hingga Jadi Miliuner'.
77 See Viva, 'Setya Novanto'.
78 See Sarwanto, 'Setya Novanto Terpilih Jadi Ketua Umum Partai Golkar'.
79 See Nugroho, 'Ternyata 6 Kasus Super Besar ini Juga Melibatkan Setya Novanto di Dalamnya'. DW, 'Jejak Korupsi Setya Novanto'.
80 See Decision of Central Jakarta District Court No 130/PID.SUS/TPK/2017/PN.JKT.PST, 17 April 2018.
81 See CTR, 'Setnov Sebut Kemendagri Ubah Sumber Biaya Proyek e-KTP'. See also Atriana, 'Ini Alur Pembahasan Anggaran Proyek e-KTP di DPR'.
82 See Lotulu, 'Siapa Penerima "Fee" Terbesar dari Kasus Korupsi e-KTP'.

83 Commission II (Komisi II) is a body in the Indonesian legislature, DPR. It is one of eleven commissions of the DPR with a scope of work centred around the country's administration and elections. It is also responsible for the state secretariat. Members of the Commission II come from all factions within DPR.
84 See Decision of the Central Jakarta District Court No. 130/PID.SUS/TPK/2017/PN.JKT.PST, 17 April 2018.
85 Ibid.
86 In line with Huntington's argument on corruption in modern states, corruption in obtaining silence, for example, may still be accepted with a reasonable objective, such as to speed up a process. Huntington, 'Modernization and corruption', pp. 253–63.
87 See Decision of the Central Jakarta District Court No. 130/PID.SUS/TPK/2017/PN.JKT.PST, 17 April 2018.
88 See Kompas, 'Artidjo Alkostar dan Vonis Berat Kasasi'.
89 Indonesia's Criminal Code divides criminal actors into two categories, namely, offender (or *dader*) and offender aide (or *mede-dader*). *Dader* and *mede-dader* are the terms used in the Netherlands from which the Criminal Code of Indonesia originated. See Indonesia's Criminal Code, Article 56.
90 See Decision of the Central Jakarta District Court No. 65/PID.SUS/TPK/2018/PN.JKT.PST, 5 December 2018.
91 Ibid.
92 See Mohammad, 'MA Perberat Hukuman Irman dan Sugiharto'. All judgments against Agung, Sugiharto, Pambudi, Nari and Naragong were based on Article 2 para. 1 of the Law No. 31 of 1999 as amended to Law No. 20 of 2001.
93 See Decision of the Supreme Court No. 430K/PID.SUS/2018, 18 April 2018.
94 See Decision of the Supreme Court No. 1998K/PID.SUS/2020, 13 July 2020. See also Sinar Harapan, 'MA Perberat Hukuman Markus Nari Jadi 8 Tahun Penjara'.
95 Decision of the Jakarta District Court is not available, but the news can be found in the media. See *Jawa Pos*, 'KPK Ajukan Banding Putusan Andi Narogong'.
96 See Decision of the Supreme Court No. 430K/Pidsus/2018, 18 April 2018.
97 See Tempo, 'Putusan Kasasi, Hukum Andi Narogong Bertambah Jadi 13 Tahun'.
98 See *Time*, Asia Edition, 24 May 1999.
99 See Decision of the Central Jakarta District Court No. 338/PDT.G/1999/PN.JKT.PST, 6 June 2000.
100 See chapter 4, p.112. See also Johnston, *Syndromes of Corruption*, pp. 177–82.
101 Lubis, 'Soeharto vs *Time*', pp. 226–69. See Fisman and Miguel, *Economic Gangsters*, pp. 22–52. See Tempo, 'Soeharto Koruptor Terkaya di Dunia'.
102 Juwono, *Melawan Korupsi*, pp. 194–7.
103 Ibid.
104 Ibid.
105 See Hendardi, 'Glorifikasi Soeharto dan Jejak Korupsi Orba'.
106 Alkostar, *Korupsi Politik Di Negara Modern*, pp. 104–5.
107 Indonesia, *Undang-Undang Hukum Acara Pidana*, Article 196, para. 1. See also Bawono and Kusumasari, 'Pengertian peradilan in absentia'.
108 Alkostar, *Korupsi Politik Di Negara Modern*, pp. 106–7.
109 Juwono, *Melawan Korupsi*, pp. 194–7, 208.
110 Ibid. See also Kumparan, 'Rentetan Kasus Hukum Tommy Soeharto'.
111 Juwono, *Melawan Korupsi*, pp. 194–7, 208.
112 See Ramdhani, 'Soeharto Gagal Jadi Pahlawan Nasional?'
113 See Topic in *Tempo*, 'Rekening Gendut Polisi' (via www.tempo.co/tag/rekening-gendut-polisi). See also Firdaus, 'Beredar Nama-Nama Jenderal Polisi yang Tersangkut Rekening Gendut'.

114 Draft of *Buku Putih* [White Paper], pp. 1–3.
115 Ibid., pp. 7–15. See also Suparman, 'KPK Lawan Kriminalisasi terhadap Bambang Widjojanto'.
116 I was with Bambang Widjoyanto as a member of a civil society group, the Coalition to Save the KPK.
117 See Artika, 'Jokowi pertimbangkan SP3 untuk Bambang Widjojanto'.
118 See *Tempo*, 'Alasan Jaksa Agung Seponering Kasus Samad dan Bambang KPK'.
119 Draft of *Buku Putih* [White Paper], pp. 16–22. See also Rahmi, 'Abraham Samad Tersangka, Pengacara: Ini Bagian dari Kriminalisasi'.
120 Lumanauw, 'KPK tahan Emir Moeis'. Emir Moeis is a senior politician from PDI-P who has served as a member of DPRE representing PDI-P.
121 Ibid. See also Rahadian, 'Kronologi Pertemuan PDIP-Abraham Samad Versi Hasto'.
122 Lumanauw, 'KPK tahan Emir Moeis', p. 17.
123 See Asril, 'Jokowi Berhentikan sementara Abraham Samad dan Bambang Widjojanto'.
124 See Waluyo, 'Jaksa Agung Deponering Kasus Abraham Samad dan Bambang Widjojanto'.
125 See Medistiara, 'Punya 2 Alat Bukti, KPK pastikan Penetapan Tersangka Novanto Sah'. See also Indonesia, *Undang-Undang Hukum Acara Pidana*, Article 183 in conjunction with Article 184.
126 See Berita Satu, 'Ada Big Fish di Balik Kasus Hukum'.
127 Someone whose name has been mentioned as involved in a corruption case may file a lawsuit claiming that he or she has been defamed and slandered. This legal threat has been frequently used. See Triyogo, 'TII: Ada 100 Kasus Ancaman Penyerangan Pelapor Korupsi Sejak 2004'.

6 Conclusion

1 Klitgaard, *Controlling Corruption*, pp. 1–12.
2 *Upeti* means tribute. In contemporary literature, *upeti* can be categorised as bribery, kickback or facilitation payment.
3 In almost every kingdom in Indonesia, one can find a history of people paying *upeti* to the monarch and his or her inner circle. See Deslatama, 'Suku Baduy Serahkan Upeti ke Gubernur Banten'.
4 Ahmed, *The Dilemma of Corruption in Southeast Asia*, p. 10. Lindsey, 'History always repeats?', p. 19.
5 Bhargava and Bolongaita, *Challenging Corruption in Asia*, pp. 209–11.
6 When I chaired Transparency International Indonesia and reported to President Yudhoyono regarding Indonesian's score in the Corruption Perceptions Index, the President told me that he wanted a score of 50 by the time he finished his term as President. Indonesia failed to achieve this.
7 See *Kompas*, 'Indeks Persepsi Korupsi Indonesia pada 2020 Turun Jadi 37, Peringkat 102 di Dunia'. See also Transparency International, 'Corruption Perceptions Index, 2020: New Zealand'.
8 King, 'Corruption in Indonesia', p. 618.
9 Moran, *Crime and Corruption in New Democracies*, p. 27.
10 Bhargava and Bolongaita, *Challenging Corruption in Asia*, pp. 217–19.
11 See Decision of the Central Jakarta District Court No. 130/PID.SUS/TPK/2017/PN.JKT.PST, 17 April 2019. See also Ulya, 'Simak, Ini Kronologi Lengkap Kasus Jiwasraya Versi BPK'.
12 Vogl, *Waging War on Corruption*, p. 88.

13 See *Nasional Kontan*, 'Daftar Terpidana Korupsi Hambalang Kian Panjang'. See also Putri, 'Saat Hakim Penasaran Berapa Uang Dikorupsi Novanto di Kasus e-KTP'.
14 Robertson-Snape, 'Corruption, collusion and nepotism in Indonesia', p. 594. See also Klitgaard, *Controlling Corruption*, pp. 13–51.
15 Legvold, 'Corruption, the criminalized state, and post-Soviet transition', pp. 95–198.
16 Huntington, 'Modernization and corruption', p. 253.
17 Ibid., p. 254.
18 Ibid., pp. 254–5.
19 Philp, 'Conceptualizing political corruption', pp. 41–57. Philp describes the dilemma of defining 'political corruption' as a legal term, given its political characteristics, but in the end he links political corruption to political failure.
20 See Economist Intelligence Unit, 'Democracy Index 2019'.
21 See Decision of the Central Jakarta District Court No. 130/PID.SUS/TPK/2017/PN.JKT.PST, 17 April 2019.
22 Legvold, 'Corruption, the criminalized state, and post-Soviet transition', pp. 196–7.
23 UNDP, *Tackling Corruption, Transforming Lives*, pp. 21–2.
24 See Sihaloho, 'Ini Alasan PDIP Tidak Mencopot Panda Nababan'.
25 King describes patrimonialism by reference to the fact that Soeharto was a 'strong man', controlling all the power of the republic. King, 'Corruption in Indonesia', pp. 603–5.
26 See Komisi Pemberantasan Korupsi [Anti-Corruption Clearing House], web.kpk.go.id/id/publikasi-data/statistik/penindakan-2. The Annual Report 2019 has not been published.
27 See *Undang-Undang Dasar 1945*, Article 18. See also Lavinda, 'Ini 4 Faktor Pemicu Amandemen UUD1945 versi JK'.
28 Indrayana, *Indonesian Constitutional Reform*, pp. 215–17.
29 Legvold, 'Corruption, the criminalized state, and post-Soviet transition', pp. 195–8.
30 See Law No. 19 of 2019 regarding Second Amendment to the Law No. 30 of 2002 regarding Corruption Eradication Commission (KPK). Indonesia, *Undang-Undang Perubahan Kedua Atas Undang-Undang Nomor 30 Tahun 2002 tentang Komisi Pemberantasan Korupsi*.
31 Scandinavian countries have always enjoyed very good scores on the Corruption Perceptions Index, always in the top 10 countries considered least corrupt. One reason for this is the character of these states: they are welfare states, where social economic equality is real. The gap between the haves and the have-nots is not steep as in other developed countries such as the United States or developing countries such as Indonesia and the Philippines.
32 Juwono, *Melawan Korupsi*, pp. 95–114, 121–46, 194–215.
33 See Nahdlatul Ulama, 'Gus Dur Pernah Usulkan Pembuktian Terbalik untuk Koruptor'.
34 Law No. 48 of 2009 on Judicial Power, Article 8, states that anyone must be presumed innocent until the court decides otherwise. Indonesia, *Undang-Undang Kekuasaan Kehakiman*, UU No. 48 Year 2009, LN. No. 157, TLN. No. 5076, Article 8. See Butt, *Corruption and Law in Indonesia*, pp. 16–17. See also Tobing, 'Tentang Sistem Pembalikan Beban Pembuktian'.
35 Law No. 31 of 1999 as amended by Law No. 20 of 2001, Article 37, para. 1: 'Defendant has a right to prove that he or she did not commit a criminal act of corruption.' Indonesia, *Undang-Undang Pemberantasan Tindak Pidana Korupsi*. See also Law No. 32 Year 2009 on Preservation and Management of Environment.
36 Yusuf, *Merampas Aset Koruptor*, p. xvi. See also Greenberg et al., *Stolen Asset Recovery*.
37 See Qur'ani, 'Aset Dirampas Tanpa Putusan Pemidanaan, Bisakah?'.

38 See Putrie, 'Asset tracing and and asset recovery'.
39 See Kejaksaan Republik Indonesia, 'Intelijen Kejagung Temukan Aset Terpidana Korupsi Rp 1,6 Triliun'.
40 See *Kompas*, 'Pemiskinan Koruptor Dinilai Lebih Efektif ketimbang Membebankan Biaya Sosial'.
41 See Ucu, 'Usulan Miskinkan Koruptor Ditolak'.

References

Books and journal articles

Ahmed, Fethi Ben Jomma. *The Dilemma of Corruption in Southeast Asia.* Kuala Lumpur: University of Malaya Press, 2005

Aidit, Dipa N. 'Mismanagement, corruption, and bureaucratic capitalist', in *Indonesian Political Thinking, 1945–1965,* ed. Herbert Feith and Lance Castles. London: Cornell University Press, 1970

Alatas, Syed Hussein. *The Problem of Corruption.* Singapore: Times Book International, 1986

Alisyahbana, Takdir S. 'The grievances of the region', in *Indonesian Political Thinking; 1945–1965,* ed. Herbert Feith and Lance Castles. London: Cornell University Press, 1970

Alkostar, Artidjo. *Korupsi Politik Di Negara Modern.* Yogyakarta: FHUII Press, 2008

Anderson, Benedict R., and Ruth T. McVey. *A Preliminary Analysis of the October 1, 1965 Coup in Indonesia.* Singapore: Equinox Publishing, 2009

Badan Pusat Statistik Provinsi Banten. *Statistik Daerah Provinsi Banten 2018.* Banten: BPS Banten, 2018. banten.bps.go.id/publication/2018/09/26/06bbec83a41878d062db3e93/statistik-daerah-provinsi-banten-2018.html

Badoh, Ibrahim Fahmi, and Abdullah Dahlan. *Korupsi Pemilu di Indonesia.* Jakarta: Indonesian Corruption Watch, Tifa, 2010

Badoh, Ibrahim Fahmi, and Lucky Diani. *Korupsi Pemilu.* Jakarta: Indonesia Corruption Watch, 2006

Bhargava, Vinay, and Emil Bolongaita. *Challenging Corruption in Asia: Case Studies and a Framework for Action.* Washington, DC: World Bank, 2004

Borsuk, Richard, and Nancy Ching. *Liem Sioe Liong's Salim Group: The Business Pillar of Suharto's Indonesia.* Singapore: Institute of Southeast Asian Studies, 2014

Brata, Roby Arya. *Why Did Anticorruption Policy Fail? A Study of Anticorruption Policy Implementation Failure in Indonesia.* Charlotte, NC: Information Age Publishing, 2014

Bull, Martin J., and James Newell. 'New avenues in the study of political corruption', *Crime, Law and Social Change*, vol. 27, 1997, pp. 169–73
Butt, Simon. *The Constitutional Court and Democracy in Indonesia*. Leiden: Brill Nijhoff, 2015
—— *Corruption and Law in Indonesia*. London: Routledge, 2012
Butt, Simon, and Tim Lindsey. *The Constitution of Indonesia: A Contextual Analysis*, Portland, OR: Hart Publishing, 2012
Caiden, Naomi. 'Shortchanging the public', *Public Administration Review*, vol. 39, no. 3, 1979, pp. 294–8
Chipkin, Ivor. 'Whither the State? Corruption, institutions and state building in South Africa', *Politikon: South Africa Journal of Political Studies*, vol. 40, 2013, pp. 211–31
Cockcroft, Laurence. *Global Corruption*, Philadelphia: University of Pennsylvania Press, 2012
Cox, Michaelene D. 'A primer in political pathologies: Corruption and its correlates', in *State of Corruption, State of Chaos: The Terror of Political Malfeasance*, ed. Michaelene Cox, New York: Lexington Books, 2008
Davidson, Jamie. 'Politics-as-usual on trial: Regional anti-corruption campaign in Indonesia', *Pacific Review*, vol. 20, no. 1, 2007, pp. 75–99
De Leon, Peter. *Thinking About Political Corruption*, New York: M.E. Sharpe, 1993
Della Porta, Donatella, and Alberto Vannucci. 'Typology of corrupt networks', in *Comparing Political Corruption and Clientelism*, ed. Junichi Kawata. Burlington, VT: Ashgate Publishing, 2006
Dhakidae, Daniel. 'Korupsi dalam Relasi Modal Negara', *Prisma*, vol. 37, 2018, pp. 1–27
Feith, Herbert. *The Decline of Constitutional Democracy in Indonesia*. London: Cornell University Press, 1962
Feith, Herbert, and Lance Castles (eds). *Indonesian Political Thinking, 1945–1965*. London: Cornell University Press, 1970
Fionna, Ulla, Siwage Dharma Negara and Hui Yew Foong. 'Indonesia in 2013, anticipating 2014', *Southeast Asian Affairs*, 2014, pp. 119–38
Fisman, Raymond, and Edward Miguel. *Economic Gangsters: Corruption, Violence, and the Poverty of Nations*. Princeton, NJ: Princeton University Press, 2008
Friedrichs, David O., and Jessica Friedrichs. 'The World Bank and crimes of globalization: A case study', *Social Justice*, vol. 29, nos 1–2, 2002, pp. 13–36
Funderburk, Charles. 'Political corruption: Causes and consequences', in *Political Corruption in Comparative Perspective: Sources, Status and Prospects*, ed. Charles Funderburk. Farnham, Surrey: Ashgate, 2012
Goodpaster, Gary. 'Reflections on corruption in Indonesia', in *Corruption in Asia: Rethinking the Governance Paradigm*, ed. Tim Lindsey and Howard Dick. Sydney: Federation Press, 2002
Greenberg, Theodore S., Linda Samuel, Wingate Grant and Larissa Gray. *Stolen*

Asset Recovery: A Good Practices Guide for Non-Conviction Based Asset Forfeiture. Washington, DC: World Bank, 2009. star.worldbank.org/sites/star/files/Non%20Conviction%20Based%20Asset%20Forfeiture.pdf

Greenhill, Kelly M. 'Kleptocratic interdependence: Trafficking, corruption, and the marriage of politics and illicit profits', in *Corruption, Global Security, and World Order*, ed. Robert I. Rotberg. Washington, DC: Brookings Institution Press, 2009, pp. 196–223

Hadiz, Vedi. *Localizing Power in Post-Authoritarian Indonesia*. Singapore: ISEAS Publishing, 2011

Hainsworth, Geoffrey. 'Rule of law, anti-corruption, anti-terrorism and militant Islam: Coping with threats to democratic pluralism and national unity in Indonesia', *Asia Pacific Viewpoint*, vol. 48, no. 1, 2007, pp. 129–44

Halaya, M. *Emergency: A War on Corruption*. New Delhi: S. Chand & Co., 1975

Hansen, Hans Krause, and Agata Stachowicz Stanusch. 'Varieties of corruption control: Introduction to special issue', *Crime Law Social Change*, vol. 60, 2013, pp. 115–26

Harris, Robert. *Political Corruption: In and Beyond the Nation State*. New York: Routledge, 2003

Harrison, Elizabeth. *Between Morality and the Law: Corruption, Anthropology and Comparative Society*. Burlington, VT: Routledge, 2004

Harvard Kennedy School Indonesia Program. *The Sum is Greater Than the Parts*. Jakarta: Gramedia Pustaka Utama, 2013

Heidenheimer, Arnold J., 'Perspectives on the perception of corruption', in *Political Corruption: A Handbook*, ed. Arnold J. Heidenheimer, Michael Johnston and Victor T. LeVine, 3rd edn. Brunswick, NJ: Transaction Books, 1989

Hellman, Joel S., Gerant Jones, Daniel Kaufmann and Mark Schankerman. *Measuring Governance Corruption and State Capture*. World Bank and European Bank for Reconstruction and Development Policy Research Working Paper, 2000

Hosen, Nadirsyah. 'The Habibie government and anti-corruption reform in Indonesia', *Asia Pacific Law Review*, vol. 12, no. 1, 2004, pp. 53–68

Huntington, Samuel. 'Modernization and corruption', in *Political Corruption: Concepts and Contexts*, ed. Arnold Heidenheimer and Michael Johnston. New Brunswick, NJ: Transaction Publishers, 2002

Indrayana, Denny. *Indonesian Constitutional Reform, 1992–2002: An Evaluation of Constitution-Making in Transition*. Jakarta: Kompas Book Publishing, 2002

—— *Jangan Bunuh KPK*. Malang: Intrans Publishing, 2016

International Council on Human Rights Policy. 'Corruption and human rights: Making the connection', Versoix, Switzerland: International Council on Human Rights Policy, 2009

Jackson, Karl D. 'The political implications of structure and culture in Indonesia', in *Political Power and Communications in Indonesia*, ed. Karl D. Jackson and Lucian W Pye. Berkeley, CA: University of California Press, 1978

Jemadu, Aleksius. *Challenges in Eradicating Corruption in the Indonesian Presidential System*, CIGI Paper no. 119. Waterloo, ON: Centre for International Governance Innovation, 2017

Jimenez, Fernando, and Miguel Cainzos. 'Political corruption in Spain', in *Corruption in Contemporary Politics*, ed. Martin J. Bull and James L. Newell. New York: Palgrave Macmillan, 2003

Johnston, Michael. *Syndromes of Corruption: Wealth, Power and Democracy*. Cambridge: Cambridge University Press, 2005

Juwono, Vishnu. *Melawan Korupsi: Sejarah Pemberantasan Korupsi di Indonesia, 1945–2014*. Jakarta: Gramedia, 2018

Kang, David C. *Crony Capitalism: Corruption and Development in South Korea and the Philippines*. Cambridge: Cambridge University Press, 2004

Kim, So Young. 'Do Asian values exist? Empirical tests of the four dimensions of Asian values', *Journal of East Asian Studies*, vol. 10, 2010, pp. 315–44

King, Dwight Y. 'Corruption in Indonesia: A curable cancer', *Journal of International Affairs*, vol. 53, no. 2, 2000, pp. 603–24

Klitgaard, Robert. *Controlling Corruption*. Berkeley, CA: University of California Press, 1988

Lapalombara, Joseph. 'Structural and institutional aspects of corruption', *Social Research*, vol. 61, no. 2, 1994, pp. 325–50

Legvold, Robert. 'Corruption, the criminalized state, and post-Soviet transition', in Robert I. Rotberg, *Corruption, Global Security, and World Order*. Washington, DC: Brookings Institution Press, 2009

Liddle, William R. *Leadership and Culture in Indonesian Politics*. Sydney: Allen & Unwin, 1996

Lindsey, Timothy. 'Black letter, black market and bad faith: Corruption and the failure of law reform', in *Indonesia in Transition: Social Aspects of Reformasi and Crisis*, ed. Chris Manning and Peter van Diermen. London: Zed Books, 2000

—— 'From rule of law to law of the rulers—to reformation', in *Indonesia Law and Society*, ed. Timothy Lindsey. Sydney: Federation Press, 1999

—— 'History always repeats? Corruption, culture and Asian values', in *Corruption in Asia: Rethinking the Governance Paradigm*, ed. Tim Lindsey and Howard Dick. Sydney: Federation Press, 2002

—— 'An overview of Indonesian law', in *Indonesia: Law and Society*, ed. Timothy Lindsey. 2nd edn, Annandale, NSW: Federation Press, 2008

Lindsey, Tim, and Mas Achmad Santosa. 'The trajectory of law reform in Indonesia: A short overview of legal system and change in Indonesia', in *Indonesia: Law and Society*, ed. Timothy Lindsey. 2nd edn, Annandale, NSW: Federation Press, 2008

Lubis, Todung Mulya. *In Search of Human Rights: Legal–Political Dilemmas of Indonesia's New Order, 1966–1990*, 2nd edn. Jakarta: Gramedia Pustaka Utama, 1993

—— 'Soeharto vs Time: Pencarian dan Penemuan Kebenaran', *Kompas*, 2001, pp. 349–444

—— *Catatan Hukum: Mengapa Saya Mencintai Negeri Ini*. Jakarta: Penerbit Buku Kompas, 2007

—— *Recrowning Negara Hukum: A New Challenge, A New Era. Policy Paper*, Melbourne: Centre for Indonesian Law, Islam and Society, Law School, University of Melbourne, 2014

—— 'Republik Mafia', *Kompass*, sains.kompas.com/read/2010/05/12/08550464/NaN?page=all

—— *Political Corruption in Indonesia*. Jakarta: CSIS, 2017

MacIntyre, Andrew. 'Investment, property rights, and corruption in Indonesia', in *Corruption: The Boom and the Bust of East Asia*, ed. J. Edgardo Campos. Manila: Ateneo De Manila University Press, 2001

Manion, Melanie. *Corruption by Design: Building Clean Government in Mainland China and Hong Kong*. Cambridge, MA: Harvard University Press, 2004

Marzuki, M. Laica. 'Pemakzulan Presiden/Wakil Presiden Menurut Undang-Undang Dasar 1945', *Jurnal Konstitusi*, vol. 7, no. 1, 2010, pp. 15–28. media.neliti.com/media/publications/112145-ID-pemakzulan-presidenwakil-presiden-menuru.pdf

Maulana, Ardian, and Hokky Situngkir. 'Dynamics of corruption eradication in Indonesia', SSRN, 17 September 2013, p. 7

Mauro, Paolo. 'World Bank researchers and the study of corruption', in *Brown Journal of World Affairs*, vol. 13, issue 2, 2007

Mietzner, Marcus. 'Party financing in post-Soeharto Indonesia: Between state subsidies and political corruption', in *Contemporary Southeast Asia: A Journal of International and Strategic Affairs*, vol. 29, issue 2, 2007, pp. 238–63

Moran, Jon. *Crime and Corruption in New Democracies: The Politics of (In)Security*. New York: Palgrave Macmillan, 2011

Morris, Stephen D. *Political Corruption in Mexico: The Impact of Democratization*. London: Lynne Rienner Publishers, 2009

Nahdlatul Ulama. 'Gus dur pernah usulkan pembuktian terbalik untuk koruptor', www.nu.or.id/post/read/36721/gus-dur-pernah-usulkan-pembuktian-terbalik-untuk-koruptor

Nasution, Adnan Buyung. *The Aspiration for Constitutional Government in Indonesia: A Socio-Legal Study of the Indonesian Konstituante, 1956–1959*. Jakarta: Pustaka Sinar Harapan, 1992

Negara, Ulla Fionna, Siwage Dharma and Hui Yew Foong. 'Indonesia in 2013, anticipating 2014', *Southeast Asian Affairs*, 2014, pp. 119–38

Nelken, David, and Michael Levi. 'The corruption of politics and the politics of corruption: An overview.' *Journal of Law and Society*, vol. 23, no. 1, 1996, pp. 1–17

Nguyen, Thang D. (ed.). *The Indonesian Dream: Unity, Diversity and Democracy in Times of Distrust*. Singapore: Marshall Cavendish, 2004

Nichols QC, Colin, Tim Daniel, Martin Polaine and John Hatchard. *Corruption and Misuse of Public Office*, Oxford: Oxford University Press, 2006

Notosusanto, Nugroho, and Ismail Saleh. *The Coup Attempt of the 'September 30 Movement' in Indonesia*. Jakarta: PT. Pembimbing Masa-Djakarta, 1968

Philp, Mark, 'Conceptualizing political corruption', in *Political Corruption: Concepts and Contexts*, ed. Michael Johnston, 3rd edn, New York: Routledge, 2002

Pompe, Sebastian. *A Study of Institutional Collapse*. Southeast Asia Program Publication. Ithaca, NY: Cornell University, 2005

Pusat Pelaporan dan Analisis Transaksi Keuangan (PPATK). *Regulasi Terbaru Di Bidang Pencegahan dan Pemberantasan Tindak Pidana Pencucian Uang dan Pendanaan Terorisme*. Jakarta, PPATK, 2012

Robertson-Snape, Fiona. 'Corruption, collusion and nepotism in Indonesia', in *Third World Quality*, vol. 20, no. 3, 1999, pp. 589–602

Rochman, Meuthia Ganie, and Rochman Achwan. 'Corruption in Indonesia's emerging democracy', *Journal of Developing Societies*, vol. 32, no. 2, 2016, pp. 159–77

Rohrohmana, Basir. 'Pidana Pembayaran Uang Pengganti Sebagai Pidana Tambahan Dalam Tindak Pidana Korupsi', *Jurmal Hukum Prioris*, vol. 6, no. 2, 2017, pp. 44–65

Rose-Ackerman, Susan. *Corruption: A Study in Political Economy*. New York: Academic Press, 1978

—— *Corruption and Government: Causes, Consequences, and Reform*. Cambridge: Cambridge University Press, 1999

—— 'Political corruption and reform in democracies: Theoretical perspectives', in *Comparing Political Corruption and Clientelism*, ed. Junichi Kawata. Burlington, VT: Ashgate Publishing, 2006

Rothe, Dawn L. 'Facilitating corruption and human rights violations: The role of international financial institutions', in *Crime Law and Social Change*, vol. 53, 2010, pp. 457–76

Sakwa, Richard. 'Russia: From a corrupt system to a system with corruption', in *Party Finance and Political Corruption*, ed. Robert Williams. New York: St Martin's Press, 2000

Schwarz, Adam. *A Nation in Waiting: Indonesia in the 1990s*. Sydney: Westview Press, 1994

Scott, James C. *Comparative Political Corruption*. Englewood Cliffs, NJ: Prentice Hall, 1972

Shore, Cris, and Dieter Haller. 'Introduction—sharp practice: Anthropology and the study of corruption', in *Corruption: Anthropological Perspectives*, ed. Cris Shore. London: Pluto Press, 2005

Simpson, Gerry J. 'Some reflections on the case concerning East Timor', in *Indonesia: Law and Society*, ed. Timothy Lindsey. Sydney: Federation Press, 1999

Stewart, Fenwick. 'Measuring up? Indonesia's Anti-Corruption Commission and the new corruption agenda', in *Indonesia: Law and Society*, ed. Timothy Lindsey. Sydney: Federation Press, 1999

Tim Penyusun Laporan Tahunan KPK. *Annual Report 2011*. Jakarta: Komisi Pemberantasan Korupsi, 2011
—— *Annual Report 2012*. Jakarta: Komisi Pemberantasan Korupsi, 2012
—— *Annual Report 2017*. Jakarta: Komisi Pemberantasan Korupsi, 2017
—— *Annual Report 2018*. Jakarta: Komisi Pemberantasan Korupsi, 2018
—— *Annual Report 2019*. Jakarta: Komisi Pemberantasan Korupsi, 2019
Thee Kian Wie, 'The Indonesian government's economic policies towards the ethnic Chinese: Beyond economic nationalism?', in *Southeast Asia's Chinese Businesses in an Era of Globalisation: Coping with the Rise of China*, ed. Lee Suryadinata. Singapore: ISEAS, 2006
Toer, Pramoedya Ananta. *Korupsi*, 2nd edn. Jakarta: Balai Pustaka, 2013
Uhlin, Anders. *Asian Values Democracy: Neither Asian Nor Democratic: Discourses and Practices in Late New Order Indonesia*. Stockholm: Center for Asia Studies, Stockholm University, 1999
United Nations Development Programme. *Tackling Corruption, Transforming Lives: Accelerating Human Development in Asia and the Pacific*. Colombo: Macmillan, 2008
Van der Eng, Pierre. 'Business in Indonesia: Old problems and new challenges', in *Business in Indonesia: New Challenges, Old Problems*, ed. M. Chatib Basri and Pierre Van der Eng. Singapore: Institute of Southeast Asian Studies, 2004
Vogl, Frank. *Waging War on Corruption*. Lanham, MD: Rowman & Littlefield, 2012
Wedeman, Andrew. *Double Paradox: Rapid Growth and Rising Corruption in China*. Ithaca, NY: Cornell University Press, 2012
Werner, Simcha B. 'The development of political corruption in Israel', in *Political Corruption: Concepts and Contexts*, ed. Arnold Heidenheimer and Michael Johnston. New Brunswick, NJ: Transaction Publishers, 2002
Winters, Jeffrey. 'Oligarchy and democracy in Indonesia', *Indonesia*, no. 96, 2013, pp. 1–23
Wolfensohn, James D. Speech delivered at the annual meeting of World Bank on 1 October 1996
Yadav, Vineeta. *Political Parties, Business Groups, and Corruption in Developing Countries*. New York: Oxford University Press, 2011
Yusuf, Muhammad. *Merampas Aset Koruptor*. Jakarta: Penerbit Kompas, 2013

Laws and regulations

Indonesia, *Instruksi Presiden tentang Aksi Pencegahan dan Pemberantasan Korupsi Tahun 2012*, Inpres no. 17 of 2011
Indonesia, *Instruksi Presiden tentang Rencana Aksi Pencegahan dan Pemberantasan Korupsi Tahun 2013*, Inpres no. 1 of 2013
Indonesia, *Keputusan Presiden Badan Pengawasan Keuangan dan Pembangunan*, Kepres no. 31 of 1983
Indonesia, *Keputusan Presiden Pembuatan Mobil Nasional*, Kepres no. 42 of 1996

Indonesia, *Ketetapan Majelis Permusyawaratan Rakyat Penyelenggara Negara yang Bersih dan Bebas Korupsi, Kolusi dan Nepotisme,* Tap MPR XI/MPR/1998 year 1998, Article 4, para. 1

Indonesia, *Ketetapan Majelis Permusyawaratan Rakyat Sementara,* Tap MPRS no. XXV/1966 of 1966

Indonesia, *Kitab Undang-Undang Pidana [Wetboek van Straftrecht],* trans. Moeljanto. Jakarta: Pradnya Paramita, 1976

Indonesia, *Peraturan Pemerintah Tata Cara Pelaksanaan Peran Serta Masyarakat dan Pemberian Penghargaan dalam Pencegahan dan Pemberantasan Tindak Pidana Korupsi,* PP no. 71 of 2000, TLN. no. 3995

Indonesia, *Peraturan Presiden Strategi Nasional Pencegahan Korupsi,* Perpres no. 54 of 2018, LN. no. 108 of 2018

Indonesia, *Peraturan Presiden Strategi Nasional Pencegahan dan Pemberantasan Korupsi Jangka Panjang Tahun 2012–2025 dan Jangka Menengah Tahun 2012–2014,* Perpres no. 55 of 2012, LN. no. 122 of 2012

Indonesia, *Peraturan Presiden tentang Strategi Nasional Pencegahan dan Pemberantasan Korupsi Jangka Panjang Tahun 2012–2025 dan Jangka Menengah Tahun 2012–2014,* Perpres no. 55 of 2012, LN. no. 122 of 2012

Indonesia, *Undang-Undang Dasar,* UUD1945

Indonesia, *Undang-Undang Badan Pemeriksa Keuangan,* UU no. 15 of 2006, LN. no. 85 of 2006, TLN. no. 4654

Indonesia, *Undang-Undang Hukum Acara Pidana,* UU no. 8 of 1981, LN. no. 76 of 1981, TLN. no. 3258

Indonesia, *Undang-Undang Kejaksaan Republik Indonesia,* UU no. 16 of 2004, LN. no. 67 of 2004, TLN. no. 4401

Indonesia, *Undang-Undang Kekuasaan Kehakiman,* UU no. 48 of 2009, LN. no. 157, TLN. no. 5076

Indonesia, *Undang-Undang Komisi Pemberantasan Korupsi,* UU no. 30 of 2002, LN. no. 137 of 2002, TLN. no. 4250

Indonesia, *Undang-Undang Komisi Yudisial,* UU no. 22 of 2004, LN. no. 89 of 2004, TLN. no. 4415

Indonesia, *Undang-Undang Tentang Kepolisian Negara Republik Indonesia,* UU no. 2 of 2002, LN. no. 2 of 2002, TLN. no. 4168

Indonesia, *Undang-Undang Mahkamah Konstitusi,* UU no. 24 of 2003, LN. no. 98 of 2003, TLN. no. 4316

Indonesia, *Undang-Undang Pemberantasan Tindak Pidana Korupsi,* UU no. 31 of 1999, LN. no. 140 of 1999, TLN. no. 3874

Indonesia, *Undang-Undang Pemberantasan Tindak Pidana Korupsi,* UU no. 3 of 1971, LN. no. 19 of 1971, TLN. no. 2958

Indonesia, *Undang-Undang Pemilihan Umum,* UU no. 7 of 2017, LN. no. 182 of 2017. TLN. no. 6109

Indonesia, *Undang-Undang Pencegahan dan Pemberantasan Tindak Pidana Pencucian Uang,* UU no. 8 of 2010, LN. no. 122 of 2010 TLN. no. 5164

Indonesia, *Undang-Undang Pengadilan dalam Lingkungan Peradilan Umum dan*

Mahkamah Agung, UU no. 13 of 1965, LN. no. 31 of 1960, TLN. no. 2767

Indonesia, *Undang-Undang Perlindungan dan Pengelolaan Lingkungan Hidup*, UU no. 32 of 2009, LN. no. 140 of 2009, TLN. no. 5059

Indonesia, *Undang-Undang Perlindungan Saksi dan Korban*, UU no. 13 of 2006, LN. no. 64 of 2006, TLN. no. 4635

Indonesia, *Undang-Undang Pers*, UU no. 40 of 1999, LN. no. 166 of 1999, TLN. no. 3887

Indonesia, *Undang-Undang Perubahan Atas Undang-Undang Nomor 2 Tahun 2008 Tentang Partai Politik*, UU no. 2 of 2011, LN. no. 8 of 2001, TLN. no. 5189

Indonesia, *Undang-Undang Perubahan atas Undang-Undang Nomor 31 Tahun 1999 tentang Pemberantasan Tindak Pidana Korupsi*, UU no. 20 of 2001, LN. no. 134 of 2001, TLN. no. 4150

Indonesia, *Undang-Undang Perubahan Kedua Atas Undang-Undang Nomor 30 Tahun 2002 tentang Komisi Pemberantasan Korupsi*, UU no. 19 of 2019, LN. no. 197 of 2019, TLN. no. 6409

Indonesia, *Undang-Undang Transfer Dana*, LN. no. 39 of 2011, TLN. no. 5204

Mahkamah Konstitusi and Dewan, Nota Kesepahaman antara Mahkamah Konstitusi Republik Indonesia dan Dewan Pers tentang Peningkatan Pemahaman Hak Konstitusional Warga Negara [Memorandum of Understanding], no. 56/PK/2019—no. 07/DP/MoU/IV/2019 (only available in Bahasa Indonesia). www.mkri.id/public/content/infoumum/kerjasama/pdf/3-186_8_%20MOU%20Dewan%20Pers.pdf

United Nations, *Convention against Corruption*, 2003

Decisions

Decision of the Central Jakarta District Court no. 338/PDT.G/1999/PN.JKT.PST, 6 June 2000

Decision of the Central Jakarta District Court no. 31/PID.B/TPK/2011/PN.JKT.PST, 21 September 2011

Decision of the Central Jakarta District Court no. 33/PID.B/TPK/2011/PN.JKT.PST, 21 September 2011

Decision of the Central Jakarta District Court no. 48/PID.B/TPK/2011/PN.JKT.PST, 19 December 2011

Decision of the Central Jakarta District Court no. 69/PID.B/TPK/2011/PN.JKT.PST, 20 April 2012

Decision of the Central Jakarta District Court no. 54/PID.B/TPK/2012/PN.JKT.PST, 7 January 2013

Decision of the Central Jakarta District Court no. 62/PID.SUS/TPK/2013/PN.JKT.PST, 11 March 2014

Decision of the Central Jakarta District Court no. 117/PID.SUS/TPK/2014/PN.JKT.PST, 1 April 2014

Decision of the Central Jakarta District Court no. 16/PID.SUS/TPK/2014/PN.JKT.PST, 23 June 2014

Decision of the Central Jakarta District Court no. 30/PID.SUS/TPK/2014/PT.DKI, 8 July 2014

Decision of the Central Jakarta District Court no. 23/PID.SUS/TPK/2014/PN.JKT.PST, 18 July 2014

Decision of Central Jakarta District Court no. 44/PID.SUS/TPK/2014/PN.JKT.PST, 1 September 2014

Decision of the Central Jakarta District Court no. 55/PID.SUS/TPK/2014/PN.JKT.PST, 24 September 2014

Decision of the Central Jakarta District Court no. 111/PID.SUS/TPK/2015/PB.JKT.PST, 16 September 2015

Decision of the Central Jakarta District Court no. 75/PID.SUS/TPK/2015/PN.JKT.PST, 27 November 2015

Decision of the Central Jakarta District Court no. 130/PID.SUS/TPK/2017/PN.JKT.PST, 17 April 2018

Decision of the Central Jakarta District Court no. 65/PID.SUS/TPK/2018/PN.JKT.PST, 5 December 2018

Decision of the Jakarta High Court no. 551/PDT/2000/PT.DKI, 16 March 2001

Decision of the Jakarta High Court no. 31/PID/TPK/2012/PT.DKI, 8 August 2012

Decision of the Jakarta High Court no. 11/PID/TPK/2013/PT.DKI, 22 May 2013

Decisions of the Jakarta High Court no. 47/PID.SUS/TPK/2014/PT.DKI, 18 September 2014

Decision of the Jakarta High Court no. 48/PID/TPK/2014/PT.DKI, 30 September 2014

Decision of the Jakarta High Court no. 57/PID/TPK/2014/PT.DKI, 15 October 2014

Decision of the Jakarta High Court no. 58/PID/TPK/2014/PT.DKI, 28 October 2014

Decision of the Jakarta High Court no. 72/PID/TPK/2014/PT.DKI, 18 November 2014

Decision of the Jakarta High Court no. 74/PID/TPK/2014/PT.DKI, 4 February 2015

Decision of the Jakarta High Court no. 03/PID/TPK/2016/PT.DKI, 26 January 2016

Decision of the Supreme Court no. 273 PK/PDT/2008, 16 April 2008

Decision of the Supreme Court no. 1393 K/PID.SUS /2012, 29 August 2012

Decision of the Supreme Court no. 2233 K/PID.SUS /2012, 22 January 2013

Decision of the Supreme Court no. 1616 K/PID.SUS /2013, 20 November 2013

Decision of the Supreme Court no. 285 K/PID.SUS /2015, 23 February 2015

Decision of the Supreme Court no. 336 K/PID.SUS/2015, 23 February 2015

Decision of the Supreme Court no. 2429 K/PID.SUS /2014, 11 March 2015
Decision of the Supreme Court no. 2427 K/PID.SUS /2014, 8 April 2015
Decision of the Supreme Court no. 1261 K/PID.SUS/2015, 8 June 2015
Decision of the Supreme Court no. 430K/PID.SUS/2018, 18 April 2018
Decision of the Supreme Court no. 1998K/PID.SUS/2020, 13 July 2020
Indonesia, *Mahkamah Konstitusi Putusan Perkara Nomor* 006/PUU-1/2003
Indonesia, *Mahkamah Konstitusi Putusan Perkara Nomor* 069/PUU-II/2004
Indonesia, *Mahkamah Konstitusi Putusan Perkara Nomor* 010/PUU-IV/2006
Indonesia, *Mahkamah Konstitusi Putusan Perkara Nomor* 012/PUU-II/2006
Indonesia, *Mahkamah Konstitusi Putusan Perkara Nomor* 16/PUU-II/2006
Indonesia, *Mahkamah Konstitusi Putusan Perkara Nomor* 019/PUU-IV/2006
Indonesia, *Mahkamah Konstitusi Putusan Perkara Nomor*19/PUU-V/2007

News and online articles

Abduh, Muhammad. 'Penghentian Penyidikan Tindak Pidana dan Penyelesaian Diluar Pengadilan Dugaan Pemerasan dan Penyalahgunaan Wewenang.' www.kompasiana.com/edhu_lontara/551c1503813311b77f9de1f9/penghentian-penyidikan-tindak-pidana-dan-penyelesaian-diluar-pengadilan-dugaan-pemerasan-dan-penyalahgunaan-wewenang?page=all

Affan, Heyder. 'Korupsi Massal di DPRD: Ada Kekuatan yang Membuat Sistem Pencegahan Tidak Berfungsi.' BBC News Indonesia. www.bbc.com/indonesia/indonesia-45464288

Afrilianti, Dwi. 'Nazaruddin Juga Sebut Menpora Terlibat dalam Kasus Wisma Atlet'. *Okezone*. news.okezone.com/read/2011/10/12/339/514492/nazaruddin-juga-sebut-menpora-terlibat-dalam-kasus-wisma-atlet

Agence France-Presse. 'Who is Prabowo Subianto?' *Rappler*. www.rappler.com/world/regions/asia-pacific/indonesia/62598-who-is-prabowo

Agus, Feri. 'Agus Rahardjo: Jangan Lagi Sebut KPK Lembaga Ad Hoc'. CNN Indonesia. www.cnnindonesia.com/nasional/20180903091110-12-327040/agus-rahardjo-jangan-lagi-sebut-kpk-lembaga-ad-hoc

Aji, M. Rosseno. 'Kasus BLBI, Mantan Kepala BPPN Dituntut 15 Tahun Penjara.' *Tempo*. nasional.tempo.co/read/1123203/kasus-blbi-mantan-kepala-bppn-dituntut-15-tahun-penjara/full&view=ok (page discontinued)

Ali, Muhammad. '5 Politikus Terjerat Korupsi Sepanjang 2015.' Liputan6. www.liputan6.com/news/read/2397562/5-politikus-terjerat-korupsi-sepanjang-2015

Amindoni, Ayomi. 'Mengapa Harga Daging Sapi di Indonesia Mahal?' BBC Indonesia. www.bbc.com/indonesia/indonesia-41264222

Amrullah, Amri. 'Kasus Suryadharma Ali, Pengamat: Ini Jadi Momentum Perbaiki Haji.' *Republika*. www.republika.co.id/berita/nasional/umum/14/05/28/n69nj9-kasus-suryadharma-ali-pengamat-ini-jadi-momentum-perbaiki-haji

Antara News. 'Aulia Pohan Tersangka Kasus Dana BI.' www.antaranews.com/berita/122210/aulia-pohan-tersangka-kasus-dana-bi

Anti-Corruption Clearing House (ACCH). 'Tindak Pidana Korupsi Berdasarkan Jenis Perkara.' acch.kpk.go.id/id/statistik/tindak-pidana-korupsi/tpk-berdasarkan-jenis-perkara

Anto, Kasihanto. 'Abraham Samad, Segeralah Deklarasi Cawapres atau Bahkan Capres!' *Pep News*. pepnews.com/2018/04/25/abraham-samad-segeralah-deklarasi-cawapres-atau-bahkan-capres/

Armenia, Resty. 'Jokowi Resmikan Gedung Rp Triliun Milik Surya Paloh.' CNN Indonesia. www.cnnindonesia.com/nasional/20150523122323-20-55194/jokowi-resmikan-gedung-rp-8-triliun-milik-surya-paloh

Artika, Putri. 'Jokowi pertimbangkan SP3 untuk Bambang Widjojanto.' *Merdeka*. www.merdeka.com/peristiwa/jokowi-pertimbangkan-sp3-untuk-bambang-widjojanto.html

Asril, Sabrina. 'Jokowi Berhentikan Sementara Abraham Samad dan Bambang Widjojanto.' *Kompas*. nasional.kompas.com/read/2015/02/18/14255131/Jokowi.Berhentikan.Sementara.Abraham.Samad.dan.Bambang.Widjojanto

Atriana, Haris Fadhil. 'Ini Alur Pembahasan Anggaran Proyek e-KTP di DPR', in *Detik News*. news.detik.com/berita/d-3442248/ini-alur-pembahasan-anggaran-proyek-e-ktp-di-dpr

Aziz, Abdul. 'Mereka Mewariskan Jabatan Politik Kepada Istrinya Sendiri.' *Tirto*. tirto.id/mereka-mewariskan-jabatan-politik-kepada-istrinya-sendiri-clbT

Aziza, Kurnia Sari. 'Kemhan dan Polri Dapat Anggaran Paling Besar pada APBN 2018'. *Kompas*. ekonomi.kompas.com/read/2017/10/26/092826726/kemenhan-dan-polri-dapat-anggaran-paling-besar-pada-apbn-2018

Banjarmasin Post. 'Korupsi Berjamaah, Ini Nama 38 Anggota DPRD Sumut Ramai-Ramai Jadi Tersangka oleh KPK.' banjarmasin.tribunnews.com/2018/03/31/korupsi-berjamaah-38-anggota-dprd-sumut-ramai-ramai-jadi-tersangka-oleh-kpk

Barbillin, Abba. 'Petinggi PT Wika Mengaku Diarahkan PT DGI dalam LelangProyek Wisma Atlet.' *Kompas Palembang*. palembang.kompas.com/read/2017/08/23/13404331/petinggi-pt-wika-mengaku-diarahkan-pt-dgi-dalam-lelang-proyek-wisma-atlet

Bari, Shamsul, and Ruhi Naz. 'Government's "zero-tolerance policy" against corruption.' *Daily Star*. www.thedailystar.net/opinion/news/governments-zero-tolerance-policy-against-corruption-1702171

Batubara, Leo. 'Edaran MA, Sinar Terang bagi Pers.' Dewan Pers. dewanpers.or.id/publikasi/opini_detail/21/Edaran_MA,_Sinar_Terang_bagi_Pers

Bawono, Adi Condro, and Diana Kusumasari, 'Pengertian peradilan in absentia.' Hukum Online. www.hukumonline.com/klinik/detail/ulasan/lt4f2e502cd0e52/pengertian-peradilan-in-absentia

BBC News Indonesia. 'Akil Mochtar divonis hukuman seumur hidup.' www.bbc.com/indonesia/berita_indonesia/2014/06/140630_vonis_akil_muchtar

—— 'Anas Urbaningrum Divonis 8 Tahun Penjara.' www.bbc.com/indonesia/berita_indonesia/2014/09/140924_vonis_anas_urbaningrum

—— 'Antasari Diberhentikan Sementara.' www.bbc.co.uk/indonesian/news/story/2009/05/090507_kpk.shtml

—— 'Kasus Setya Novanto "Pelesiran", Dua Petugas Lapas Sukamiskin Dijatuhi Hukuman, Kepala Lapas Tak Bersalah.' www.bbc.com/indonesia/indonesia-48645909

—— 'Ketua DPD Irman Gusman Ditetapkan Sebagai Tersangka Setelah Operasi Tangkap Tangan KPK.' www.bbc.com/indonesia/berita_indonesia/2016/09/160917_indonesia_dpd_kpk

—— 'Menteri ESDM Jero Wacik Resmi Tersangka.' www.bbc.com/indonesia/berita_indonesia/2014/09/140903_jero_wacik_tersangka

—— 'Nazaruddin Diperiksa Penyidik KPK.' www.bbc.com/indonesia/berita_indonesia/2011/08/110818_narzaruddinquestioned

—— 'Nazaruddin Resmi Tersangka Kasus Suap.' www.bbc.com/indonesia/berita_indonesia/2011/06/110630_nazaruddincharge

—— 'Rekomendasi Tim Pencari Fakta.' www.bbc.com/indonesia/forum/2009/11/091123_tim8

—— 'Setya Novanto dihukum 15 tahun, denda Rp 500 juta, dicabut hak politik 5 tahun.' www.bbc.com/indonesia/indonesia-43876177

BBC United Kingdom. 'Indonesian taxman Gayus Tambunan jailed for corruption.' www.bbc.co.uk/news/world-asia-pacific-12224782.

Berita Satu. 'Ada Big Fish di Balik Kasus Hukum.' www.beritasatu.com/hukum/6402/ada-big-fish-di-balik-kasus-hukum

—— 'Kabur ke Luar Negeri, Beratkan Nazaruddin.' www.beritasatu.com/nasional/40407/kabur-ke-luar-negeri-beratkan-nazaruddin

—— 'Perusahaan Nazaruddin untuk Bermain di Tender Pemerintah.' www.beritasatu.com/hukum/43724-perusahaan-nazaruddin-untuk-bermain-di-tender-pemerintah.html

Budilaksono, Imam. 'Gerinda: Prabowo-ARB Miliki Kedekatan Khusus.' Antara News. www.antaranews.com/berita/756731/gerindra-prabowo-arb-miliki-kedekatan-khusus

Celebes, Jong. 'Konglomerasi Media Massa, Siapa Menguasai Apa?' *Kompasiana.* www.kompasiana.com/abutahir/5655cd6a8223bd97098b45bc/konglomerasi-media-massa-siapa-menguasai-apa?page=all

Chaterine, Rahel Narda. 'Kejagung Dapat Tambahan Anggaran Rp 350 M untuk Bangun Gedung Utama.' *Detik News,* news.detik.com/berita/d-5181702/kejagung-dapat-tambahan-anggaran-rp-350-m-untuk-bangun-gedung-utama

CNN Indonesia. 'Orang Dekat Akil Mochtar Divonis 4,5 Tahun Penjara.' www.cnnindonesia.com/nasional/20200312185006-12-482976/orang-dekat-akil-mochtar-divonis-45-tahun-penjara

CTR. 'Setnov Sebut Kemendagri Ubah Sumber Biaya Proyek e-KTP.' CNN Indonesia. www.cnnindonesia.com/nasional/20180413145903-12-290599/setnov-sebut-kemendagri-ubah-sumber-biaya-proyek-e-ktp

Damhuri, Elba. 'Mengapa Idrus Marham Jadi Tersangka?' Republika. www.

republika.co.id/berita/nasional/news-analysis/18/08/26/pe13ki440-mengapa-idrus-marham-jadi-tersangka

Databoks. '1% Orang Terkaya Indonesia Menguasai 46% Kekayaan Penduduk.' databoks.katadata.co.id/datapublish/2018/10/30/1-orang-terkaya-indonesia-menguasai-46-kekayaan-penduduk

Denny, Charlotte. 'Soeharto, Marcos and Mobutu head corruption table with $50bn scams.' *Guardian*. www.theguardian.com/world/2004/mar/26/indonesia.philippines

Deslatama, Yandhi. 'Suku Baduy Serahkan Upeti ke Gubernur Banten.' *Liputan6*. www.liputan6.com/lifestyle/read/2051364/suku-baduy-serahkan-upeti-ke-gubernur-banten

Detik News. 'Jokowi Berhentikan Sementara Abraham Samad dan BW karena Jadi Tersangka.' news.detik.com/berita/2836722/jokowi-berhentikan-sementara-abraham-samad-dan-bw-karena-jadi-tersangka

—— 'Kronologi Chandra and Bibit Menuju Tahanan Rutan Bareskrim.' news.detik.com/berita/d-1231430/kronologi-chandra--bibit-menuju-tahanan-rutan-bareskrim

—— 'Kronologi Kasus Mulyana Versi BPK.' news.detik.com/berita/346216/kronologi-kasus-mulyana-versi-bpk

—— 'Nazaruddin Sebut Lagi Anas Otak Kasus Korupsi Wisma Atlet.' news.detik.com/berita/d-1764577/nazaruddin-sebut-lagi-anas-otak-kasus-korupsi-wisma-atlet

—— 'Polisi Perpanjang Penahanan Antasari Azhar Hingga 31 Agustus.' news.detik.com/berita/d-1175762/polisi-perpanjang-penahanan-antasari-azhar-hingga-31-agustus

—— 'Rokhmin Divonis 7 Tahun Penjara.' news.detik.com/berita/d-808249/rokhmin-divonis-7-tahun-penjara

—— 'Said Agil Jadi Tersangka Korupsi, Tetangga Juga Terkaget-Kaget.' news.detik.com/berita/384018/said-agil-jadi-tersangka-korupsi-tetangga-terkaget-kaget

—— 'SBY Minta Timtas Tipikor Sedikit Bicara Banyak Bekerja.' news.detik.com/berita/d-355487/sby-minta-timtas-tipikor-sedikit-bicara-banyak-bekerja

—— 'Sudah Divonis Bersalah Aulia Pohan Jelas Koruptor.' news.detik.com/berita/1426329/sudah-divonis-bersalah-aulia-pohan-jelas-koruptor

—— 'Sudah Jelas Bersalah, Aulia Pohan Jelas Koruptor.' news.detik.com/read/2010/08/24/061730/1426329/10/sudah-divonis-bersalah-aulia-pohan-jelas-koruptor

—— 'Susi "Kurir Suap Akil Mochtar" Dihukum 7 Tahun Penjara.' news.detik.com/berita/d-2840644/susi-kurir-suap-akil-mochtar-dihukum-7-tahun-penjara

—— 'Total Uang Akil Mochtar yang Disita KPK Senilai Rp 7,2 M'. news.detik.com/berita/d-2377495/total-uang-akil-mochtar-yang-disita-kpk-senilai-rp-72-m

DW. 'Jejak Korupsi Setya Novanto—Dari Limbah Beracun Hingga e-KTP.' www.dw.com/id/jejak-korupsi-setya-novanto-dari-limbah-beracun-hingga-e-ktp/a-18923831

Economist. 'Democracy's enemy within.' 31 August 2019. www.economist.com/weeklyedition/2019-08-31

Economist Intelligence Unit. 'Democracy Index 2019: A year of democratic setbacks and popular protests.' www.eiu.com/topic/democracy-index

Erdianto, Kristian. 'Bakal Terpilih Lagi, Megawati Perpanjang Rekor Ketum Parpol Terlama.' *Kompas.* nasional.kompas.com/read/2019/08/02/13270711/bakal-terpilih-lagi-megawati-perpanjang-rekor-ketum-parpol-terlama

Erwanti, Marlinda Oktavia. 'Hary Tanoe: Perindo Hadir untuk Bantu Bangun Bangsa.' *Detik News.* news.detik.com/berita/d-3929562/hary-tanoe-perindo-hadir-untuk-bantu-bangun-bangsa

Evani, Fuska Sani. 'Jusuf Kalla: Indonesia Juara Dunia Penjarakan Orang.' *Berita Satu.* www.beritasatu.com/nasional/394903/jusuf-kalla-indonesia-juara-dunia-penjarakan-orang

Fadhil, Haris. 'JK Sebut Pemberantasan Korupsi Belum Berhasil, KPK Bicara Komitmen.' *Detik News.* news.detik.com/berita/d-4645913/jk-sebut-pemberantasan-korupsi-belum-berhasil-kpk-bicara-komitmen

—— 'KPK Tangani 178 Kasus Korupsi di 2018, Terbanyak Libatkan Legislatif.' *Detik News.* news.detik.com/berita/4350420/kpk-tangani-178-kasus-korupsi-di-2018-terbanyak-libatkan-legislatif

Fahmi, Ismail, 'Luthfi Tampik Ijonkan Proyek Kementan untuk Danai PKS.' Bisnis.com. kabar24.bisnis.com/read/20130717/17/151387/luthfi-tampik-ijonkan-proyek-kementan-untuk-danai-pks

Farisa, Fitria Chusna. 'Tak Ada Batas Pengeluaran Dana Kampanye Pemilu.' *Kompas.* nasional.kompas.com/read/2018/08/23/14513351/tak-ada-batas-pengeluaran-dana-kampanye-pemilu

Fatmawati, Nur Indah. 'KPK Soal Artidjo Pension: Beliau Contoh Baik Berantas Korupsi.' *Detik News.* news.detik.com/berita/d-4032431/kpk-soal-artidjo-pensiun-beliau-contoh-baik-berantas-korupsi

—— 'Kronologi OTT Kasus Suap Gubernur Bengkulu.' *Detik News.* news.detik.com/berita/d-3538058/kronologi-ott-kasus-suap-gubernur-bengkulu

Febrian, Ramdan. 'The bittersweet love story of Pak Harto and Ibu Tien.' VOI. voi.id/en/memori/6940/the-bittersweet-love-story-pak-harto-and-ibu-tien

Finance Detik. 'Harga Daging Sapi di 3 Negara ini Jauh Lebih Murah dari RI.' finance.detik.com/berita-ekonomi-bisnis/d-2843071/harga-daging-sapi-di-3-negara-ini-jauh-lebih-murah-dari-ri

Firdaus, Febriana. 'KPK Tetapkan Gubernur Sumut Gatot dan istri Mudanya sebagai Tersangka.' *Rappler.* www.rappler.com/indonesia/100814-kpk-tetapkan-gubernur-sumut-gatot-istri-sebagai-tersangka

Firdaus, Firdaus. 'Ini Penyebab Rusdiharjo Divonis Rendah.' *Tribunnews.* www.

tribunnews.com/nasional/2012/01/31/ini-penyebab-rusdiharjo-divonis-rendah

Firdaus, Randy Ferdi. 'Beredar Nama-Nama Jenderal Polisi yang Tersangkut Rekening Gendut.' *Merdeka*. www.merdeka.com/peristiwa/beredar-nama-nama-jenderal-polisi-yang-tersangkut-rekening-gendut.html

Firmanto, Danang. 'Revisi UU KPK, Sejumlah Indikasi Pelemahan KPK.' nasional.tempo.co/read/858914/revisi-uu-kpk-sejumlah-indikasi-pelemahan-kpk/full&view=ok

Forbes Press Release. 'Wealth of tycoons on Forbes Indonesia Rich List reaches a record $129 billion.' *Forbes*. www.forbes.com/sites/forbespr/2018/12/12/wealth-of-tycoons-on-forbes-indonesia-rich-list-reaches-a-record-129-billion/#561b939572d3

Gabrillin, Abba. 'Kewenangan SP3 bagi KPK Dikhawatirkan Diperjualbelikan.' *Kompas*. nasional.kompas.com/read/2016/02/11/12115271/Kewenangan.SP3.bagi.KPK.Dikhawatirkan.Diperjualbelikan

—— 'Ruki, Sejak 2005, Saya Sinyalir ada "Corruptor Fight Back".' nasional.kompas.com/read/2017/07/07/15301021/ruki.sejak.2005.saya.sinyalir.ada.corruptor.fight.back

Gatra, Sandro. 'Antasari Azhar Bebas Bersyarat, Ini Perjalanan Kasusnya.' *Kompas*. nasional.kompas.com/read/2016/11/10/05300091/antasari.azhar.bebas.bersyarat.ini.perjalanan.kasusnya

Gecko Project, The. 'Ghost in the machine.' thegeckoproject.org/ghosts-in-the-machine-4acb5c5236cc

Guanto, E.S. 'Tumpak, Mas Achmad Santosa, dan Waluyo Pimpinan KPK Sementara.' *Tempo*. nasional.tempo.co/read/200925/tumpak-mas-achmad-santosa-dan-waluyo-pimpinan-kpk-sementara/full&view=ok

Guritno, Tatang. 'Kejanggalan Tes Wawasan Kebangsaan Pegawai KPK yang Jadi Sorotan.' *Kompas*. nasional.kompas.com/read/2021/05/17/06273661/kejanggalan-tes-wawasan-kebangsaan-pegawai-kpk-yang-jadi-sorotan?page=all

Habibie, Nur. 'Data 2004–2018: 104 Kepala Daerah Tersandung Korupsi, Paling Banyak di Jawa Timur.' *Merdeka*. www.merdeka.com/peristiwa/data-2004-2018-104-kepala-daerah-tersandung-korupsi-paling-banyak-di-jawa-timur.html

Hakim, Rakhmat Nur. 'KPK Ajukan Rp 985 Miliar untuk Anggaran 2019.' *Kompas*. nasional.kompas.com/read/2018/06/08/07160291/kpk-ajukan-rp-985-miliar-untuk-anggaran-2019

Hamzah, Herdiansyah. 'Urgensi Penyidik Independen KPK.' *Kompasiana*. www.kompasiana.com/herdiansyah/54fd2b51a33311902050f9cb/urgensi-penyidik-independen-kpk

Harian Jogja. 'JK Sebut Jumlah Kasus Korupsi Belum Berhasil Ditekan, Begini Tanggapan KPK.' news.harianjogja.com/read/2019/07/31/500/1009131/jk-sebut-jumlah-kasus-korupsi-belum-berhasil-ditekan-begini-tanggapan-kpk

Hendardi. 'Glorifikasi Soeharto dan Jejak Korupsi Orba.' *Berita Satu*. www.

beritasatu.com/opini/6227/glorifikasi-soeharto-dan-jejak-korupsi-orba

Hidayat, Faiq, and Haris Fadhil, 'Terbukti Korupsi e-KTP, Setya Novanto Divonis 15 Tahun Penjara', *Detik News*, news.detik.com/berita/d-3987879/terbukti-korupsi-e-ktp-setya-novanto-divonis-15-tahun-penjara

Hukum Online. 'Divonis Delapan Tahun Penjara, Mantan Dirut Jamsostek Ngamuk.' www.hukumonline.com/berita/baca/hol14793/divonis-delapan-tahun-penjara-mantan-dirut-jamsostek-ngamuk/

—— 'Hakim: Penyidik Independen KPK Bertentangan dengan Hukum.' www.hukumonline.com/berita/baca/lt55647f2f3cb3c/hakim--penyidik-independen-kpk-bertentangan-dengan-hukum

—— 'KPK Geledah Rumah di Depok Terkait Kasus Sutan Bhatoegana.' www.hukumonline.com/berita/baca/lt541b0328011ef/kpk-geledah-rumah-di-depok-terkait-kasus-sutan-bhatoegana

—— 'KPK Memang Dirancang Superbody Sedari Awal.' www.hukumonline.com/berita/baca/hol22416/kpk-memang-dirancang-isuperbodyi-sedari-awal

—— 'KPK Tetapkan Abdullah Puteh sebagai Tersangka Korupsi.' www.hukumonline.com/berita/baca/hol10616/kpk-tetapkan-abdullah-puteh-sebagai-tersangka-korupsi

—— 'Mau Tahu Biaya Penanganan Perkara Korupsi? Simak Angka dan Masalahnya.' www.hukumonline.com/berita/baca/lt5733f0ea01aea/mau-tahu-biaya-penanganan-perkara-korupsi-simak-angka-dan-masalahnya

—— 'Pilih Antasari sebagai Ketua KPK, DPR Dihujani Kritik.' www.hukumonline.com/berita/baca/hol18126/pilih-antasari-sebagai-ketua-kpk-dpr-dihujani-kritik

—— 'Senin, Presiden Lantik Pimpinan KPK.' www.hukumonline.com/berita/baca/hol9395/senin-presiden-lantik-pimpinan-kpk

Hutomo, Aryo Putranto Sapto. 'Kasus Suap Gugatan Pilkada Lebab, Atut Didakwa Menyap Akil.' *Merdeka*. www.merdeka.com/peristiwa/kasus-suap-gugatan-pilkada-lebak-atut-didakwa-menyuap-akil.html

Ibrahim, Gibran Maulana. 'Nur Mahmudi Tersangka Korupsi, Fahri Hamzah Berkicau Soal Sosoknya.' *Detik News*. news.detik.com/berita/d-4191114/nur-mahmudi-tersangka-korupsi-fahri-hamzah-berkicau-soal-sosoknya

ICAC. 'Brief history.' www.icac.org.hk/en/about/history/index.html

Ihsanuddin. 'Minta Dukungan, SBY Janjikan Surya Paloh Jabatan Menteri.' *Kompas*. nasional.kompas.com/read/2014/03/10/2307155/Minta.Dukungan.SBY.Janjikan.Surya.Paloh.Jabatan.Menteri

Indonesia Corruption Watch. 'Korupsi KPU; MA Kurangi Hukuman Nazaruddin Sjamsuddin.' antikorupsi.org/id/news/korupsi-kpu-ma-kurangi-hukuman-nazaruddin-sjamsuddin

Indonesia Investments. 'Korupsi di Indonesia.' www.indonesia-investments.com/id/bisnis/risiko/korupsi/item235

Infoplease. 'World's ten most corrupt leaders.' www.infoplease.com/top-ten-worlds-ten-most-corrupt-leaders

Institute for Criminal Justice Reform. 'Times vs H.M. Soeharto (PK).'

Available only in Bahasa Indonesia. icjr.or.id/times-vs-h-m-soeharto-pk
Investor Daily Indonesia. 'KPK Tahan Tujuh Anggota DPRD Riau.'
  id.beritasatu.com/home/kpk-tahan-tujuh-anggota-dprd-riau/52565
Irish Times. 'Mobutu leaves legacy of chaos and corruption.' www.irishtimes.
  com/news/mobutu-leaves-legacy-of-chaos-and-corruption-1.104463
Jawa Pos. 'KPK Ajukan Banding Putusan Andi Narogong.' www.jawapos.com/
  nasional/hukum-kriminal/03/01/2018/kpk-ajukan-banding-putusan-
  andi-narogong/
—— 'Selain Gayus Tambunan, Ini Sederet Kasus Suap Melibatkan Pegawai
  Pajak.' www.jawapos.com/nasional/hukum-kriminal/04/03/2021/selain-
  gayus-tambunan-ini-sederet-kasus-suap-melibatkan-pegawai-pajak
JG News Channel. 'Former lawmaker Angelina Sondakh denies intimidation
  in Hambalang case.' jakartaglobe.id/news/former-lawmaker-angelina-
  sondakh-denies-intimidation-in-hambalang-case/
Kejaksaan Republik Indonesia. 'Intelijen Kejagung Temukan Aset Terpidana
  Korupsi Rp1,6 Triliun.' www.kejaksaan.go.id/berita.php?idu=1&id=14370
Komisi Pemberantasan Korupsi [Anti-Corruption Clearing House]. web.kpk.
  go.id/id/publikasi-data/statistik/penindakan-2
—— 'Beranda KPK.' www.kpk.go.id/id/
—— 'Lahirnya Komisi Pemberantasan Korupsi KPK.' www.sejarah-negara.
  com/2016/03/lahirnya-komisi-pemberantasan-korupsi-kpk.html
—— 'Laporan Akuntabilitas (LAKIP) KPK 2018.' www.kpk.go.id/id/
  publikasi/laporan/laporan-akuntabilitas-kinerja/768-laporan-akuntabilitas-lakip-
  kpk-2018
—— 'Siaran Pers Capaian Kinerja KPK di Tahun 2018.' www.kpk.go.id/id/
  berita/siaran-pers/717-capaian-dan-kinerja-kpk-di-tahun-2018
—— 'Press release: Capaikan dan Kinerja di Tahun 2018.' www.kpk.go.id/id/
  berita/siaran-pers/717-capaian-dan-kinerja-kpk-di-tahun-2018
Komisi III DPR. 'Anggaran Kejagung 2020 Sebesar Rp. 6,725 Triliun.' www.
  dpr.go.id/berita/detail/id/24904/t/Anggaran+Kejagung+2020+Sebesar+R
  p+6%2C725+Triliun
Kompas. '2017, Kejagung Selamatkan Uang Negara RP 734 M dari Kasus
  Pidana Khusus.' nasional.kompas.com/read/2018/01/09/17011791/2017-
  kejagung-selamatkan-uang-negara-rp-734-m-dari-kasus-pidana-khusus
—— 'Andi Mallarangeng Didakwa Korupsi Rp 4 Miliar dan 550.000 Dollar
  AS.' nasional.kompas.com/read/2014/03/10/1458227/Andi.Mallarangeng.
  Didakwa.Korupsi.Rp.4.Miliar.dan.550.000.Dollar.AS
—— 'Angelina Sondakh Divonis 4,5 Tahun Penjara.' nasional.kompas.com/
  read/2013/01/10/16300431/Angelina.Sondakh.Divonis.4.5.Tahun.Penjara
—— 'Artidjo Alkostar dan Vonis Berat Kasasi.' www.kompas.com/topik-
  pilihan/list/3261/artidjo-alkostar-dan-vonis-berat-kasasi
—— 'Burhanuddin Abdullah Divonis Lima Tahun.' nasional.kompas.com/
  read/2008/10/29/12144047/Burhanuddin.Abdullah.Divonis.Lima.Tahun
—— 'Indeks Persepsi Korupsi Indonesia pada 2020 Turun Jadi 37, Peringkat

102 di Dunia'. nasional.kompas.com/read/2021/01/28/14120521/indeks-persepsi-korupsi-indonesia-pada-2020-turun-jadi-37-peringkat-102-di
—— 'Infografik: 29 Kepala Daerah Terjerat kasus Korupsi Sepanjang 2018.' nasional.kompas.com/read/2018/12/27/08512001/infografik-29-kepala-daerah-terjerat-kasus-korupsi-sepanjang-2018
—— 'Ini Detail Kasus Dugaan Korupsi Pajak yang Diduga Menjerat Hadi Poernomo.' nasional.kompas.com/read/2014/04/21/1929221/Ini.Detail. Kasus.Dugaan.Korupsi.Pajak.yang.Menjerat.Hadi.Poernomo
—— 'Jalan Panjang Revisi UU KPK, Ditolak Berkali-kali hingga Disahkan.' nasional.kompas.com/read/2019/09/17/16171491/jalan-panjang-revisi-uu-kpk-ditolak-berkali-kali-hingga-disahkan?page=all
—— 'Kaleidoskop 2016: 10 Kelapa Daerah Tersangka Korupsi.' nasional. kompas.com/read/2016/12/12/09232571/kaleidoskop.2016.10.kepala. daerah.tersangka.korupsi.?page=all
—— 'Patrialis Akbar Divonis 8 Tahun Penjara.' nasional.kompas.com/read/ 2017/09/04/12302181/patrialis-akbar-divonis8-tahun-penjara
—— 'Pemiskinan Koruptor Dinilai Lebih Efektif ketimbang Membebankan Biaya Sosial.' nasional.kompas.com/read/2016/09/15/09463981/ pemiskinan.koruptor.dinilai.lebih.efektif.ketimbang.membebankan.biaya. sosial?page=all
—— 'Petahana yang Kembali Terpilih Jadi Pimpinan KPK.' nasional.kompas. com/read/2019/09/13/09045851/alexander-marwata-petahana-yang-kembali-terpilih-jadi-pimpinan-kpk
—— 'Syamsul Arifin-Gatot Pujo Nugroho Resmi Menang.' nasional.kompas. com/read/2008/04/25/01372720/syamsul.arifin-gatot.pujo.nugroho.resmi. menang
—— 'Tiga Jabatan SBY di Partai Demokrat.' nasional.kompas.com/read/ 2010/06/25/14382552/Tiga.Jabatan.SBY.di.Partai.Demokrat
KPK Pers Conference. 'Capaian dan Kinerja KPK di Tahun 2018.' www.kpk. go.id/id/berita/siaran-pers/717-capaian-dan-kinerja-kpk-di-tahun-2018
Kulsum, Umi. 'Tahun 2018, KPK Serap Anggaran Rp 744 Miliar.' *Nasional Kontan*. nasional.kontan.co.id/news/tahun-2018-kpk-serap-anggaran-rp-744-miliar
Kumoro, Heru Sri. 'Mantan Ketua MK Akil Mochtar Divonis Seumur Hidup.' *Kompas*. nasional.kompas.com/read/xml/2014/06/30/2203501/Mantan. Ketua.MK.Akil.Mochtar.Divonis.Seumur.Hidup
Kumparan. 'Kaleidoskop 2019: 5 Kasus Korupsi dengan Nilai Terbesar.' kumparan.com/kumparannews/kaleidoskop-2019-5-kasus-korupsi-dengan-nilai-terbesar-1sWzDbLTGiv
—— 'Rentetan Kasus Hukum Tommy Soeharto.' kumparan.com/ kumparannews/rentetan-kasus-hukum-tommy-soeharto/2
—— 'Menilik Kembali Gurita Dinasti Politik Banten.' kumparan.com/@ kumparannews/menilik-kembali-gurita-dinasti-politik-banten
Kurnia, Tommy. 'Daftar Terbaru 150 di Indonesia 27 Juli 2018.' *Liputan6*.

m.liputan6.com/bisnis/read/3600690/daftar-terbaru-150-orang-terkaya-di-indonesia-27-juli-2018

Lavinda. 'Ini 4 Faktor Pemicu Amandemen UUD1945 versi JK.' *Kabar 24 Bisnis*. kabar24.bisnis.com/read/20151207/15/499297/ini-4-faktor-pemicu-amandemen-uud-1945-versi-jk

Lestari, Sri. 'ICW, Vonis Bebas Terdakwa Kasus Korupsi Meningkat.' BBC News Indonesia. www.bbc.com/indonesia/berita_indonesia/2016/02/160207_indonesia_korupsi

Lifepal. 'Dari Jualan Ikan Asin Hingga Jadi Bos TV, Ini Kisah Inspiratif Surya Paloh.' www.moneysmart.id/surya-paloh-di-balik-kesuksesan-menjadi-bos-media-grup-memiliki-kisah-hidup-yang-inspiratif/

Liljas, Per, 'Here's why some Indonesians are spooked by this presidential contender.' *Time*. time.com/2836510/prabowo-subianto-human-rights-indonesia-elections/

Liputan6. 'Profil Andi Malarangeng.' www.liputan6.com/news/read/278017/profil-andi-malarangeng

—— '12 Tahun Lalu, Soeharto Menang Lawan Majalah Time.' www.liputan6.com/news/read/4049227/12-tahun-lalu-soeharto-menang-lawan-majalah-time

Litigasi. 'Turut Serta Melakukan Kejahatan Dapat Dihukum.' litigasi.co.id/turut-serta-melakukan-kejahatan-dapat-dihukum

Lopez, Linette. 'How dead oligarch Boris Berezovsky impoverished himself fighting Putin and losing a lawsuit against his old friend.' *Business Insider*. www.businessinsider.com/how-boris-berezovsky-lost-his-fortune-2013-3?r=US&IR=T

Lotulu, Garry Andrew. 'Siapa Penerima "Fee" Terbesar dari Kasus Korupsi e-KTP.' nasional.kompas.com/read/2017/03/10/06060031/siapa.penerima.fee.terbesar.dari.kasus.korupsi.e-ktp.?page=all

Lumanauw, Novy. 'KPK tahan Emir Moeis.' *Berita Satu*. www.beritasatu.com/nasional/125095/kpk-tahan-emir-moeis

Maharani, Dian. 'Luthfi Hasan Ishaaq Divonis 16 Tahun Penjara.' *Kompas*. nasional.kompas.com/read/2013/12/09/2106550/Luthfi.Hasan.Ishaaq.Divonis.16.Tahun.Penjara

—— 'Rudi Rubiandini Divonis 7 Tahun Penjara.' *Kompas*. nasional.kompas.com/read/2014/04/29/1343545/Rudi.Rubiandini.Divonis.7.Tahun.Penjara

Masykuri, Romel. 'Potret Oligarki Politik di Madura.' *Review Buku*. www.academia.edu/29006134/Review_Buku_Potret_Oligarki_Politik_di_Madura

Medistiara, Yulida. 'Punya 2 Alat Bukti, KPK pastikan Penetapan Tersangka Novanto Sah.' *Detik News*. news.detik.com/berita/d-3653857/punya-2-alat-bukti-kpk-pastikan-penetapan-tersangka-novanto-sah

Merdeka. 'Kasus Luthfi Hasan Ishaaq. KPK Periksa Sekretaris Mentan.' www.merdeka.com/tag/k/kasus-suap-daging/kasus-luthfi-hasan-ishaaq-kpk-periksa-sekretaris-mentan.html

Mohammad, Yandi. 'MA Perberat Hukuman Irman dan Sugiharto.' *Beritagar*. beritagar.id/artikel/berita/ma-perberat-hukuman-irman-dan-sugiharto

Movanita, Ambaranie Kemala Movanita. 'Kasus Simulator SIM, KPK periksa Empat Polisi.' *Kompas*. nasional.kompas.com/read/2015/08/26/11320391/Kasus.Simulator.SIM.KPK.Periksa.Empat.Polisi

—— 'Komisioner KPK: Saya Takut Kena Laknat Bung Hatta kalau Membiarkan Korupsi.' *Kompas*. nasional.kompas.com/read/2016/02/18/19291191/Komisioner.KPK.Saya.Takut.Kena.Laknat.Bung.Hatta.kalau.Membiarkan.Korupsi

Mubarok, Dinul. 'Inilah Alasan polisi Jadikan Bibit dan Chandra Tersangka.' *Tempo*. nasional.tempo.co/read/198331/inilah-alasan-polisi-jadikan-bibit-dan-chandra-tersangka

Nasional Kontan. 'Daftar Terpidana Korupsi Hambalang Kian Panjang.' nasional.kontan.co.id/news/daftar-terpidana-korupsi-hambalang-kian-panjang

No Man's Land, 'KPK: Lembaga Permanen atau Lembaga Ad Hoc?' bh4kt1.wordpress.com/2012/10/03/331/

Novianti, Diah. 'Kontroversi Seputar Terpilihnya Antasari Azhar Sebagai Ketua KPK.' Antara News. www.antaranews.com/berita/85953/kontroversi-seputar-terpilihnya-antasari-azhar-sebagai-ketua-kpk

Noviyanto. 'PDIP Sepakat KPK Dibubarkan.' *Lensa Indonesia*. www.lensaindonesia.com/2011/08/04/pdip-sepakat-kpk-dibubarkan.html

Nugroho, Adi. 'Ternyata 6 Kasus Super Besar ini Juga Melibatkan Setya Novanto di Dalamnya.' *Boombastis*. www.boombastis.com/kasus-setya-novanto/51218

Nugroho, Kukuh Bhimo. 'Berbagai Skandal yang Membelit Setya Novanto.' *Tirto*. tirto.id/berbagai-skandal-yang-membelit-setya-novanto-b5M6

Nugroho, Rony Ariyanto. 'Dinasti Politik Ratu Atut Setelah Delapan Tahun Berkuasa.' *Kompas*. nasional.kompas.com/read/2013/12/18/0729208/Dinasti.Politik.Ratu.Atut.Setelah.Delapan.Tahun.Berkuasa?page=all

Nurita, Dewi. 'Begini Kronologi Kasus Setya Novanto.' *Tempo*. nasional.tempo.co/read/1041781/begini-kronologi-kasus-setya-novanto

Nurrizki, Adinda. 'Prabowo Subianto Pimpin Partai Gerindra.' *Merah Putih*. merahputih.com/post/read/prabowo-subianto-pimpin-partai-gerindra

Office of Assistance to Deputy Cabinet Secretary for State Documents and Translation. 'Zero tolerance for corruptors hiding their money abroad, President Jokowi says.' Setkab. setkab.go.id/en/zero-tolerance-for-corruptors-hiding-their-money-abroad-president-jokowi-says/

Oke News. 'Akil Mochtar Tidak Menyesal Dihukum.' news.okezone.com/read/2014/07/01/339/1006377/akil-mochtar-tidak-menyesal-dihukum-seumur-hidup

Paat, Yustinus. 'ICW: Di Tahun 2015, Jumlah Tersangka kasus Korupsi Sebanyak 1328 Orang.' *Berita Satu*. www.beritasatu.com/hukum/249898-icw-di-tahun-2014-jumlah-tersangka-kasuskorupsi-sebanyak-1328-orang.html

Pangaribuan, Luhut. 'Tentang PK (Peninjauan Kembali).' Hukum Online. www.hukumonline.com/klinik/detail/ulasan/lt4a0bd93d0f7ac/tentang-pk-peninjauan-kembali-/

Perkasa, Anugerah. 'Harta 40 Orang Terkaya Makin "Gendut" di Rezim SBY dan Jokowi.' www.cnnindonesia.com/nasional/20180330011157-20-287008/harta-40-orang-terkaya-makin-gendut-di-rezim-sby-dan-jokowi

Permana, Dany. 'Kisah Hidup Setya Novanto, dari Tukang Beras, Model Hingga Jadi Miliuner.' *Kompas*. nasional.kompas.com/read/2017/11/21/14561161/kisah-hidup-setya-novanto-dari-tukang-beras-model-hingga-jadi-miliuner?page=all

Prabowo, Dani. 'Novel Baswedan: Ini Kriminalisasi.' *Kompas*. nasional.kompas.com/read/2015/05/03/14574081/Novel.Baswedan.Ini.Kriminalisasi

Priyambodo, R.H. 'Terbukti Korupsi, Komjen Suyitno Landung Divonis 18 Bulan Penjara.' *Antara News*. www.antaranews.com/berita/44142/terbukti-korupsi-komjen-suyitno-landung-divonis-18-bulan-penjara

Publica News. 'Kesimpulan Pansus Hak Angket Sebut KPK Superbody.' www.publica-news.com/berita/nasional/2017/08/22/12323/kesimpulan-pansus-hak-angket-sebut-kpk-superbody.html

Purwanti, Puput. '3 Contoh Politik Oligarki di Indonesia.' *Hukamnas*. hukamnas.com/contoh-politik-oligarki-di-indonesia

Puspita, Ratna. 'LIPI: Oligarki Parpol Perburuk Kualitas Demokrasi di Indonesia.' *Republika*. www.republika.co.id/berita/nasional/politik/18/12/11/pjkf8l428-lipi-oligarki-parpol-perburuk-kualitas-demokrasi-indonesia

Putra, Lutfy Mairizal. 'Ini Poin-Poin dalam RUU yang Dinilai Akan Memperlemah KPK.' *Kompas*. nasional.kompas.com/read/2017/03/31/20480011/ini.poin-poin.dalam.ruu.yang.dinilai.akan.memperlemah.kpk?page=all

Putri, Zunita. 'Saat Hakim Penasaran Berapa Uang Dikorupsi Novanto di Kasus e-KTP.' *Detik News*. news.detik.com/berita/d-4731102/saat-hakim-penasaran-berapa-uang-dikorupsi-novanto-di-kasus-e-ktp

Putrie, Irene, 'Asset tracing and and asset recovery', jurnal.kpk.go.id/Dokumen/SEMINAR_ROADSHOW/01-Asset-Recovery-Irene-Putrie.pdf

Putsanra, Dipna Videlia. 'Ratu Atut Divonis 5,5 Tahun Bui dalam kasus Korupsi Alkes.' *Tirto*. tirto.id/ratu-atut-divonis-55-tahun-bui-dalam-kasus-korupsi-alkes-cs7U

Qur'ani, Hamalatul. 'Aset Dirampas Tanpa Putusan Pemidanaan, Bisakah?' Hukum Online. www.hukumonline.com/berita/baca/lt5cc2bfdb0fbdc/aset-dirampas-tanpa-putusan-pemidanaan--bisakah/

R Antares, P. [sic] 'Elit Demokrat yang Terjerat kasus Korupsi Besar.' *Tagar*. www.tagar.id/elit-demokrat-yang-terjerat-kasus-korupsi-besar

Rafie, Barratut Taqiyyah. 'Begini Cerita Lengkap Soal Korupsi Berjamaan 41 Anggota DPRD Malang.' *Kontan*. nasional.kontan.co.id/news/begini-cerita-lengkap-soal-korupsi-berjamaah-41-anggota-dprd-malang

Rahadian, Lalu. 'Kronologi Pertemuan PDIP-Abraham Samad Versi Hasto.' CNN Indonesia. www.cnnindonesia.com/nasional/20150122162359-20-26587/kronologi-pertemuan-pdip-abraham-samad-versi-hasto

Rahmi, Novrieza. 'Abraham Samad Tersangka, Pengacara: Ini Bagian dari Kriminalisasi.' Hukum Online. www.hukumonline.com/berita/baca/lt54e2e7402f70d/abraham-samad-tersangka--pengacara--ini-bagian-dari-kriminalisasi/

Ramdhani, Jabbar. 'Soeharto Gagal Jadi Pahlawan Nasional?' *Detik News.* news.detik.com/berita/d-3929510/soeharto-gagal-jadi-pahlawan-nasional

Rastika, Icha. 'Ditahan KPK, Atut Menangis.' *Kompas.* nasional.kompas.com/read/2013/12/20/1746234/Ditahan.KPK.Atut.Menangis

—— 'Wafid Muharam tetap Divonis 3 Tahun Penjara.' *Kompas.* nasional.kompas.com/read/2012/04/19/17442234/Wafid.Muharam.Tetap.Divonis.Tiga.Tahun.Penjara

Reily, Michael. 'Ada 19 Kasus Korupsi Selama 2017, KPK Cetak Rekor OTT Terbanyak.' *Kata Data.* katadata.co.id/berita/2017/12/27/ada-19-kasus-korupsi-selama-2017-kpk-cetak-rekor-ott-terbanyak

Republika. 'Kasus Gayus Tambunan Pengaruhi Kepercayaan Wajib Pajak.' www.republika.co.id/berita/ekonomi/makro/13/10/01/mtzen4-kasus-gayus-tambunan-pengaruhi-kepercayaan-wajib-pajak

—— 'Rugikan Negara Rp 33,7 Miliar Bachtiar Chamsyah Hanya Divonis 1,8 Tahun.' nasional.republika.co.id/berita/breaking-news/hukum/11/03/22/171392-rugikan-negara-rp-33-7-m-bachtiar-chamsyah-hanya-divonis-1-8-tahun

Revianur, Aditya. 'Hukuman Mantan Mendagri Hari Sabarno Jadi 5 Tahun.' *Kompas.* nasional.kompas.com/read/2012/10/17/22093474/Hukuman.Mantan.Mendagri.Hari.Sabarno.Jadi.5.Tahun

RFE/RL. 'Global banks reported $2 trillion in suspicious transactions over two decades, new report shows.' www.rferl.org/a/global-banks-reported-2-trillion-in-suspicious-transactions-over-two-decades-new-report-shows/30848790.html

Ridwan, Muhammad. 'Diganjar 18 Tahun Penjara, Mantan Presiden PKS Akhirnya Ajukan PK.' *Jawa Pos.* www.jawapos.com/nasional/hukum-kriminal/16/12/2020/diganjar-18-tahun-penjara-mantan-presiden-pks-akhirnya-ajukan-pk/

Rimbawana, A.S. 'Sejarah Upaya Pelemahan KPK: Dari Cicak vs Buaya Hingga Teror.' *Tirto.* tirto.id/sejarah-upaya-pelemahan-kpk-dari-cicak-vs-buaya-hingga-teror-eho9

Risalah, Dian Fath. 'Ini Daftar Lengkap 19 OTT KPK Sepanjang 2017.' *Republika.* www.republika.co.id/berita/nasional/hukum/18/01/01/p1vv1h409-ini-daftar-lengkap-19-ott-kpk-sepanjang-2017

Rizqo, Kanavino Ahmad. 'Anggaran Kejaksaan 2018 Capai Rp 6,4 T, Jaksa Agung: Alhamdulillah.' *Detik News.* news.detik.com/berita/d-3702699/

anggaran-kejaksaan-2018-capai-rp-64-t-jaksa-agung-alhamdulillah
Rodzi, Fakhrur. 'Tiga Kali Gubernur Riau Korupsi, Ada Apa Dengan Riau?' *Riau Online*. www.riauonline.co.id/riau/kota-pekanbaru/read/2016/04/25/tiga-kali-gubernur-riau-korupsi-ada-apa-di-sini
Safitri, Dewi. 'Pemerintah masih teruskan penyuap Gayus.' BBC Indonesia. www.bbc.com/indonesia/berita_indonesia/2010/12/101222_mafiahukum'
Sandbrook, Jeremy. 'The 10 most corrupt world leaders of recent history.' *Integritas*. integritas360.org/2016/07/10-most-corrupt-world-leaders/
Santoso, Audrey. 'Polri Tangani 1.472 Kasus Korupsi Selama 2017, 1.028 Selesai.' *Detik News*. news.detik.com/berita/d-3790172/polri-tangani-1472-kasus-korupsi-selama-2017-1028-selesai
Saputra, Andi. 'PK Suryadharma Ali Ditolak, Tetap Dibui 10 Tahun karena Korupsi Haji.' *Detik News*. news.detik.com/berita/d-4524884/pk-suryadharma-ali-ditolak-tetap-dibui-10-tahun-karena-korupsi-haji
Sari, Maya Ayu Puspita. '8 Upaya Pelemahan KPK oleh DPR Menurut Catatan ICW.' *Tempo*. nasional.tempo.co/read/885616/8-upaya-pelemahan-kpk-oleh-dpr-menurut-catatan-icw
Sarwanto, Abi. 'Setya Novanto Terpilih Jadi Ketua Umum Partai Golkar.' CNN Indonesia. www.cnnindonesia.com/nasional/20160517071332-32-131204/setya-novanto-terpilih-jadi-ketua-umum-partai-golkar
Setyawan, Agus. 'Nazaruddin "Bekingi" PT DGI Garap Wisma Atlet Palembang.' CNN Indonesia. www.cnnindonesia.com/nasional/20170823134410-12-236681/nazaruddin-bekingi-pt-dgi-garap-wisma-atlet-palembang
Sihalolo, Markus Junainto. 'Ini Alasan PDIP Tidak Mencopot Panda Nababan', *Berita Satu*. www.beritasatu.com/nasional/175828/ini-alasan-pdip-tidak-mencopot-panda-nababan
Sinar Harapan. 'MA Perberat Hukuman Markus Nari Jadi 8 Tahun Penjara.' www.sinarharapan.co/hukum/read/20121/ma_perberat_hukuman_markus_nari_jadi_8_tahun_penjara
Sindo News. 'Konsep KPK Dibentuk Ad Hoc, Tak Perlu Dipermanenkan.' nasional.sindonews.com/read/1241893/13/konsep-kpk-dibentuk-bersifat-adhoc-tak-perlu-dipermanenkan-1506045208
—— 'Pengamat Setuju KPK Harus Dipermanenkan.' nasional.sindonews.com/read/1052410/13/pengamat-setuju-keberadaan-kpk-harus-dipermanenkan-1444635277
Sitompul, Juven Martua. 'Kasus Ratu Atut, KPK Periksa Pihak Swasta.' *Merdeka*. www.merdeka.com/peristiwa/kasus-ratu-atut-kpk-periksa-pihak-swasta.html
Sofwan, Rinaldy. 'Ulang Tahun ke-69 Polri dan Penanganan Korupsi Kakap.' CNN Indonesia. www.cnnindonesia.com/nasional/20150701073417-12-63476/ulang-tahun-polri-ke-69-dan-penanganan-korupsi-kakap
Stefanie, Christie. 'Pro Kontra DPR di Pasar Dewan Pengawas KPK.' CNN Indonesia. www.cnnindonesia.com/nasional/20160212211731-32-110669/

pro-kontra-dpr-di-pasal-dewan-pengawas-kpk

Suparman, Fana. 'KPK Lawan Kriminalisasi terhadap Bambang Widjojanto.' *Berita Satu*. www.beritasatu.com/nasional/243231/kpk-lawan-kriminalisasi-terhadap-bambang-widjojanto

Suriyanto. 'Kontroversi Gayus Tambunan: Hobi Pelesir Saat Dipenjara.' www.cnnindonesia.com/nasional/20150921104505-12-79976/kontroversi-gayus-tambunan-hobi-pelesir-saat-dipenjara

Taher, Andrian Pratama. 'Catatan Kinerja KPK di 2017: Data Kasus dan Latar Belakang Koruptor.' *Tirto*. tirto.id/catatan-kinerja-kpk-di-2017-data-kasus-dan-latar-belakang-koruptor-cCn5

Tempo. '20 Tahun Pembunuhan Hakim Agung Syafiuddin yang Melibatkan Tommy Soeharto.' nasional.tempo.co/read/1487431/20-tahun-pembunuhan-hakim-agung-syafiuddin-yang-melibatkan-tommy-soeharto

—— 'Akbar Tandjung Divonis 3 Tahun di Pengadilan Tinggi.' nasional.tempo.co/read/1127/akbar-tandjung-divonis-3-tahun-di-pengadilan-tinggi

—— 'Alasan Jaksa Agung Seponering Kasus Samad dan Bambang KPK.' nasional.tempo.co/read/750731/alasan-jaksa-agung-seponering-kasus-samad-dan-bambang-kpk

—— 'Burhanuddin Abdullah: Kasus BLBI Kewengangan Penegak Hukum.' www.tempo.co/read/news/2006/02/22/05674346/Burhanuddin-Abdullah--Kasus-BLBI-Kewenangan-Penegak-Hukum

—— 'Daftar Kader Partai Demokrat yang Terlibat Korupsi.' nasional.tempo.co/read/784106/daftar-kader-partai-demokrat-yang-terlibat-korupsi/full&view=ok

—— 'DPR dan TNI Akan Bereaksi Kalau Dekrit Keluar.' nasional.tempo.co/read/28768/dpr-dan-tni-akan-bereaksi-kalau-dekrit-keluar

—— 'Fahri Hamzah Sarankan KPK Dibubarkan, Pukat UGM: Logikanya Kacau.' nasional.tempo.co/read/888846/fahri-hamzah-sarankan-kpk-dibubarkan-pukat-ugm-logikanya-kacau

—— 'Hasil Hitung Cepat, Anak Bupati Lebak Unggul.' nasional.tempo.co/read/509112/hasil-hitung-cepat-anak-bupati-lebak-unggul/full&view=ok

—— 'Ini Kejanggalan Penetapan Novel Baswedan sebagai Tersangka.' nasional.tempo.co/read/645153/ini-kejanggalan-penetapan-novel-baswedan-sebagai-tersangka/full&view=ok

—— 'Kasus Bruneigate dan Buloggate Bisa Dibuka Lagi.' nasional.tempo.co/read/29691/kasus-bruneigate-dan-buloggate-bisa-dibuka-lagi/full&view=ok

—— 'Kasus Wisma Atlet, Saksi: Nazaruddin Tersohor di Dunia Konstruksi.' nasional.tempo.co/read/902473/kasus-wisma-atlet-saksi-nazaruddin-tersohor-di-dunia-konstruksi

—— 'Nazaruddin Ditangkap di Kolombia.' nasional.tempo.co/read/350601/nazaruddin-ditangkap-di-kolombia/full&view=ok

—— 'Peran Andi dan Anas di Wisma Atlet Mulai Diusut.' nasional.tempo.co/read/353740/peran-andi-dan-anas-di-wisma-atlet-mulai-diusut/full&view=ok

—— 'Proyek Wisma Atlet Dinilai Sudah Direkayasa Sejak Awal.' nasional. tempo.co/read/346479/proyek-wisma-atlet-dinilai-sudah-direkayasa-sejak-awal/full&view=ok

—— 'Putusan Kasasi, Hukum Andi Narogong Bertambah Jadi 13 Tahun.' nasional.tempo.co/read/1130018/putusan-kasasi-hukuman-andi-narogong-bertambah-jadi-13-tahun

—— 'Soeharto Koruptor Terkaya di Dunia.' nasional.tempo.co/read/41026/soeharto-koruptor-terkaya-di-dunia

—— 'Surya Eka Perkasa corporate secretary: No grounds for the charges.' en.tempo.co/read/531520/surya-eka-perkasa-corporate-secretary-no-grounds-for-the-charges

—— 'Terbukti Terima Suap, Irman Gusman Dihukum 4,5 Tahun.' nasional.tempo.co/read/848246/terbukti-terima-suap-irman-gusman-dihukum-45-tahun

—— 'Theo Toemion Divonis 6 Tahun.' nasional.tempo.co/read/82614/theo-toemion-divonis-6-tahun

—— 'UU Pemilu, Jangan Ada Lagi Dana Siluman Partai.' nasional.tempo.co/read/387975/uu-pemilu-jangan-lagi-ada-dana-siluman-partai

Thoha, Achmad Siddik. 'Korupsi Berjamaah Berjamaan, Sebuah Istilah yang Tidak Pantas.' *Kompasiana*. www.kompasiana.com/achmadsiddikthoha/55118c028133110c4cbc6293/korupsi-berjamaah-sebuah-istilah-yang-tidak-pantas

Tirto. 'Profile Muhammad Nazaruddin.' amp.tirto.id/m/muhammad-nazaruddin-Y

Tobing, Letezia. 'Tentang Sistem Pembalikan Beban Pembuktian.' www.hukumonline.com/klinik/detail/ulasan/lt513ff99d6eedf/tentang-sistem-pembalikan-beban-pembuktian/

Transparency International, 'Corruption Perceptions Index 2020', cpi.transparency.org/cpi/2020

—— 'Corruption Perceptions Index [2021].' www.transparency.org/research/cpi/overview

—— 'Corruption Perceptions Index 2019.' cpi.transparency.org/cpi/2019

—— 'Global Corruption Barometer 2009.' www.transparency.org/whatwedo/publication/global_corruption_barometer_20091

—— 'Seize Mobutu's wealth or lose your own money, Western governments told.' www.transparency.org/news/pressrelease/seize_mobutus_wealth_or_lose_your_own_money_western_governments_told

Transparency International Indonesia. 'Global Corruption Barometer 2017.' riset.ti.or.id/global-corruption-barometer-2017/

Tri/Apr. 'Yahya Harahap dapat dituntut.' Hukum Online. www.hukumonline.com/berita/baca/hol3281/font-size1-colorff0000bkasus-suap-hakim-agungbfontbryahya-harahap-dapat-dituntut-

Tribun Medan. 'Daftar Nama-Nama 38 Anggota DPRD Sumut yang Tersangka KPK masa Penahanan Diperpanjang.' medan.tribunnews.com/2018/10/09/

daftar-nama-nama-38-anggota-dprd-sumut-yang-tersangka-kpk-masa-penahanan-diperpanjang

Tribun News. 'ICW Minta Jaksa Agung Berani Tangkap Koruptor Kakap.' www.tribunnews.com/nasional/2014/11/28/icw-minta-jaksa-agung-berani-tangkap-koruptor-kakap

—— 'Ini 8 Kepala Daerah yang Dijerat KPK Sepanjang 2017.' www.tribunnews.com/nasional/2017/10/25/ini-8-kepala-daerah-yang-dijerat-kpk-sepanjang-2017

—— 'Jaksa Agung Bentuk Satgas Khusus Tangani Kasus Korupsi Besar.' www.tribunnews.com/nasional/2014/12/18/kejaksaan-agung-bentuk-satgas-khusus-tangani-kasus-korupsi-besar

—— 'Kisah Pelarian Nazaruddin Sebelum Tertangkap di Kolombia.' www.tribunnews.com/nasional/2011/08/08/kisah-pelarian-nazaruddin-sebelum-tertangkap-di-kolombia

—— 'Sebut Korupsi Ibarat Kanker Bagi Negara, Artidjo Alkostar: Saya Ingin Hukum Mati Koruptor.' www.tribunnews.com/nasional/2018/06/06/sebut-korupsi-ibarat-kanker-bagi-negara-artidjo-alkostar-saya-ingin-hukum-mati-koruptor

Triyogo, Arkhelaus Wisnu. 'TII: Ada 100 Kasus Ancaman Penyerangan Pelapor Koruosi Sejak 2004.' *Tempo*. nasional.tempo.co/read/1043972/tii-ada-100-kasus-ancaman-penyerangan-pelapor-korupsi-sejak-2004/full&view=ok

Ucu, Karta Raharja. 'Usulan Miskinkan Koruptor Ditolak.' *Republika*. republika.co.id/berita/n05cwr/usulan-miskinkan-koruptor-ditolak

Ulya, Fika Nurul. 'Simak, Ini Kronologi Lengkap Kasus Jiwasraya Versi BPK.' *Kompas*. money.kompas.com/read/2020/01/09/063000926/simak-ini-kronologi-lengkap-kasus-jiwasraya-versi-bpk?page=all

Umah, Annisatul. 'Jokowi Curiga: 30 Tahun RI Tak Bangun Kilang Minyak, Ada Apa?' CNBC Indonesia. www.cnbcindonesia.com/news/20191211113926-4-122133/jokowi-curiga-30-tahun-ri-tak-bangun-kilang-minyak-ada-apa

Utomo, Tri Widodo W Utomo. 'Politik Dinasti dalam Pemerintah Daerah.' Knowledge Sharing Forum. www.slideshare.net/triwidodowutomo/politik-dinasti-dalam-pemerintahan-daerah

Viva. 'Kisah kejatuhan Gus Dur dari kursi presiden.' www.viva.co.id/berita/nasional/117600-kisah-kejatuhan-gus-dur-dari-kursi-presiden

—— 'Setya Novanto', www.viva.co.id/siapa/read/78-setya-novanto

Wahyu, Yohan. 'Cegah Korupsi Jadi Budaya.' *Kompas*. kompas.id/baca/riset/2018/12/10/cegah-korupsi-jadi-budaya/

Walker, Shaun. 'Mikhail Khodorkovsky on life after prison and Russia after Putin.' *Guardian*. www.theguardian.com/world/2014/dec/26/mikhail-khodorkovsky-life-after-prison-russia-after-putin

Waluyo, Andylala. 'Jaksa Agung Deponering Kasus Abraham Samad dan Bambang Widjojanto.' VOA Indonesia. www.voaindonesia.com/a/jaksa-agung-deponering-kasus-abraham-samad-dan-bambang-widjojanto-/3219269.html

Wardah, Fathiyah. 'KPK tetapkan Miranda Goeltom sebagai Tersangka.' VOA Indonesia. www.voaindonesia.com/a/kpk-tetapkan-miranda-goeltom-sebagai-tersangka-138125233/104026.html

Warta Kota. 'Update Survei: 7 Parpol Tak Lolos Ambang Batas Parlemen Pemilu 2019, Ini Daftar Partai Gagal.' wartakota.tribunnews.com/2019/03/21/update-survei-7-parpol-tak-lolos-ambang-batas-parlemen-pemilu-2019-partai-hanura-dipilih-09

—— 'Ingat Rani Juliani Caddy Golf yang Terlibat Kasus Antasari? Kabarnya Terkini Mengejutkan.' wartakota.tribunnews.com/2017/01/03/ingat-rani-juliani-caddy-golf-yang-terlibat-kasus-antasari-kabarnya-terkini-mengejutkan

Wedhaswary, Inggeried Dwi. 'Dinasti Politik Lokal Semakin Meluas.' *Kompas*. nasional.kompas.com/read/2013/03/06/09172396/dinasti.politik.lokal.semakin.meluas

Welianto, Ari. 'KPK: Sejarah dan Tugas Pokoknya.' www.kompas.com/skola/read/2020/01/05/080000269/kpk-sejarah-dan-tugas-pokoknya?page=all

West, Palti, 'KPK Harusnya Dipermanenkan, Bukan Dihilangkan', *Kompasiana*, www.kompasiana.com/paltihutabarat/5618b0934123bdf713f2001d/kpk-harusnya-dipermanenkan-bukan-dihilangkan

Wicaksono, Bagus Ary. 'PKI Dibubarkan Tahun 1966, PDI Lahir 1973 Hasil Fusi Lima Partai, Versi PDIP Lahir Tahun 1970.' *Nusa Daily*. nusadaily.com/culture/pki-dibubarkan-tahun-1966-pdi-lahir-1973-hasil-fusi-lima-partai-versi-pdip-lahir-tahun-1970.html

Wicaksono, Satrio, 'Muhammad Nazaruddin; Kutu Loncat yang Bikin Gerah.' *Anti Korupsi*. www.antikorupsi.org/id/article/muhammad-nazaruddin-kutu-loncat-yang-bikin-gerah

Winarto, Yudho. 'Skandal Bank Bali: Kongkalikong Berbau Politik.' *Liputan Khusus Perbankan*. lipsus.kontan.co.id/v2/perbankan/read/325/Skandal-Bank-Bali-kongkalingkong-berbau-politik

World Bank. 'G-20 high level principles on beneficial ownership transparency.' star.worldbank.org/sites/star/files/g-20_high-level_principles_beneficial_ownership_transparency.pdf

Zhafira, Arnidhya Nur, 'KPK terus Lanjutkan Usut Kasus Korupsi BLBI.' *Sumut Antara News*, sumut.antaranews.com/berita/234300/kpk-terus-lanjutkan-usut-kasus-korupsi-blbi

Index

Page numbers including 'n' indicate endnotes.

Abdulgani, Roeslan 43
Abdullah, Burhanuddin 11, 65
Abdullah, Rizal 143–4, 145–6
abuse of power 17, 48, 50–1, 100
  allegations against Soeharto 154–7
Actions for Prevention and Eradication of Corruption (2013) 33
active corruption 40–1
ADB (Asian Development Bank) 14, 166
Agung, Made Oka Mas 152
Agustinus, Andi (Andi Narogong) 150, 151–3
Aidit, D.N. 42
Akbar, Patrialis 68, 71
Alam, Nur 70
Ali, Suryadharma 69, 147
Alisyahbana, Sutan Takdir 41–2
Alkostar, Artidjo 69, 152
Andayani, Susi Tur 137–40
Angraini, Diah 150–1
anti-corruption legislation 6, 17–19, 44, 47–50, 55, 73, 170–1
  corruption types stipulated 191
  Criminal Code 40–1, 47
  Law No. 30 of 2002 (KPK Law) *see* KPK Law (No. 30 of 2002) and amendments
  Law No. 31 of 1999 (Eradication of Criminal Acts of Corruption Act) 4, 6, 17–18, 59, 75–6, 78, 138–40, 145–6, 171
anti-corruption measures 6–9, 40–1, 73, 92, 94–5, 170–3
  asset forfeiture 171–2
  Habibie government 59, 85
  Jokowi government 32–3, 69, 107
  Megawati Soekarnoputri government 61–3
  Soeharto government 50–2, 54–5
  Soekarno government 44–50
  state agencies 8–9
  Wahid government 60–1, 85
  Yudhoyono government 32–3, 63–4, 66–7, 78–84, 107
  see also corruption in Indonesia; KPK (Komisi Pemberantasan Korupsi, Corruption Eradication Commission); United Nations Convention against Corruption (UNCAC)
anti-corruption movement 9, 58
  public support for KPK 66, 73, 75, 79, 82, 84–5, 91, 100, 107, 108
Arifin (Wismet Atlet Procurement Committee representative) 144
Arifin, Syamsul 30
Arto, Sugih 51

Index 233

Asian cultures
  corruption scores 2, 164
  values 15, 163
  see also Indonesia (state)
Asian Development Bank (ADB) 14, 166
Asian financial crisis 3, 56, 62
asset forfeiture 171–2
Attorney General's Office 5, 7–8
  anti-corruption measures 65–6
  budget 96, 97
  corruption cases handled 9, 11, 12, 31, 89, 96
  corruption in 5, 98, 106
  relationship with KPK 93–9, 160–1
  role 96
Atut, Ratu see Chosiyah, Ratu Atut
Azhar, Antasari 65, 66, 81, 88

Badan Pemeriksa Keuangan (BPK, Financial Audit Body) 8–9
Badan Pemeriksa Keuangan Pemerintah (BPKP, Financial and Development Audit Body) 8, 9
Badan Pengawasan Kegiatan Aparatur Negara (Bapekan, State Apparatus Supervisory Agency) 46–7
Badan Penyehatan Perbankan Nasional (BPPN or IBRA, National Banking Restructuring Agency) 62
Bakri, Aburizal 122, 125, 126
Bakri Group 34
Bank Bali case 58–9, 149
Bank Century case 82, 161, 165, 188n24
Bank Indonesia 11, 30, 65, 99
Banten Province 113–14, 135–40
Bapekan (State Apparatus Supervisory Agency) 46–7
Basirun, Nurdon 72
Baswedan, Novel 106, 158
Batoegana, Sutan 67
beef trade 26, 34, 68, 147, 179n112
Berezovsky, Boris Abraham 129

Bhargava, Vinay 27
Bhatoegana, Sutan 67, 69
Bintih, Hambit 133
black corruption, defined 16
Board of Supervisors (of KPK) 86, 89, 91, 102, 104–5, 147
Bolongaita, Emil 27
bottom-up corruption, defined 16
BPK (Badan Pemeriksa Keuangan, Financial Audit Body) 8–9
BPKP (Badan Pemeriksa Keuangan Pemerintah, Financial and Development Audit Body) 8, 9
BPPN (Badan Penyehatan Perbankan Nasional, or IBRA, National Banking Restructuring Agency) 62
bribery 6, 22, 64, 68, 70–1, 94, 113, 151–3, 164, 169
  case summaries 135–40, 150–3
  KPK case numbers 9–10, 30
  Law No. 31 of 1999 provisions 17
  UNCAC provisions 18, 19, 32
  see also gift-giving practices
Budiono 62
Bulog 52, 54, 61
business corruption see corporate corruption
businessmen, Indonesian 34–5, 41–2, 121–2; see also oligarchs and oligarchies
Butt, Simon 74, 94–5

Cahyo, Irvanto Hendra Pambudi 151, 152
Cambodia, corruption score 2
Century Bank case see Bank Century case
Chamsyah, Bachtiar 30, 68
Chasan, Tubagus Chaeri Wardana 137–9
Chevron case 31
China, corruption cases 11
Chinese political oligarchs 124
Chinese-Indonesian business families 121–2

Chosiyah, Ratu Atut 69, 113–14, 135–40, 149, 161, 162, 168
collective corruption (*korupsi berjamaah*) 128, 142, 145–6, 150–3, 164
Commission of Four (Komisi Empat) 51–2, 54
commissions (kickbacks) *see* bribery; kickbacks
Committee for Retooling the State Apparatus (Paran) 47
conflicts of interest 6, 17, 18, 19, 30, 33, 127; *see also* political corruption
Constitution (1945) and amendments 4–5, 61, 169
Constitutional Court 5, 80, 161
   corruption 35, 68, 133
   false testimony alleged 158–9
   Justices 11, 30, 35, 68, 71, 133, 137–9
   KPK Law challenges 101–3, 106, 157–8
corporate corruption 31–2, 34–5, 54, 60, 118–21, 123, 129–30, 141–2
corruption 19–28, 111–13, 167
   categories of corrupt states 22–3, 115–17, 169–70
   corrupt world leaders (top ten) 111–12
   costs of 27–8
   definitions and types 14–19
   in Indonesia *see* corruption in Indonesia
   modernisation and 26, 166–7
   origin of term 15
   weak governance and 24, 112, 113, 118, 120, 167
Corruption Eradication Commission *see* KPK (Komisi Pemberantasan Korupsi, Corruption Eradication Commission)
Corruption Eradication Team (Tim Pemberantasan Korupsi) 51
corruption in Indonesia 2, 19–28, 91–2, 110–17, 127–31, 161–73

   case numbers 9–13, 69–72, 87
   case summaries 33–6, 133, 135–57
   cases handled *see* KPK (Komisi Pemberantasan Korupsi, Corruption Eradication Commission); *and* cases handled *under* Attorney General's Office; police; *and* Supreme Court
   in colonial times 39–40, 74
   costs of 27–8, 69
   cultural notion of 38–40, 41, 128, 163–4
   foreign elements 24–5, 31, 120–1
   gift-giving practices 15, 37–9, 40
   historical perspective 37–44, 72–3, 77
   level of 2–3, 73, 74, 115–17, 164–5
   in local administration 69–71, 74, 113–14, 116–17, 127, 128, 168
   within military forces 46, 60, 62, 64
   see also anti-corruption legislation; anti-corruption measures; bribery; corporate corruption; judicial corruption; oligarchs and oligarchies; political corruption
Corruption Perceptions Index (CPI) 2, 73, 83–4, 111, 116, 164
crimes of globalisation 23, 24, 32; *see also* transnational criminal organisations (TCOs)
Criminal Code anti-corruption provisions 40–1, 47
Criminal Procedure Code (KUHAP, Kitab Undang-Undang Hukum Acara Pidana) xiii, 95, 105, 161
criminal states 22, 31, 49–50, 115, 169
criminalisation of officials 106–7, 158–62
criminalised states 22–3, 28, 50, 56, 115–16, 117–18, 169–70

Dahuri, Rokhmin 64
Dalam, Jusuf Muda 51
Damayanti 70
Darusman, Marzuki 156

death penalty 84
  opposition to xii–xiii
decentralisation of authority 116–17, 120, 127, 168
Della Porta, Donatella 21
Democrat Party *see* Partai Demokrat (Democrat Party)
Democratic Party of Struggle *see* Partai Demokrasi Indonesia—Perjuangan (PDI-P, Democratic Party of Struggle)
democratic values jeopardised by corruption 26, 27–8
demonstrations *see* student activism
Dhakidae, Daniel 39–40
Djarum Group 122
Djoyohadikusumo, Hasyim 122, 125
Djoyohadikusumo, Soemitro 43, 179n108
drug trafficking 24, 32
Duaji, Susno 82, 83, 106

East Timor referendum 76, 175n14
economic development and corruption 26, 166–7
E-KTP scam *see* electronic identification card (E-KTP) scam
Election Commission (KPU, Komisi Pemilihan Umum) 64, 100, 131, 137, 138
elections
  electoral reform 58
  general elections 59
  presidential 59, 63, 184n93
electoral corruption 20, 133, 135–40; *see also* political corruption
electronic identification card (E-KTP) scam 35, 147, 150–3, 165, 167–8
embezzlement 17, 18, 19, 32, 35, 112, 113
Endang, Kombes 158
energy sector 26, 34–5
Eradication of Acts of Money Laundering (Law No. 8 of 2010) 6

Eradication of Criminal Acts of Corruption Act (Law No. 31 of 1999) 4, 6, 17–18, 59, 75–6, 78, 171
  violation charges 138–40, 145–6
  see also anti-corruption measures
European Bank for Reconstruction and Development 23
extortion 6, 17, 18, 19

facilitation payments *see* bribery; kickbacks
Fattanah, Ahmad 68
Fauzi, Gamawan 150–1
Financial and Development Audit Body (BPKP, Badan Pemeriksa Keuangan Pemerintah) 8, 9
Financial Audit Body (BPK, Badan Pemeriksa Keuangan) 8–9
Financial Transaction Reports and Analysis Center (PPATK, Pusat Pelaporan dan Analisis Transaksi Keuangan) 8
food security 26
  beef trade corruption 26, 34, 68, 147, 179n112
freedom of the press xii, 4, 9, 57–8, 76
'functional corruption' concept 119
Funderburk, Charles 25

G30S coup (Gerakan 30 September, Movement of 30 September) 50, 51, 181n17, 194n63
gas and oil sector 26, 34–5
Gayus Tambunan case 26
Gerindra (political party) 125
Ghalib, Andi 155
gift-giving practices 15, 37–9, 40, 163–4
  legal prohibition 18, 40–1
  see also bribery
globalisation 23, 24, 32; *see also* transnational criminal organisations (TCOs)

Golkar Party 35, 59, 126, 135, 137, 147, 148–9, 151, 184n91
Gondokusumo, Djody 42
Goodpaster, Gary 27
governance
   Constitution 4–5, 61, 169
   rule by law instead of rule of law 50, 111
   separation of powers principle 45, 48, 56, 102
   supremacy of law 170, 172
   weak governance and corruption 24, 112, 113, 118, 120, 167
   see also presidential power; state capture corruption
governmental agencies 6, 33, 50–1, 52, 68, 80, 142, 169, 170
   corrupt officials 5, 15, 29–30, 43, 44, 54–5, 64–5, 72, 79–80, 116–17, 120, 128, 132, 142–8, 151–3
   petty corruption 15
   see also grand corruption; judicial corruption; KPK (Komisi Pemberantasan Korupsi, Corruption Eradication Commission); political corruption; state auxiliary agencies; state-owned enterprises
governors 64, 69, 71, 113–14, 135–40, 168
grand corruption 19, 26–7, 29, 52, 72, 128, 148
   case handling 89, 94, 95–8; *see also* KPK (Komisi Pemberantasan Korupsi, Corruption Eradication Commission)
   case summaries 33–6
   defined 15
   political corruption and 27, 35–6, 162, 164–5, 166–8
Greenhill, Kelly M. 23–4, 31
grey corruption, defined 16
Guided Democracy period 45–50; *see also* Soekarno government
Gultom, Miranda 30, 68

Gunawan, Budi 106, 158, 160
'Gus Dur' *see* Wahid, Abdurrahman (Gus Dur)
Gusman, Irman 70

Habibie, B.J. 4, 58–9, 75–6, 77, 154–5
Habibie government 58–9, 73, 75–6, 85, 154–5
Hambalang sports facility projects 31, 35, 148, 165
Hamzah, Amir 137–40
Hamzah, Chandra 66, 81–4, 106
Harahap, Chairuman 151
Harahap, Yahya 61
Hardjapamekas, Erry Riyana 78
Harmoko 4
Harris, Robert 25
Hartono, Michael and Robert Budi 122
Haryadi, Siti Hediyati 125
Hasan, Muhammad (Bob) 60, 156–7
Hatta, Muhammad 37, 52
Heidenheimer, Arnold J. 16
Hellman, Joel S. 118–19
Hong Kong Independent Commission Against Corruption (ICAC) 5, 7
human trafficking 24, 32
Huntington, Samuel 26, 119, 151, 166

IBRA (National Banking Restructuring Agency) 62
identity system *see* electronic identification card (E-KTP) scam
Idris, Mohamad El 143, 144, 145–6
IKAHI (Ikatan Hakim Indonesia, Indonesian Judges' Association) 45
IMF (International Monetary Fund) 14, 166
Independent Commission Against Corruption (ICAC), Hong Kong 5, 7
Indonesia (state)
   Constitution 4–5, 61, 169

Index   237

corruption *see* corruption in Indonesia
  as criminalised state 50, 56, 115–16
  decentralisation 116, 120, 127, 168
  independence 40
  integralistic state concept 50–6
  presidential power 45, 48–9, 50, 56
  rebellions and state of emergency 45–6
  rulers and power in colonial period 37–9
  separation of powers principle 45, 48, 56, 102
  see also governance; *and specific governments:* Habibie government; Jokowi government; Megawati Soekarnoputri government; Soeharto government; Soekarno government; Wahid government; Yudhoyono government
Indonesian Communist Party (PKI) 42, 182n42, 194n63
Indonesian Corruption Eradication Commission *see* KPK (Komisi Pemberantasan Korupsi, Corruption Eradication Commission)
Indonesian Corruption Watch (ICW) 69, 70, 189n45
Indonesian Judges' Association (IKAHI, Ikatan Hakim Indonesia) 45
Indonesian tycoons 122; *see also* oligarchs and oligarchies
Indonesian-Chinese conglomerates 121–2
Indrayana, Denny 106, 108
integralistic state 50–6
International Monetary Fund (IMF) 14, 166
Irman 150, 152–3
Ishaaq, Luthfi Hasan 26, 30, 34, 68, 147, 178n73
Ismudjoko 58, 155

Jemadu, Alexius 93, 99, 108

Johnston, Michael 129
Jokowi xvi–xvii, 84
Jokowi government 84–5, 125, 126, 149, 158, 159
  anti-corruption measures 32–3, 69, 107
  cabinet ministers prosecuted 11
  infrastructure development 117
Judicial Commission (Komisi Yudisial, KY) 5, 8, 100, 131, 132, 161, 169
judicial corruption 27, 30, 35, 61, 68, 71, 105, 133, 137–40
judicial independence 44–50, 56
Junaedi, Achmad 63–4

KAK (Komite Anti Korupsi, Anti-Corruption Committee) 52
Kalla, Jusuf 117, 126
Kang, David C. 15–16
Karmawan, Wawan 144
Kartasasmita, Syafiuddin 60, 157
Kasmin 137–40
Khodorkovsky, Michael 129
kickbacks 21, 22, 31, 113, 150; *see also* bribery
Kitab Undang-Undang Hukum Acara Pidana (KUHAP, Criminal Procedure Code) xiii, 95, 105, 161
KKN (*korupsi, kolusi and nepotisme*) *see* corruption; corruption in Indonesia; nepotism
kleptocratic interdependence 23–4
kleptocratic states *see* criminalised states
Klitgaard, Robert 14–15
Komando Tertinggi Retooling Alat Revolusi (Kotra, Supreme Command for Retooling the Revolutionary Apparatus) 47
Komisi Empat (Commission of Four) 51–2, 54
Komisi Pemberantasan Korupsi (KPK) *see* KPK (Komisi Pemberantasan Korupsi, Corruption Eradication Commission)

Komisi Pemeriksa Kekayaan Pejabat Negara (KPKPN, State Official Asset Auditing Commission) 95–6
Komisi Pemilihan Umum (KPU, Election Commission) 64
Komisi Yudisial (KY, Judicial Commission) 5, 8, 100, 131, 132, 161, 169
Komite Anti Korupsi (KAK, Anti-Corruption Committee) 52
Konsorsium Astragraphia 151
Konsorsium Murakabi 151
Konsorsium PNRI 151
korupsi, origin of term 15; *see also* corruption; corruption in Indonesia
korupsi berjamaah (collective corruption) 128, 142, 145–6, 150–3, 164
Kotra (Komando Tertinggi Retooling Alat Revolusi, Supreme Command for Retooling the Revolutionary Apparatus) 47
KPK (Komisi Pemberantasan Korupsi, Corruption Eradication Commission) 5, 7
  achievements 29–36
  Board of Supervisors 86, 89, 91, 102, 104–5, 147
  budget 96–7
  case summaries 33–6, 62, 64–5, 133, 135–57
  cases handled (number) 9–12, 30–1, 69–72, 87, 95
  Commissioners 78, 81–2, 83, 84, 87–8, 98, 103–4
  Commissioners criminalised 106–7, 158–62
  constitutional body proposal 108–9
  establishment 5–7, 61–2, 76, 77–8
  grand corruption focus 26–7, 89, 97
  investigative processes 80–1, 90–1
  legal standing *see* KPK Law (No. 30 of 2002) and amendments
  mission 2–3
  political context 107–9
  powers 7, 29, 63, 71–2, 85–93, 102
  public support for 66, 73, 75, 79, 82, 84–5, 91, 100, 107, 108
  recovery of funds 29–30
  relationships with law enforcement agencies 65–7, 80–4, 86–7, 91, 93–9, 105–7, 158–61
  role 5–7, 30, 63, 76, 78, 89–90, 92
  strengthening proposed 108–9, 170–2
  weakening of 71–2, 80, 84, 89, 93, 99, 100–8, 157–60, 170
KPK Law (No. 30 of 2002) and amendments 29, 63, 74, 84–91, 99, 108, 161
  challenges to 101–3, 106, 157–8
  key changes 71–2, 80, 85, 86, 92, 97, 102–5, 170
  promulgation of 61–2, 77–8
  recruitment of investigators 105–6
KPKPN (Komisi Pemeriksa Kekayaan Pejabat Negara, State Official Asset Auditing Commission) 95–6
KPU (Komisi Pemilihan Umum, Election Commission) 64
Krisis Moneter (monetary crisis, *Krismon*) 3–4
KUHAP (Kitab Undang-Undang Hukum Acara Pidana, Criminal Procedure Code) xiii, 95, 105, 161
Kusdinar, Deddy 146
Kusumah, Mulyana W. 64
KY (Komisi Yudisial, Judicial Commission) 5, 8, 100, 131, 132, 161, 169

Landung, Suyitno 64
Laos, corruption score 2
law enforcement agencies 170–2
  corruption in 5, 64, 71, 98, 106, 158
  inadequacies 60–1
  investigative teams 79–80
  relationships with KPK 65–7, 80–4, 86–7, 91, 93–9, 105–7, 158–61

see also Attorney General's Office; judicial corruption; judicial independence; KPK (Komisi Pemberantasan Korupsi, Corruption Eradication Commission); police

Law No. 3 of 1971, on corruption eradication 55

Law No. 8 of 2010, Eradication of Acts of Money Laundering 6

Law No. 30 of 2002, on KPK *see* KPK Law (No. 30 of 2002) and amendments

Law No. 31 of 1999, Eradication of Criminal Acts of Corruption Act 4, 6, 17–18, 59, 75–6, 78, 171
violation charges 138–40, 145–6
see also anti-corruption legislation

Legvold, Robert 16, 22–3, 28, 44, 49, 56, 115–16, 169

Lie Hok Thay 43

Liem, Feriyana 159

Lindsey, Tim 48–9

LPSK (Lembaga Perlindungan Saksi dan Korban, Witness and Victim Protection Agency) 8

Lubis, Mochtar 43

Lubis, Todung Mulya
biographical details ix–xiv, xvi–xvii, 59, 67, 78, 79
Tim Lima 81
Time trial 56–7, 154
Transparency International 83–4
and Widjoyanto 158–9

Maamun, Anas 69

Mahmudi, Nur 68

Majelis Permusyawaratan Rakyat Republik Indonesia (MPR, People's Consultative Assembly) 58, 59, 108, 154, 155

Malarangeng, Andi 22, 30, 67, 146–8

Malari incident (15 January Calamity) 54

Malaysia, corruption score 2

Manullang, Mindo Rosalina 143, 144, 145–6

Marcos, Ferdinand 112, 129

Marham, Idrus 71

Marjono, Eko 158

Matalata, Andi 81

Maulana, Ardian 109

media enterprises 124, 126

Megawati Soekarnoputri government 59, 61–3, 77–8

Mietzner, Marcus 20–1, 28, 147

military, corruption within 46, 60, 62, 64

Mochtar, Akil 30, 35, 68, 133, 137–40, 149

modernisation and corruption 26, 166–7

Moeis, Emir 30, 160

Moeljatno 47

money-laundering 6, 32, 113, 127, 167
anti-money-laundering measures 8, 17, 18, 73, 169
cases handled by KPK 9–10, 29, 30
in UNCAC definition of corruption 18, 19

MPR (Majelis Permusyawaratan Rakyat Republik Indonesia, People's Consultative Assembly) 58, 59, 108, 154, 155

Muharam, Wafid 143, 144, 145–8

Mukti, Ridwan 71

Munawar, Said Agil 63

municipal administration *see* decentralisation of authority; political corruption

Murdaya, Hartati 67

Myanmar, corruption score 2

Nababan, Panda 30

Nahrowi, Imam 72

Najamuddin, Agusrin 67

Nari, Markus 152, 153

Narogong, Andi (Andi Agustinus) 150, 151–3

Nasdem (political party) 126
Nasution (General) 46–7, 182n42
Nasution, Adnan Buyung (Presidential Adviser) 81
National Banking Restructuring Agency (IBRA) 62
National Commission of Human Rights 132
National Strategy to Prevent Corruption (2018) 6, 33
Nazaruddin, Muhammad 30, 31, 67, 140–8, 161, 162, 178n73
nepotism 38, 56, 113–15, 127; *see also* political dynasties; Soeharto family
New Order (*Orde Baru*) regime 3–4, 34, 50–6, 70, 121–2, 126, 134, 149
Noor, Teuku Bagus Mokhamad 146
Novanto, Setya 35, 120, 147, 148–53, 161, 162, 164, 184n91
Nugroho, Gatot Pudjo 69
Nurbaiti, Nunun 30
Nurhayati, Wa Ode 30

Octavia, Iti 137
oil and gas sector 26, 34–5
Old Order *see* Guided Democracy period
oligarchs and oligarchies 33–5, 113–15, 121–30, 135–40, 168, 169–70; *see also* wealth
Ombudsman 95–6, 100, 131
Operasi Budhi (Operation Budhi) 47
Operasi Tangkap Tangan (OTT, Operation Red-handed) 70, 71, 73
Operasi Tertib (Opstib or Operation Order) 55
Orde Baru see New Order (*Orde Baru*) regime
organised crime *see* transnational criminal organisations (TCOs)

Paloh, Surya 126
Pambudi, Irvanto Hendra *see* Cahyo, Irvanto Hendra Pambudi
Panggabean, Tumpak Hatorangon 78, 82
Panigoro, Arifin 122
Paran (Panitia Retooling Aparatur Negara, Committee for Retooling the State Apparatus) 47
parliamentarians, corrupt *see* political corruption
Parmono, Didik 98
Partai Demokrasi Indonesia—Perjuangan (PDI-P, Democratic Party of Struggle) 59, 61, 124–5, 160
Partai Demokrat (Democrat Party) 22, 31, 35, 67–8, 125, 135, 140, 141–8, 151
Partai Keadilan Sejahtera (PKS, Prosperous Justice Party) 22, 34, 68, 126, 147
Partai Persatuan Pembangunan (PPP) 126, 141, 147
Partai Sosialis Indonesia 43
passive corruption 40, 41
Pekuneg (Pengawasan Keuangan Negara, State Finance Supervision) 51
People's Consultative Assembly (MPR, Majelis Permusyawaratan Rakyat Republik Indonesia) 58, 59, 108, 154, 155
Perhutani 52
Permai Group 143
Pertamina 52, 54, 182n39
petty corruption 11, 13, 15, 72, 89, 128, 164–5
Philippines 129
PKB (political party) 126
PKI (Indonesian Communist Party) 42, 182n42, 194n63
PKS *see* Partai Keadilan Sejahtera (PKS, Prosperous Justice Party)
Pohan, Aulia 11, 65, 99
police 5, 7–8
  anti-corruption measures 65–6
  budget 96, 97

corruption cases handled 9, 11, 13, 64, 89, 95–6
corruption in 5, 64, 98, 106, 158
inadequacies of law enforcement agencies 60–1
investigative processes 79–80
relationship with KPK 65–7, 81–4, 86–7, 91, 93–9, 105–7, 158–61
role 95
political corruption 19–28, 30–1, 42, 67–8, 90, 130, 161–73
and business 117–21, 132, 141–53, 164–5
as business activity 25
case summaries 133, 135–57
electoral corruption 20, 133, 135–40
examples 30, 33–6, 41–4, 51, 62, 69–71, 87
grand corruption and 27, 35–6, 162, 164–5, 166–8
interconnectivity 117–21, 132, 134, 146–7, 161
jeopardises values of democracy 27–8
manifestations of 25–6
political interference 104, 161–2
political dynasties 113–14, 124–7, 130, 135–40, 168, 169–70; *see also* nepotism
political parties 124–7, 130, 147
family enterprises 124–5
financing 20–2, 31, 122–4, 125, 141–2, 146–7, 167
law on 76
oligarchies 114–15, 124–6, 127
see also Golkar Party; Partai Demokrasi Indonesia—Perjuangan (PDI-P, Democratic Party of Struggle); Partai Demokrat (Democrat Party); Partai Keadilan Sejahtera (PKS, Prosperous Justice Party)
politicians prosecuted 11–12, 30, 67–8, 70–2, 87, 140–53

Pompe, Sebastian 44–5, 49
PPATK (Pusat Pelaporan dan Analisis Transaksi Keuangan, Financial Transaction Reports and Analysis Center) 8
PPP (Partai Persatuan Pembangunan) 126, 141, 147
Prasetya, Rudy Indra 71
presidential power 45, 46, 48–51, 134
abuse of power (allegations against Soeharto) 154–7
see also governance
Presidents
election procedures 59, 63, 184n93
term 5
see also specific governments: Habibie government; Jokowi government; Megawati Soekarnoputri government; Soeharto government; Soekarno government; Wahid government; Yudhoyono government
Press Law *see* freedom of the press
private sector corruption *see* corporate corruption
Procedures for People's Participation and Awards for Prevention and Eradication of Corruption 77
procurement cases 9, 10, 30, 51, 64, 71, 116, 142–8; *see also* corporate corruption
prosecutors *see* Attorney General's Office
PT Duta Graha Indah Tbk 142–3, 146, 148
'public corruption' concept 22, 116
Purba, Parlin 71
Purnomo, Hadi 69
Purwadi, Dudung 143
Pusat Pelaporan dan Analisis Transaksi Keuangan (PPATK, Financial Transaction Reports and Analysis Center) 8
Puteh, Abdullah 64

Putra, Hutomo Mandala (Tommy
    Soeharto) 60, 156–7

Rajasa, Hatta 82
Rasul, M. 78
Ratu Atut *see* Chosiyah, Ratu Atut
Ratulangi, Sam 40
Reformasi (Reform) movement 4–5,
    7, 9, 113, 117, 122–4, 130, 149
  Constitutional Court 68
  and corruption eradication 73, 75–6,
    85, 92, 109, 116, 134, 165
  and decentralised government
    116–17, 127, 169
regional administration *see*
    decentralisation of authority
Regional People's Representative
    Assembly 5
Rianto, Bibit Samad 66, 81–4, 106
Roem, Muhammad 43
Rose-Ackerman, Susan 14
Rubiandini, Rudi 26, 30, 34
Ruki, Taufikurahman 78, 81
Rusdihardjo 65
Russia 115, 128–9, 134

Sabarno, Hari 30, 68
Sakwa, Richard 134
Saleh, Chairul 51
Salim Group 130
Samad, Abraham 98, 106, 158, 159–60
Samad, Imran 159
Santosa, Mas Achmad 82
Sanusi, Mohammad 70
Saragih, Eni Maulani 71
separation of powers principle 45, 48,
    56, 102
Singapore, corruption score 2
Sinivasan, Marimutu 60
Situngkir, Hokky 109
SKK Migas 30, 34
smuggling 24, 46, 115
social decay, corruption as factor in
    26–7, 28

Soedomo 55
Soeharto
  abuse of powers charges 154–7
  corruption 58, 60, 110–11, 112, 153–7
  defamation case against *Time* xii,
    56–7, 111, 153–4
  resignation 56, 58
Soeharto, Tommy (Hutomo Mandala
    Putra) 60, 156–7
Soeharto family 3, 52–3, 55, 56, 58,
    60, 111, 148–9, 153–4, 155, 156–7
Soeharto government 3–4, 34, 50–6,
    70, 74, 154–5
  corruption 3, 51–6, 110–11, 115–16,
    129–30, 164–5
  New Order (*Orde Baru*) 3–4, 34,
    50–6, 121–2, 126, 134, 149
Soekarno 42, 125
Soekarno government 44, 45–50, 74
Soekarnoputri, Megawati 59, 61–3,
    77–8, 125
Soepomo 50
Soeprapto 42
Sondakh, Angelina 30, 67, 142–3, 146,
    161n138
sports facility projects 22, 31, 35, 142–8
State Apparatus Supervisory Agency
    (Bapekan) 46–7
state auxiliary agencies 5, 6, 8, 32, 73,
    100, 131
state capture corruption 16–17, 23,
    34–5, 69, 72, 117–21, 130–1, 168–9;
    see also criminalised states
state integrity and security 27–8
State Official Asset Auditing
    Commission (KPKPN, Komisi
    Pemeriksa Kekayaan Pejabat Negara)
    95–6
state revenues (taxes) 26
  cases handled by KPK 26, 33–4
state-owned enterprises 82, 98
  corruption within 3, 47, 49, 52, 53,
    54, 60, 63–4
  see also governmental agencies

student activism 4, 50–1, 52–4
Subianto, Prabowo 125
Sudiartana, I Putu 70
Sudiwardono 71
Sugiharto 152–3
Sumardi, Ade 137
Sumarlin, J.B. 55
Sunaryadi, Amin 78
Supandji, Hendarman 63
Supreme Command for Retooling the Revolutionary Apparatus (Kotra) 47
Supreme Court 94, 156
  corruption cases handled 13, 62, 65, 69, 139, 145, 148, 152
  judges 132
  Time magazine case xii, 56–7, 111, 153–4
  see also judicial corruption
Suroso, Machfud 146
Suryana, Dewi 71
Suryo (General) 51
Susilo, Djoko 30, 98, 106
Suswono 22
Sutanto 64
Sutowo, Ibnu 46
Syamsuddin, Nazaruddin 64
Syarif, Laode Muhammad 37, 72

Taman Miniatur Indonesia Indah (Taman Mini) project 53
Tambunan, Guyas 33–4
Tanjung, Akbar 62, 184n91
Tanumihardja, Gatot 46
taxes *see* state revenues (taxes)
TCOs (transnational criminal organisations) 24–5, 31, 120–1
telephone conversation interception 86, 91, 102–3, 104
Texmaco 60
Thailand, corruption score 2
Tim Delapan (Team of Eight) 66–7, 82–4
Tim Gabungan Pemberantasan Tindak Pidana Korupsi (TGPTK, Combined Team for Corruption Eradication) 60–1, 95–6
Tim Lima (Team of Five) 81–2
Tim Pemberantasan Korupsi (Corruption Eradication Team) 51
Tim Pemberantasan Tindak Pidana Korupsi (Timtas Tipikor, Team to Eradicate Corruption), 63–4
Time magazine, defamation case brought by Soeharto xii, 56–7, 111, 153–4
Timtas Tipikor (Coordination Team for Corruption Eradication) 79
Tjandra, Joko 66
Tjokroadisurjo, Iskaq 41–2
Toemion, Theo 64
Toer, Pramoedya Ananta 1–2
top-down corruption, defined 15–16
transnational criminal organisations (TCOs) 24–5, 31, 120–1
Transparency International 2, 56, 73, 83–4, 111, 116, 171, 189n45
  Corruption Perceptions Index (CPI) 2, 73, 83–4, 111, 116, 164
Trias Politika see separation of powers principle
tribute (*upeti*) 163–4; *see also* bribery; gift-giving practices

Umar, Haryono 81
United Nations Convention against Corruption (UNCAC) 6, 18–19, 32
United Nations Development Programme
  most common forms of corruption (list) 18
  'state capture' definition 16–17
Uno, Sandiaga 122, 125
upeti (tribute) 163–4; *see also* bribery; gift-giving practices
Urbaningrum, Anas 35, 67, 141, 146–8

Vannucci, Alberto 21
Volksraad 40

Wacik, Jero 67, 69
Wahid, Abdurrahman (Gus Dur) 59–61, 67, 126
Wahid government 59–61, 77, 85, 155–6
Wahyuni, Neneng Sri 143, 145
Waluyo 82
wealth 29, 44, 92, 121–2, 165, 168
   illegal wealth confiscation proposals 171, 172
   Marcos 112, 129–30
   Soeharto 56, 111, 112
   see also oligarchs and oligarchies
white corruption, defined 16
Wibisono, Jusuf 43
Widiatmoko, Ari 158
Widjoyanto, Bambang 106, 158–9, 160
Widjoyo, Anggoro 66
Widodo, A.S. 81
Widodo, Joko *see* Jokowi
Widodo government *see* Jokowi government
Wilopo 51

wiretaps (telephone conversation interception) 86, 91, 102–3, 104
Wisma Atlet sports facility project 22, 31, 35, 142–8
Witness and Victim Protection Agency (LPSK, Lembaga Perlindungan Saksi dan Korban) 8
Wolfensohn, James 112–13
World Bank 14, 23, 118, 166

Yadav, Vineeta 21
Yasin, Muhammad 81
Yudhoyono, Susilo Bambang 11, 65, 66–7, 69, 99, 125–6, 141, 147
Yudhoyono government 63, 69, 78, 125
   anti-corruption measures 32–3, 66–7, 78–84, 107
   cabinet ministers prosecuted 11, 67
   presidential aides corruption 67
   see also Partai Demokrat (Democrat Party)
Yusuf, Irwandi 71

Zainal, Rusli 30
Zola, Zumi 71
Zulkarnain, Nazaruddin 66